MAPPING JEWISH LOYALTIES
IN INTERWAR SLOVAKIA

THE MODERN JEWISH EXPERIENCE

Deborah Dash Moore and Marsha L. Rozenblit, *editors*
Paula Hyman, *founding coeditor*

MAPPING JEWISH LOYALTIES

IN INTERWAR SLOVAKIA

REBEKAH KLEIN-PEJŠOVÁ

Indiana University Press

Bloomington and Indianapolis

This book is a publication of

INDIANA UNIVERSITY PRESS
Office of Scholarly Publishing
Herman B Wells Library 350
1320 East 10th Street
Bloomington, Indiana 47405 USA

iupress.indiana.edu

Manufactured in the United States of America

Library of Congress Cataloging-in-Publication Data

Klein-Pejšová, Rebekah, [date] author.
Mapping Jewish loyalties in Interwar Slovakia / Rebekah
Klein-Pejšová.
    pages cm. – (The modern Jewish experience)
  Includes bibliographical references and index.
  ISBN 978-0-253-01554-9 (cloth : alkaline paper) — ISBN
978-0-253-01562-4 (ebook) 1. Jews–Slovakia–History–20th
century. 2. Jews–Czechoslovakia–History–20th century.
3. Slovakia–Ethnic relations. 2. Czechoslovakia–Ethnic
relations. I. Title.
  ML420.H25B76 2015
  782.42168092—dc23
  [B]

                              2014021653

1 2 3 4 5 20 19 18 17 16 15

For Zora and Milena

Our Jews are clever enough to seek the right path, and I think they will find it, even if they have not yet given any indication of their decision to do so.

—Vavro Šrobár, minister plenipotentiary for Slovakia, 1920

Contents

Acknowledgments

I F THIS IS a book about changing borders and how people's lives are remade within them, then so, too, do its origins reveal the profound influence of transformed geopolitical realities on my own. The long journey toward this book began when I studied in Budapest as an exchange student from Bard College at Eötvös Loránd Tudományegyetem (ELTE) in 1993, encouraged by Karen Greenberg, Leon Botstein, and friends in Bard's exceptional Program in International Education—always striving for true reciprocity. It was a period of great openness, mutuality, excitement, and discovery that I will always cherish. I decided then to write my senior project on late nineteenth-century Dualist Era Hungary Jewry—the "Golden Age of Hungarian Jewry." My sage adviser, David Kettler, recommended that I make it "more interesting" by extending my period of study through the postwar chaos and anti-Semitic legislation, which I did. In the process I became acquainted with Indiana University Press, the first academic press of which I was cognizant, through William O. McCagg's *A History of Habsburg Jews, 1670–1918.*

Later I wrote my MA thesis at the Central European University in Budapest on the comparative responses of Jews in Austria-Hungary to the early Zionist movement, in order to understand the appeal, or lack thereof, the concept had for Jews in Vienna, Prague, and Budapest. This was a formative period in all respects, where scholarly growth and "common socialization" went hand in hand. I am grateful to have had the opportunity to work with Péter Hanák, Viktor Karády, and András Gerő. The variations in Jewish culture, society, politics, and levels of integration became clearer to me after I moved to Prague and learned that for Jews there the interwar period was their "Golden Age" and President Masaryk was their hero.

After a tour-guiding stint and work at the Jewish Museum in Prague, I went to Columbia University to study the distance between these two narratives, to compare the experience of Hungarian and Czech Jews in relation to each other and to the surrounding society. I wanted to understand the ruptures and continuities across the cataclysm of the First World War. The answer, of course, was Slovakia. I wrote this book because I wanted to know what happens after empire, after the borders change; how Jews closely tied to Hungary's prewar successes also experienced its failure, and whether they, too, had a chance at another "Golden Age" in Czechoslovakia before it disintegrated.

xi

My heartfelt gratitude goes to István Deák for guidance and inspiration from the moment I set foot on Columbia's campus. Michael Stanislawski, my sponsor, provided crucial direction and perspective. My special thanks must go to Bradley Abrams, devoted mentor and scholarly community builder, and to Nancy Sinkoff, whose invaluable assistance eased my transition to academic mom and who models how to keep this maximalism in balance. My sincere appreciation goes to Hillel Kieval, Marsha Rozenblit, Mark von Hagen, Mark Mazower, Attila Pók, Yeshayahu Jelínek, András Kovács, András Bozóki, Ivan Sanders, Karen Barkey, Rebecca Kobrin, Paul Hanebrink, and Benjamin Frommer for their support, encouragement, and stimulating conversation. I wish to thank Carol Rounds for Hungarian language training at Columbia as well as Jana Navrátilová and L'ubica Banášová of the Institute of Language and Academic Preparation for Foreign Students (UJOP) of Comenius University in Bratislava for Slovak language training. I enjoyed valuable conversations with Ivan Kamenec, Eva Kowalská, Elena Mannová, and Will Kymlicka at crucial stages in my research.

The research and writing for this book were generously supported by a number of institutions to whom I am sincerely indebted. First and foremost my thanks are due to the East Central Europe Center and Harriman Institute at Columbia for the Meier Fellowship, the Junior Fellowship, and summer travel grants. Foreign Language and Area Studies (FLAS) fellowships in the summer of 1999 for Czech and academic year 2001–2002 for Hungarian allowed me to improve my language skills and carry out archival research. Funding from the Center for Historical Social Sciences at Columbia and a fellowship from the Hungarian Európa Intézet in 2002 enabled me to continue my research and engage with a vibrant scholarly community in Budapest. Accommodations at the dorm of the Slovak Academy of Sciences in Bratislava greatly facilitated my research at the Slovak National Archives and the City Archives of Bratislava. I am grateful for the award of the ACLS Dissertation Completion Fellowship in East European Studies in the academic year 2005–2006. My thanks also go to the Institute for Israel and Jewish Studies at Columbia for an award of a fellowship from 2004 to 2007.

I acknowledge with gratitude the assistance of the chief archivist, Dr. Lajos Gecsényi, and all of the staff in the K148 section of the Hungarian National Archives, the librarians at the Szécsenyi National Library, at the Hungarian Academy of Sciences, and at the Central European University. I am indebted to chief archivist Dr. Peter Magura and his staff at the Slovak National Archives for their rapid and painless delivery of materials, the staff of the Archive of the City of Bratislava, and the library of the Slovak Academy of Sciences. I wish to express my thanks to the archive of the Ministry of Foreign Affairs in the Czech Republic and to the librarians at the Klementinum, the Czech National Library. The staff of the Dorot Jewish Division of the New York Public Library was invaluable for its assistance as were the YIVO Institute for Jewish Research and the Center for

Jewish History in New York City overall. It was a joy to use the rich collections of Columbia University and the Jewish Theological Seminary and to write in various corners of Butler Library.

My heartfelt thanks go to Dee Mortensen at Indiana University Press for taking on this project and extending to me the honor and privilege of joining the distinguished circle of IUP authors. Marsha Rozenblit and Deborah Dash Moore, whose work I have long admired, accepted the book for the pathbreaking Modern Jewish Experience series. My sincere thanks go out to all the editors and anonymous readers who have provided valuable feedback at every stage, finding errors and helping me think deeply about what I really want to say. Any remaining errors in the text are my own. Many thanks go to my colleagues at Purdue University, especially to Charles Ingrao, Whitney Walton, Laurel Weldon, Aaron Hoffmann, Dan Frank, and the Jewish Studies Program, which is also generously subsidizing indexing costs. The work/family balance would not have been achieved without the help of Sadete Zykollari in New York and Burgett's Learning Center here in West Lafayette, Indiana, which crucially understands the time question.

Throughout the research and writing of this book, I have been fortunate to enjoy the collegiality and companionship of a vibrant and formidable far-flung community: Constantin Iordachi, Éva Bicskei, Marius Turda, Péter Ápor, Mihály Szilagy-Gál, Peter Šoltés, Kate Antonova, Veronica Aplenc, Kim Zarecor, Tatjana Lichtenstein, Jan Láníček, Anna Gedrich, Julia Gray, Orsolya Illés, Anna Terfy, Norma Musih, and Dani Szpruch. My special appreciation goes to Michael Miller, Maroš Borský, Jared Manasek, Ruth Ellen Gruber, and Eva Derman of the Society for the History of Czechoslovak Jews. Thank you Myra Waterbury: we broke on through.

I thank my parents and sister with love for their understanding, support, and pride through all the years.

Finally, I reserve my deepest gratitude and appreciation for one who insists on anonymity and truth, without whom none of this would be possible, not least of all our daughters, Zora and Milena, who have grown up with this book for their entire young lives so far. Yes.

Note on Place-Names and List of Place-Name Equivalents

AN ALREADY DENSE map of alternate place-names for many towns and cities in the Habsburg Monarchy was further complicated by the geopolitical shifts following the First World War. Most places in the Habsburg Monarchy were supplied with German names by the administration in the Viennese capital. Hungarian authorities likewise provided Magyar names for places. Speakers of the many other vernaculars, too, preferred to use names for places in their own languages. After the First World War, as a general rule, the successor states—Poland, Czechoslovakia, Romania, Yugoslavia—used the place-names preferred by the newly dominant nationalities, manifesting the new status quo.

Place-name usage is sensitive and contested. In a book devoted to examining the transfer of political loyalties from Hungary to Czechoslovakia among the Jewish population in the newly defined territory of Slovakia, it is crucial to be clear up front about the method used for determining place-name usage throughout the text. I generally use the post-1918 nomenclature, since the body of the book focuses on the interwar period. For example, the capital of Slovakia is called Bratislava throughout the text. The exception is the introduction, which deals largely with the pre–World War I development of the Jewish population in the northern counties of the Kingdom of Hungary that would later become Slovakia. In the introduction I use the contemporary nomenclature of common usage among the Jewish population in order to avoid anachronism. Therefore, the city that would later be known as Bratislava is called by its German name, Pressburg, rather than its Magyar name, Pozsony.

What follows is a list of Slovak, German, and Magyar place-name equivalents for locations in Slovakia mentioned in this book. Other places commonly known by English names, like Vienna, Prague, and Budapest, are referred to as such.

SLOVAK	GERMAN	MAGYAR
Banská Bystrica	Neusohl	Besztercebánya
Bardejov	Bartfeld	Bártfa
Bratislava	Pressburg	Pozsony
Hlohovec	Freistadt an der Waag	Galgóc
Košice	Kaschau	Kassa
Lučenec	Lizenz	Losonc
Michalovce	Großmichel	Nagymihály
Nitra	Neutra	Nyitra
Nové Zámky	Neuhäusel	Érsekújvár
Parkaň (Šturovo)	Gockern	Párkány
Piešťany	Pistyan	Pőstyén
Považská Bystrica	Waagbistritz	Vágbeszterce
Prešov	Eperies	Eperjes
Prievidza	Priwitz	Privigye
Rimavská Sobota	Großsteffelsdorf	Rimaszombat
Ružomberok	Rosenberg	Rózsahegy
Šahy	Eipelschlag	Ipolyság
Trenčín	Trentschin	Trencsén
Trenčianske Teplice	Trentschinteplitz	Trencsénteplic
Turčiansky Svätý Martin	Turz-Sankt Martin	Turócszentmárton
Vrbové	Werbau	Verbó
Žilina	Sillein	Zsolna

MAPPING JEWISH LOYALTIES
IN INTERWAR SLOVAKIA

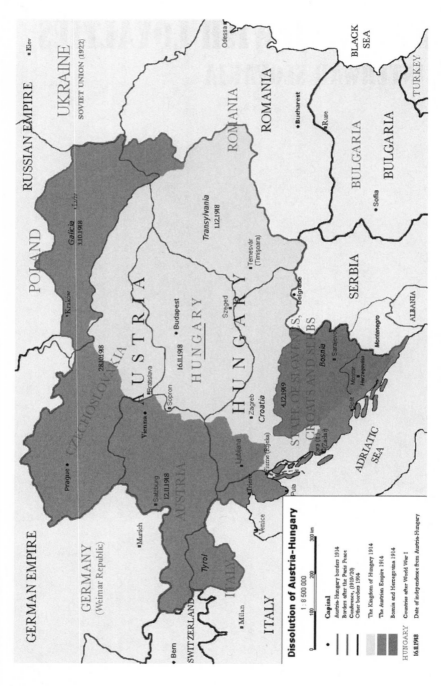

Successor states to Austria-Hungary after World War I. *Courtesy of Wikimedia Commons.*

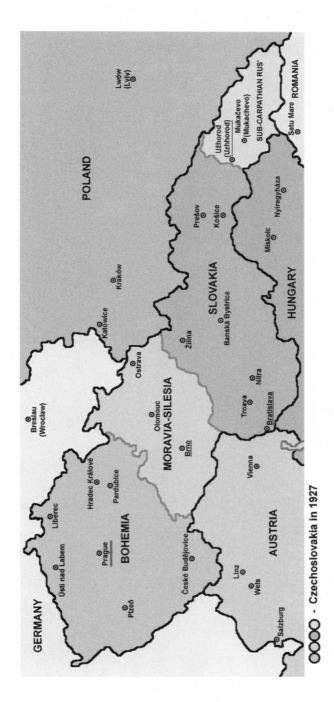

OOOO - Czechoslovakia in 1927

Interwar Czechoslovakia and neighboring states. *Courtesy of Wikimedia Commons.*

Introduction: Seek the "Right Path"

The Jews of Slovakia in Remapped
Post–World War I East Central Europe

Borders change. Lives are remade. When the First World War ended, the four empires that long determined the shape of state and social relations within and beyond their borders—the Habsburg, the German, the Russian, and the Ottoman—had dissolved. A state system based on the principle of national self-determination took their place in east central Europe, in which citizenship and state belonging were seen through a national lens. The map was complicated. In the movement from empire to nation-state, the entirely new country of Czechoslovakia was born, arising from the successful wartime argument made by Tomáš Garrigue Masaryk, Edvard Beneš, and Milan Štefánik in exile abroad that the Czechs and Slovaks comprised two branches of the same Slavic nation. Yet Czechoslovakia was in fact a multinational state, with significant German and Hungarian national minorities who challenged the state's legitimacy and whose kin states threatened its borders.

Czechoslovakia consisted not only of Bohemia, Moravia, and part of Silesia, established political units that had been constituent lands within "Austria" in the prewar Austro-Hungarian Monarchy, but also of Slovakia and Subcarpathian Ruthenia, neither of which had previously existed as distinct entities.[1] Both emerged as separate bounded territories created from the former northern counties of the prewar Kingdom of Hungary with the establishment of Czechoslovakia. Slovakia was fiercely contested from the outset, being crucial to the creation and existence of independent Czechoslovakia and, at the same time, an object of interwar rump Hungary's irredentist obsessions. Not so Subcarpathian Ruthenia, considered "one of the most backward regions in all Europe," which the Entente powers granted to Czechoslovakia in September 1919 largely because "no one else was interested," giving the state a common border with Romania.[2] The military struggle for Slovakia drew to a close with the signing of the Treaty of Trianon between Hungary and the Entente powers in early June

1920. Slovakia's population turned toward a capital in Prague rather than in Budapest.

Czechoslovak authorities were convinced that the 135,000 Jews in the newly defined and uneasily controlled territory of Slovakia were "one hundred percent Magyarized" before the First World War.[3] Yet they trusted that the far-reaching Hungarian assimilation they saw among the Jews there could cease with the collapse of the Habsburg Monarchy. In a February 1920 interview in neighboring Vienna, just thirty-five miles due west following the Danube from Slovakia's capital, Bratislava, Czechoslovakia's minister plenipotentiary for Slovak affairs, Vavro Šrobár, expressed his confidence that Jews in Slovakia would be "clever enough to seek the right path" in the state, "even if they had not yet given any indication of their decision to do so."[4]

This book is a story of how Jews in Slovakia sought the "right path" in interwar Czechoslovakia. It is an examination of Jewish reorientation within the borders of a radically remapped post–World War I east central Europe at the intersection of state and society. The Jewish population in Slovakia, abruptly dislocated from an established set of behaviors and expectations, now confronted the challenge of relocating their political loyalty from Hungary to Czechoslovakia—and proving they had done so. Fearful that Jews there may be potential accomplices to the interwar Hungarian government's goal of reacquiring Slovakia, the state continuously carried out investigations to determine if this transfer had indeed occurred, shifting the markers it defined as indicators of citizen loyalty as well as its techniques of observation over time to reflect the ascendancy of irredentist threats to Czechoslovakia over domestic sociocultural tensions. Focus on Slovakia, its very existence a phenomenon of interwar state building, captures the complexities of the movement from empire to nation-state in a hostile and fragile state system.

Jewish reorientation turned on the question of political loyalty, the central pillar of the Jewish relationship with the state. Relations between Jews and the state are crucial for how Jewish history develops, its shape and content, how it is written and rewritten. Pierre Birnbaum and Ira Katznelson underscore the importance of the state in their authoritative study of the Jewish emancipation process, writing, "It is clear that as Jews managed to map and travel the pathways of emancipation, the nature of the state they confronted proved pivotal, shaping the character of antisemitism, the qualities of economic development, the contours of the class structure, the development of the public arena, and the constitution of civil society."[5] Bound up in Jewish emancipation was a transformed loyalty relationship with the state that would exert influence on all of these areas, including a new basis for political belonging and its corollary, a new basis for Jewish exclusion. The questioning of Jewish loyalty to the state runs like a red thread through modern Jewish history from the Dreyfus Affair to the accusation of Jewish dual loyalties following the establishment of the State of Israel. Napoleon's twelve questions addressed to the Assembly of Jewish Notables, which he convened in 1806 in order to better understand the Jewish relationship to the French state and to their fellow citizens, has been called "the first serious loyalty test administered to the Jews by a modern state," where "the stakes were enormous."[6]

Proving individual and collective Jewish loyalty to the state is a fixture of post-emancipation modern Jewish history. Sorting out strategies for affirming citizenship and state belonging through loyalty is the first step in the Jewish search for security, well-being, advancement, and survival. Loyalty precedes identity in modern Jewish history. Identity arises from the loyalty relationship with the state.

Hungary

Understanding how Jews in Slovakia mapped and traveled the pathways of their reorientation from Hungary to Czechoslovakia after the First World War means first tracing the development of Jewish state and social relations within Hungary, concentrating on those relations in its northern counties. Jews migrated to the future territory of Slovakia from Bohemia, Austria, and Germany as early as the eleventh century and founded the first Jewish community in Pressburg in the late thirteenth century. Their migrations and settlements from the seventeenth through nineteenth centuries, however, had the most significant influence on the subsequent growth of regional Jewish communal and cultural networks as well as their state and social relations. The official end of the Ottoman occupation of Hungary in 1699 marked a pivotal turn in the development of Hungarian Jewry.

During the 150-year Ottoman occupation (1541–1699), the Habsburg-controlled northern and western parts of the Kingdom of Hungary (Slovakia, Subcarpathian Ruthenia, western Transdanubia, and Croatia) became known as Royal Hungary.[7] Fleeing the battles and destruction in central Hungary, the Hungarian nobility and their Hungarian-speaking subjects, along with Croatians, Magyars, and Serbs, moved to the mountainous north. Religious exiles—Protestants and other non-Catholics from Moravia, Bohemia, and Lower Austria—arrived in waves to western and northwestern Royal Hungary during the Thirty Years' War, aiding the region's economic growth and demographic recovery from Ottoman raids and anti-Habsburg insurrections. Walachians, too, migrated to the eastern Carpathians, mixing and settling with the Rusyn population.[8]

By the end of the Ottoman occupation, nearly all Hungarian Jews lived in northwestern Royal Hungary. A large number of Jews from Vienna had migrated up the Danube after the anti-Jewish violence of 1679 (connected with the outbreak of bubonic plague in Vienna that year[9]), and Moravian Jews founded a number of communities in Royal Hungary as the Habsburg armies drove the

Turks out of central Hungary.[10] Most Jews lived in Pressburg and on aristocratic estates along the western border. A further influx of Moravian Jews followed the restrictive marriage laws passed in 1726–1727. Moravian Jews found emigration from Moravia across the border to the renewed neighboring Kingdom of Hungary an appealing response to these marriage laws, or familiants, for Moravian Jewish sons who wished to marry legally without converting to Catholicism.[11]

A new, energetic immigration wave began in the early 1780s from Galicia southward into Hungary shortly after Joseph II issued his Edicts of Toleration. The Habsburgs acquired Galicia in the course of the three partitions of Poland from 1772 through 1795. The Galician economy suffered depression following Habsburg annexation, and Hungary seemed to be a land of opportunity in comparison. This led to a rapid increase in the Hungarian Jewish population from about 83,000 in 1787 to about 130,000 in 1805. Based to a large extent on immigration influx, the Hungarian Jewish population grew by approximately 40 to 50 percent every twenty years until 1880, when immigration from Galicia slowed down. At that time the Hungarian Jewish population stood at 624,700. It reached 910,000 by 1910.[12] Encouraged by the Hungarian aristocracy, Jews migrating to northern Hungary from Moravia, Galicia and Bukovina, and Lower Austria tended to settle near the borders of the states from which they had come. They maintained religious, communal, and linguistic ties with Jewish communities across the borders.[13] At the end of the eighteenth century, most Jews in Hungary lived in villages and on estates belonging to the aristocracy. They were also permitted to settle in cities under royal rule as well as in market towns that were wholly or partly on aristocratic estates. The Hungarian Jews were useful residents, working as merchants, supplying necessary goods from abroad, and consuming agricultural surplus. They paid their Toleration Tax, initiated during the reign of Maria Theresa, to Vienna until the 1830s, when the vast changes to economic, political, and cultural conditions brought about by heightened tensions between the royal Austrian and independent Hungarian governments began.[14]

During the 1830s and 1840s, known as Hungary's Reform Period, leading Hungarian liberal politicians spearheaded the transformation of the Jews' legal position as part of the overall push for the modernization and Magyarization of the state. They saw the Jewish population as exceptionally valuable for developing trade and finance within the modern capitalist economy they wished to create, a sharp turn away from entrenched feudal social and economic patterns. Jews in Hungary experienced increasing economic success performing a vital role in a "backward" economy characterized by a large peasant population, a politically powerful and substantial nobility, and a predominantly nonnative urban population.[15] Jewish status in Hungary became a staple of parliamentary debate. In 1839 and 1840 the "Reform Diet" enacted a law that virtually removed long-standing residency restrictions: Jews could settle nearly anywhere in the state, except for a few mining towns, and even found new communities.[16] At the same time the diet ruled Magyar to be the official language in the Kingdom of Hungary and the exclusive language of government, replacing Latin.[17]

Grateful for their new freedom of movement, broader economic opportunities, and cooperative arrangement with the Hungarian nobility, many Jews in Hungary learned Hungarian, which was also viewed as their support for independent Hungarian liberal political ambitions. They embarked on the pervasive trend of Magyarizing the German-sounding names their ancestors had taken on after legislation passed in the 1780s under Joseph II. Yet they found that their economic usefulness and Hungarian language acquisition in addition to the German, Judeo-German, or Yiddish they spoke would not be enough to become truly integrated into Hungarian society. They would also have to reform—modernize and Magyarize—Judaism itself. For this reason, argues Jacob Katz, there were greater assimilationist demands on the Jews than on the other non-ethnic Magyar peoples in the Kingdom of Hungary.[18] József Eötvös, later minister of religion and education, and the great Hungarian statesman Ferenc Deák mapped a path for their Jewish friends to follow toward emancipation: put an end to Jewish immigration into Hungary and do away with Orthodoxy.[19] Jews in Hungary thus began the process of accommodating to these demands in an era of shifting and modernizing patterns of religious practice among the Jews in east central Europe.

The Hungarian Revolution of 1848 against Habsburg rule tied Jews in Hungary closer to the Hungarian national cause. They enthusiastically supported the revolt both financially and militarily.[20] Even the traditional rabbis in Pressburg, the center of Hungarian Orthodoxy and bulwark against reform in the legacy of Rabbi Moses Sofer (popularly known as the Hatam Sofer[21]), came to join the Hungarians when violent outbreaks against the Jewish community were carried out by the local population.[22] Slovak national agitators did not accept the Hungarian revolutionary leader Lajos Kossuth's model of a Hungarian political nation and its accompanying Magyarization policy. They struggled against the Hungarian Revolution on Vienna's side, wishing to maintain the geographically rather than nationally understood Kingdom of Hungary, or Lands of St. Stephen's Crown— what they called *Uhorsko*—and seeking autonomy within that framework.[23] Hungarian authorities viewed the participation of Slovak volunteers fighting for the Habsburgs as treason. Theirs was an anti-Habsburg struggle, whereas the Slovak one was predominantly pro-Habsburg, and even Russophile. Hungarian leaders feared Russian expansion and sought to stamp out "Pan-Slavic" and other anti-Magyar domestic movements.[24] Hungarian ill feeling toward Russia grew as the Russian army of Tsar Nicholas I aided the just enthroned Habsburg emperor Franz Josef in defeating Hungary in its war for independence.[25]

Just before the Hungarian surrender to the Russians at Világos in August 1849, the revolutionary Hungarian National Assembly granted emancipation to the Jews of Hungary. The act bound the Jewish population to the defeated revolution. As the Habsburgs reincorporated Hungary into the realm, they levied a heavy fine on the Jews. Later, however, they returned the monies to the Jewish communities for cultural and educational activities, which took place under the neo-absolutist government's pressure and supervision.[26] The goal was to re-entrench German language and culture among the Jews, whose deep connection to it had been swept over by reform-era Hungarian language acquisition and allegiance to the revolution. German-language Jewish schools were rapidly established and frequently taught by Jews coming from Bohemia and Moravia.[27]

By 1858 there were 308 modern German-language Jewish schools in Hungary, 131 of which were in Pressburg, just a short railway ride from the Viennese capital.[28] Pressburg was the focal point of the northwestern counties of the country known as the *Oberland,* between the northwestern border with Moravia and Lower Austria to the Tatra Mountains. Here Jewish contact with the surrounding society steadily increased, and Jewish communities made use of the opportunities presented by the schools. In the northeastern counties of the country, however, known as the *Unterland* (later eastern Slovakia and Subcarpathian Ruthenia), the Jewish population avoided the new school system by employing private tutors or sending their children to non-Jewish high schools rather than forsake their traditional educational institutions. Most Jews in the Unterland had migrated down from Galicia and spoke Yiddish, and many brought a Hasidic lifestyle with them. They tended to remain tied to the agricultural economy, unlike Jews in Hungary's west, who conspicuously benefited from Vienna's introduction of important avenues of new capitalist enterprise to Hungary in the 1850s, especially the railroads. It was an era of great economic and industrial innovation. German linguistic and cultural orientation and economic opportunity heightened Vienna's pull on the Hungarian Jews.[29]

A decade later Hungarian Jews were immersed in an era of "intense social change," characterized by rapid modernization, economic growth, and institutional innovation following the constitutional reform known as the Austro-Hungarian Compromise, or *Ausgleich,* of 1867, which had quickly led to their formal re-emancipation by the again sovereign Hungarian parliament.[30] The Ausgleich created the Dual Monarchy of Austria-Hungary: a union of the Austrian Empire and the Kingdom of Hungary, in which both countries had separate governing bodies but shared a head of state and three common ministries (foreign affairs, war, and finance). The Austrian emperor also served as the king of Hungary. Prussia's crushing victory over Austria in 1866 had compelled Vienna to accede to Hungarian demands in order to fortify the empire. The ruling Magyar elite now enjoyed power beyond the dreams of any other national or social group within Austria-Hungary.[31] Any Czech national hopes for a reformed federalist empire were unequivocally dashed. Poles, too, shared resentment over this unanticipated development.[32] Despite its rise in political power, however, the Magyar elite lacked a centralized administration and remained small and financially weak. And it ruled over a vast heterogeneous kingdom where ethnic Magyars were a minority among peoples whose mother tongues included Romanian, Ruthenian, Croatian, Serbian, German, and Slovak.[33]

Jews throughout Hungary found themselves enabled and encouraged to form a mutually beneficial relationship with the Hungarian government as it pursued swift modernization and absorption of the non-Magyar population after 1867. The government found it imperative to fortify the ethnic Magyar position in the country by increasing Magyar numbers and by repressing perceived threats to their rule through a policy of Magyarizing non-Magyar ethnic groups. Jews seemed especially valuable for this proposition, given their history of support for the Hungarian national movement, lack of territory, and absence of an anti-Magyar national movement of their own.[34] The Hungarian government offered the Jews protection from popular antisemitism and cleared a path for their social mobility through education and religious equality. In return it expected the Jews' loyalty to the Hungarian national state, marked by political support, cultural Magyarization, and social assimilation that included the renunciation of Jewish cultural, behavioral, and religious "peculiarities."[35]

Hungarian Jews overwhelmingly, and with gratitude, adopted a strategy of unwavering allegiance to the Hungarian government. They substituted Magyar —since 1867 the official language of Hungary—for German in their process of secondary acculturation.[36] Expressions of Jewish loyalty ranged from simply declaring Magyar as their mother tongue on the census, which was essential for securing a slim Magyar majority in the Kingdom of Hungary, to outright identification with the Magyar nation through sincerely speaking Magyar as their mother tongue, changing their names to Magyar ones, affiliation with Neolog Judaism, intermarriage, or even conversion.[37] It is important to acknowledge the difference. Unlike collective identification, or an understanding of the self and the collective as inseparable, loyalty can be defined as following through on a known set of expectations or holding up one's end of the bargain.[38] Jewish support enabled the Hungarian government to pursue nationalizing ambitions while taking advantage of Jewish expertise to modernize the economy, creating economic independence from Austria. It was the "golden age" of Hungarian Jewry.

Expectations of religious modernization and Magyarization proved more internally divisive. In 1868 a country-wide Hungarian Jewish Congress organized by Hungary's minister of religion and education, József Eötvös, took place, through which he intended to create a unified, centralized body to handle Jewish affairs throughout the state modeled on Napoleon's consistory. Instead the congress worked to harden deepening fault lines within the Hungarian Jewish population regarding religious practice and worldview. Its most significant legacy is the religious split within Hungarian Jewry: the division between the Neolog (or congress, a moderate form of Reform Judaism), Orthodox, and Status Quo Ante (similar to Neolog in its efforts toward linguistic acculturation, but maintaining the traditional piety of the Orthodox[39]) branches of Judaism in Hungary. The split became official in 1871 when Franz Josef recognized Orthodoxy as a separate Jewish religion.[40]

Neolog Judaism, in contrast to Orthodoxy, is peculiar to Hungary, where it developed as a means of fulfilling Magyar social assimilationist expectations that were rooted in the reform era. It encompassed no radical changes to the traditional liturgy, but allowed for use of an organ and moved the speaker's podium (*bimah*) from the center to the front of the synagogue, as in Reform congregations in Germany. Neolog Jews referred to themselves as Hungarians of the Jewish religion or Hungarians of the Mosaic faith.[41] An imaginary diagonal line drawn from the northwest of the country at Pressburg to the southeast at Brassó (Braşov) describes the geographic dimensions of the religious split. Most regions to the north of the line were predominantly Orthodox, while most regions to the south of it were predominantly Neolog. Status Quo Ante communities were fewer and more diverse.[42] Jewish communities in the territories of the post–World War I successor states that had been part of prewar Hungary—that is, Transylvania (Romania) and Vojvodina (Yugoslavia), in addition to Slovakia (Czechoslovakia)—saw carryover of their prewar Hungarian Jewish institutions despite the fundamental changes in the geopolitical landscape. That cross-border communal legacy presented serious challenges to the Jewish relationship with the postwar state.[43]

The Magyarization process was uneven among the Jews in the Kingdom of Hungary. While exceptionally effective overall, the degrees of Magyarization were tied to broader environmental and demographic factors. Political loyalty and linguistic acculturation were the easiest to accommodate. Social assimilation was a more challenging and problematic endeavor, however, because it demanded that Jews give up "undesirable" Jewish cultural, behavioral, and, especially, religious distinctions. The religious split within Hungarian Jewry most decisively influenced Magyarization patterns. Neolog Jews, not unexpectedly, tended to be the most deeply Magyarized. By 1910 sermons were delivered in Hungarian in most Neolog synagogues. Orthodox Jews also broadly accommodated linguistic Magyarization, but Hungarian-language sermons in Orthodox synagogues were uncommon. Linguistic Magyarization among the Orthodox was more likely to occur in urban rather than rural settings, especially in strongly ethnic Magyar environments. Nevertheless, Hungarian language usage was not exclusive. Hungarian Jews tended to remain bilingual, usually in German and Hungarian, or in Yiddish and Hungarian in the northeast of the country.[44]

In areas where Jews lived among a non-Magyar majority, Magyarization was slower and incomplete; the opposite was true in Magyar-dominated regions.[45] Magyarization ran most deeply and comprehensively among Jews in Budapest and within the borders of central Hungary, where there was the densest ethnic Magyar concentration in the state as well as the highest numbers of Neolog Jews.[46] On the other end of the spectrum, Magyarization among the Jews in rural and agricultural northeastern Hungary (later Subcarpathian Ruthenia) was far from thorough, where the traditional Jewish population tended to speak Yiddish and the same Rusyn language as the local peasant population. Nor was Magyar language usage widespread in urban centers there, save for a minority of businessmen and professionals.[47] Jews in the territory of Slovakia experienced high levels of Magyarization at varying rates of accommodation, usually according to the Orthodox patterns noted above, for this Orthodox-majority Jewish population.[48]

As Hungarian Jews politically, culturally, and socially traveled the path of Magyarization, they experienced economic and social advancement and the rapid rise of a Hungarian Jewish middle class. Magyarization was the prerequisite for economic and social advancement or the pursuit of an administrative career in any field in post-Ausgleich Hungary. Hungarian Jews saw an occupational turnaround as they participated in this arrangement. Their livelihoods were no longer overwhelmingly bound to traditional occupations like trade, petty lending, and small business. In addition to industry and banking, in which some Hungarian Jews had experienced great success in the neo-absolutist 1850s, they also moved into newly accessible middle-class fields like the liberal professions of medicine, education, law, journalism, and the civil service.[49]

Jewish occupational advancement and relations with the surrounding society were deeply affected by Hungary's push for industrial development in its northern counties, the Slovak region. Nearly one-third of Hungary's manufacturing budget went to the area, where it had important tax tariff concessions. Jews engaged in the rapid expansion of the Budapest-oriented railway network.[50] They were active as well in the liquor distilling industry, either renting existing distilleries from the nobility or founding new ones. They led the sawmill and lumber industry, furniture and toy manufacturing, and also the construction industry, especially in brickworks and slate production. Jewish manufacturing concerns in the food industry included fruit and vegetable production and distribution, as well as cheese and sugar.[51] In addition, Jewish merchants were chiefly responsible for introducing traditional Slovak regional products like homespun cotton, embroidery, cheese, wines, and liquors to international markets.[52]

Jewish youth in the Slovak region had the feeling that "Magyarization gives you wings," while Slovak youth felt it "clipped" theirs.[53] The nationality policies of the Hungarian government in Budapest fueled terrible resentment among the non-Magyar, non-Jewish ethnic groups, who saw a "paradoxical situation" arise with Magyarization. Although Jews benefited economically, culturally, and socially from it, Magyarization suppressed the political and intellectual development of other peoples and heightened tensions between them and the Jewish population. It acted to raise their national consciousness. Magyarization gave national contours to entrenched medieval religious anti-Jewish sentiment combined with more recent economic and social antisemitism. The pervasive new stereotype of the Jew as "Magyarizer" joined the traditional image of the Jew as exploiter, usurer, and innkeeper. Slovak national agitators lamented Hungarian state policies that stunted Slovak political and intellectual development and robbed them of potential national elites.[54]

The influential British historian and political activist R. W. Seton-Watson brought the position of Slovaks, Romanians, and southern Slavs ("Yugoslavs") in Austria-Hungary to international attention, later encouraging the establishment of Czechoslovakia and Yugoslavia. In his lectures and writings he detailed Hungarian policies that were intended to assimilate the nonethnic Magyar population, largely through educational institutions. He surveyed the prohibition of Slovak language instruction in all secondary schools, universities, and religious seminaries, and even its steady removal from primary schools. The three Slovak-language gymnasia founded in the 1860s were dissolved in 1875 for allegedly fostering Pan-Slavism as the Hungarian government intensified its Magyarization policy. The Hungarian authorities shut down the Matica Slovenska (Slovak Cultural Association), the center of Slovak cultural activity, on the same charges. Slovak was excluded from the government administration, public offices, railways, and post offices. The Hungarian government sought to silence the Slovak-language press; it also prohibited Slovak assembly or association and prevented proportional Slovak representation in parliament.[55] No more than twenty Slovak representatives entered the Hungarian parliament between 1847 and 1910, and no Slovak delegation included more than seven.[56]

A number of Jews in northern Hungary expressed sympathy for the Slovak national movement and attempted to use their very limited influence to aid the Slovak national cause. Several Jews were among the founding members of the Matica Slovenska in 1863, and the two Jewish members of the Hungarian parliament, Moritz Wahrman and Eduard Horn, tried to prevent the closure of the three Slovak-language gymnasia in 1874.[57] However, their efforts came to naught in a system where one could not even use the Slovak language to buy a train ticket, letters with the addresses written in Slovak were not delivered, and fines were levied if a cart going to market bore the Slovak name of a village.[58]

At the same time Slovaks bitterly watched as Jewish representation in Hungarian business, finance, and the professions increased. Their belief that Jews served as exponents of a repressive Hungarian regime merged with long-standing religious and social prejudices to provide fertile ground for the growth of modern antisemitism in prewar Hungary. Nascent Slovak Catholic clerical politics were both anticapitalistic and anti-Jewish, drawing on a concept of the "Jewish Question" as it spread from Germany to east central Europe in the 1870s. Slovak publicists declared the need for "economic antisemitism" to help Slovaks emancipate themselves.[59] "We curse the Jews," wrote the journalist and Slovak national activist Fedor Houdek, "but we continue to support them: If you need something—you go buy it from the Jews; you need legal defense—you go to the Jewish lawyer; you need a doctor—you go to the Jew; the grocer needs goods—you go buy them from the Jewish supplier. . . . In this way we will never take even one step forward."[60] Slovak literature, folktales, and polemics painted the Jew as the "king of the inn," responsible for alcoholism in the villages, happily working as informers to the Hungarian authorities and as their proxies.[61] Nearly a week of widespread anti-Jewish riots broke out in Pressburg in connection with the Tisza-Eszlár blood libel affair in 1882, and again before the conclusion of the ensuing trial in 1883, related to other outbreaks throughout the country.[62]

A broad Hungarian Catholic opposition organized itself politically in a passionate struggle against the proposed and ultimately successful laws passed by the Hungarian parliament in 1895 on civil marriage and "reception" of Judaism as a religion equal with Christianity. The liberal laws extended full legal equality for Hungarian Jews, completing their 1867 emancipation. Headed by the country's lay Catholic magnates, the lower clergy, and the Catholic intelligentsia, the opposition responded by establishing the Magyar Katholikús Néppárt, or Hungarian Catholic People's Party, instituting political Catholicism in Hungary.[63]

Slovak Catholic priests split from the Hungarian Catholic People's Party in the early 1900s. Their Slovenská Ľudová Strana, or Slovak People's Party, officially came into being in November 1918, one month after the creation of Czechoslovakia from its prewar configuration as simply the People's Party. Led by Andrej Hlinka until his death in August 1938, the People's Party drew strong support among the peasants and the urban poor, civil servants, and members of the intelligentsia. It conducted anti-Jewish agitation based on well-known economic and political arguments, arguing that Jewish capital ruled over the Slovaks.[64] Economic arguments dominated the pre- and postwar anti-Semitic literature. Popular works by the Slovak writer and literary critic Svetozár Hurban-Vajanský in the 1880s and 1890s cultivated the concept of the Jew as rich exploiter. The People's Party circulated leaflets urging local peasants not to buy from the Jews, but to become shopkeepers themselves.[65]

With the establishment of Czechoslovakia, Slovak national leaders, the Slovak press, and the local population wanted to see evidence that times had changed. They wanted to see a significant reduction in Jewish economic influence in Slovakia. They also wanted proof that the Jewish population acknowledged the new postwar status quo, marked by Jews speaking Slovak—not Magyar—in schools, businesses, coffeehouses, in the synagogue, on the street, and among themselves. The new government administrators in Slovakia used their authority to curb "Jewish privilege," by which they especially meant liquor licenses, in the broader framework of "economic overrepresentation."[66] When accused of anti-Jewish bias in administering land reform in his district, the chief constable of Prievidza (Privigye) in western Slovakia replied, "There will only be balance if we suppress the Jews a little, so they wouldn't be higher than the Christian Slovaks. . . . They must suffer punishment for their sins."[67] The socioeconomic and politically grounded antisemitism tied to prewar Hungary's nationality policies and their legacies in the interwar Czechoslovak state would later transform into a new, more radical "Jewish Question" in the 1930s, bound up with a broadly popular Slovak autonomist movement and energized by the Nazi rise to power in Germany.

Czechoslovakia

Territorial separation from Hungary in the aftermath of the First World War brought with it the challenge of reorganizing Jewish communal space and networks for the greatest proportion of Czechoslovakia's Jewish population. It catalyzed a reconstitution of Jewish community infrastructure and demographics within the framework of dauntingly new and inverted state and social relations. Jews in Slovakia began to cautiously remap their belonging to the territory, gradually coming to understand their relation to it as "Slovak Jews." They would successfully adapt economically to the changed conditions, pursue politics loyal to the Czechoslovak state, and to a certain extent acquire the state language, but they would not and could not join the Slovak cultural nation.

Bratislava replaced Budapest as the seat of territory-wide institutions that were essential for administering the Slovak Jewish community. Košice (Kassa, Kaschau) became the second largest city in Slovakia and grew dramatically in importance as a regional center and immigration magnet.[68] The Jewish population of Košice expanded significantly, growing from 8,792 in 1921 to 11, 504 in 1930 (out of a total population of 70,117). This increase included the settlement of two important Hasidic rebbes and their courts in the city, which formed a de facto separate division within Košice's Orthodox community after 1918.[69] In 1921 the Jewish population in Slovakia stood at 135,819 (or 4.53 percent of the total). In absolute numbers this was more than 10,000 greater than in Bohemia (79,777, or 1.19 percent of the total), Moravia (37,989, or 1.43 percent), and Silesia (7,317, or 1.09 percent) combined. Only Subcarpathian Ruthenia, which like Slovakia had been part of prewar Hungary, had a more concentrated Jewish population. At 93,341, or 15.39 percent of the total, it more than three times outweighed Slovakia's Jewish population ratio to the surrounding inhabitants. Nevertheless, the number of Jews in Slovakia was 40,000 greater than in Subcarpathian Ruthenia, making it the most populous Jewish region of Czechoslovakia.[70]

According to the 1921 Czechoslovak census, a total of 354,342 Jews by religion lived in Czechoslovakia. Jews in Bohemia and Moravia were concentrated in the Czechoslovak capital city of Prague and Moravia's capital, Brno (Brünn), as well as in other larger cities and industrial and commercial centers. Few Jews lived in the countryside. This was a highly urbanized Jewish population, although Jews in Moravia and Silesia lived in smaller cities than Jews in Bohemia. Nearly 50 percent of Bohemian Jews lived in Prague (35,463), and more than 25 percent of Moravian Jews lived in Brno (11,003).[71] Jews in Bohemia and Moravia worked predominantly in the fields of business, finance, and communication (approximately 60 percent), while their second highest occupational representation lay in the fields of industry and crafts, at 22.6 and 28.5 percent, respectively. In these two western provinces of the state, marginally more than 14 percent of the Jewish working population was employed in public services and the professions.[72]

Jewish residency patterns in Slovakia were spread between cities, towns, and rural villages. The leading Czechoslovak demographer of his time, Antonín Boháč, wrote in his analysis of the 1921 census that the Jews in Slovakia formed a substantial national minority, at least four times as numerous as in the historic Czech lands. While close to 12 percent of Slovak Jews lived in the Slovak capital, Bratislava, they were also a significant presence in all the cities and towns in all regions of the territory.[73] Slovak Jewish occupational patterns were similar to those in Bohemia and Moravia, with the difference that Jewish visibility in the bourgeoisie and in the professions was conspicuously higher because of the patterns of economic modernization and nationalities policies in prewar Hungary discussed above. Despite the fact that the Jewish lower-middle and working classes were considerably larger in Slovakia and Subcarpathian Ruthenia than in Bohemia and Moravia, Jewish shopkeepers, businessmen, and industrialists stood out much more prominently in the popular local consciousness, since, unlike the Czech lands, these former Hungarian territories lacked a substantial native bourgeoisie. Jewish representation in the professions was indeed disproportionately high. As late as the end of the 1930s, 40 percent of the doctors in Slovakia were Jewish.[74]

Jews in Subcarpathian Ruthenia were mainly rural village and small-town Jews, predominantly Yiddish-speaking, and practiced either traditional Judaism or a Hasidic lifestyle in this mountainous borderland region, which was characterized by its ethnic and confessional heterogeneity and economic impoverishment.[75] Many Jews there settled in villages along or near the Latorytsia River valley, a principal immigration route for Jews coming from Galicia, where lay the Jewish-majority city Mukachevo (Mukacheve, Munkács, Muncaci, Mukaczewo, Mukačevo, Munkatsch), the only exception to the rural residency pattern.[76] Subcarpathian Ruthenia had the largest Jewish agricultural peasant population in Europe. Jews there also worked as day laborers, craftsmen, storekeepers, kosher butchers, and innkeepers. Jewish beggars, smugglers, yeshiva students, and other people engaged in *luftgescheften* ("living off the air") were a common presence in the villages and towns of Subcarpathian Ruthenia.[77]

The legacies of ethno-national politics in Austria-Hungary had a profound influence on shaping the circumstances under which Jews entered newly established Czechoslovakia. The persistent afterlife of Magyarization policy drew the most important distinction between conditions shaping Jews' potential for political and cultural integration into the state and surrounding society in Bohemia and Moravia in contrast to Slovakia—and to a lesser extent Subcarpathian Ruthenia. Their process of integration was by no means unproblematic or straightforward. The Czechoslovak government questioned the extent to which Jews would become loyal citizens of the state. This was especially true for Jews in Slovakia who had experienced high levels of Magyarization as citizens of the Kingdom of Hungary, although the issue also arose to a certain extent for German-speaking Jews in Bohemia and Moravia and even for Jewish nationalists.[78]

Although Jews of all stripes espoused full allegiance to the state as the common denominator of the Czechoslovak political culture they developed, and gradually felt a collective identification with it through the Czech and Slovak languages, the ease or difficulty of their integration varied dramatically by province.[79] Comparing their prospects across the state underscores the strikingly complex situation faced by the Jews in Slovakia. Integration is not a one-way street; its success depends on a set of civic and linguistic preconditions that open the door for reciprocity between two distinct groups. In the Jewish case, successful integration requires that the receiving group espouse broader civic values rather than exclusively defined national or religious ones. The language and culture of the receiving group also needs prestige and power to make its acquisition a desirable goal.[80]

For Jews in Bohemia and Moravia, these conditions were present and aided the relatively smooth integration of Jews into Czech society. Already by 1900 more than 54 percent of Bohemian and Prague Jews had declared Czech as their language of daily use on the census.[81] The historically strong Czech Jewish movement found satisfaction in the establishment of Czechoslovakia. Leaders of the movement encouraged Jews to further pursue their acculturation into the state's now dominant majority culture.[82] Jews who had previously declared German as their primary language on the census steadily opted for Czech instead, primarily because of the Czech government's sympathies for Zionism and their later opposition to Nazism in Germany. It is important here to remember, too, that at least before the Nazi rise to power in 1933, the Hungarian irredentist threat was more acute than the German one. The main fault line within the Jewish community lay between the Czech Jewish and Zionist nationality concepts.[83]

Kateřina Čapková explains the domestic and international, social and political reasons for the strength of reciprocity between the Czechs and Jews in the interwar republic. Above all, the low level of antisemitism in Bohemia and Moravia accounts for this circumstance: a result of an anticlerical attitude among the intelligentsia and general population; the presence of a strong native bourgeoisie and well-organized proletariat; economic prosperity; and the legacy of a more flexible and tolerant Austrian political tradition, unlike in Hungary, Russia, or Romania. After the wave of anti-Jewish violence in 1918 through 1919 that accompanied the change of regimes throughout the country had subsided, a period of relative calm followed in which integration could occur. Czech political ambitions were generally fulfilled with the peace treaties, and Czech leaders felt they could sit down to negotiations with the Jewish Council. This was also in the best interest of the Czechoslovak government with respect to the international community, which wanted to see evidence of the state's democratic behavior. The authority, position, and sterling international reputation of President Tomáš Garrigue Masaryk as a moderate Western-oriented nationalist was crucial for creating a Czechoslovak political culture that was supportive of Jewish national rights and unwelcoming for antisemitism. Czech society itself was quite secular among both the Christian and Jewish populations and experienced high levels of intermarriage.[84]

In Slovakia, by contrast, the civic and linguistic conditions necessary for Jewish cultural and political integration into the Slovak cultural nation were missing.[85] Magyarization policies carried out in the Kingdom of Hungary deformed relations between the Jews and the non-Magyar ethnic groups, with serious implications for the Jewish position in post–World War I successor states. The Slovak national movement viewed the Jews as a foreign element that was diametrically opposed to Slovak interests. That perceived opposition, it has been argued, was the single most important—and dangerous—factor in the failure of reciprocity between the two groups in the interwar years.[86]

The keys to the door of reciprocity between Jews in Slovakia and the Slovak cultural nation were missing. As it evolved from the mid-nineteenth century forward, the Slovak national movement was strongly tied to the Catholic Church and espoused exclusivist rather than broader civic values. Slovak society before the interwar period, through evident historical circumstance, did not have a non-clerical elite that could open the door for Jewish cultural integration. Furthermore, the Slovak language lacked prestige and power, reflecting the repression of Slovak national culture. Slovak language and culture simply had little appeal as avenues of acculturation. When Slovak became a state language with the creation of Czechoslovakia, Slovak national leaders and the Slovak press expressed the expectation that Jews in Slovakia would rapidly acculturate, and even assimilate, to the Slovak nation—just as they had earlier Magyarized and so aided the Magyars in achieving their national aspirations. A negligible Slovak Jewish assimilationist movement called Sväz Slovenských Židov (the Union of Slovak Jews) did indeed appear in the late 1920s led by the Bratislava physician Hugo Roth. Based on the success of the Czech Jewish example, Roth argued for raising Jewish children in Slovakia in the spirit of the Slovak nation, its language and culture.[87] The movement collapsed shortly after his resignation as head in May 1934 in an increasingly anti-Semitic environment.[88]

Even though Jews in Subcarpathian Ruthenia, like Jews in Slovakia, had experienced Magyarization as citizens of the prewar Kingdom of Hungary, the success of the policy was only partial. This predominantly rural, impoverished, traditional, and unassimilated Jewish population, argues Slovak Jewish historian Yeshayahu Jelínek, remained Yiddish-speaking and maintained a religious and pious lifestyle. They declared Hungarian as their mother tongue on the Hungarian census out of loyalty to the prewar state regardless of their actual linguistic proficiency or attachment to the language. The surrounding cultures, too, had little appeal for them.[89]

Once in Czechoslovakia, Jews in Subcarpathian Ruthenia wanted to keep to themselves and avoid the problems involved with associating with one nationality or another. They were well aware of the Czechoslovak administration's intense desire to steer the Jews in the formerly Hungarian areas of the state away from any connections with the Magyars, as well as of interwar Hungary's anti-Semitic orientation. They generally lacked interest in declaring themselves as Rusyns, who were far less nationally aware than the Slovaks, or as Czechs, due to lack of familiarity with that western Slavic language. Jews in Subcarpathian Ruthenia overwhelmingly were staunch enemies of Jewish nationalism but wholly identified as members of a separate Jewish nation, of the Jewish people.[90] The region became the site of educational experimentation in Czechoslovakia, where the Prague government set up schools that successfully competed with other Slovak-, Hungarian-, German-, Rusyn-, and even Hebrew-language institutions to bring Subcarpathian Ruthenia into the "Czech cultural orbit." Nevertheless, Jews there remained distant from nationality and national consciousness.[91]

Jewish Nationality

It is true that Jews in the territory of Slovakia fit the pattern of Jewish reciprocity with the prewar Magyar governing elite, a theme that dominates the scholarship on Hungarian and Habsburg Jewish history, and experienced high levels of Magyarization in the Kingdom of Hungary.[92] It is a recurring error, however, to regard the Jewish population throughout the entire prewar Hungarian state as a wholly "Magyarized," undifferentiated body. Jelínek lays the blame for misrepresenting Slovak Jews in this manner largely at the feet of Hungarian and Hungarian Jewish historians, who wanted "sometimes justly and sometimes by force" to see the Jews in Upper Hungary as "Magyars." Additionally, he faults Czech Jewish historians for promoting a thesis of a united "Czechoslovak Jewry," similar to the thesis of a united "Czechoslovak nation," and a united Hungarian Jewry. Only a handful of scholars have studied Jews in the territory of Slovakia on their own terms and within a separate historiography.[93] Jelínek argues throughout his body of work on Slovak Jewry that they constitute a separate ethnic group, which we may discern primarily through differentiating their behavior, customs, habits— in sum, their identities—from their coreligionists in Hungary's central plain.[94]

My work departs from this view in approaching the emergence of a separate Slovak Jewry as a phenomenon tied to conditions created by the movement from empire to nation-state. There was no "Slovak Jewry" until Slovakia itself became a defined, bounded territorial unit created from the former northern counties of prewar Hungary in the aftermath of the First World War. Slovak Jews came to define themselves geographically rather than nationally, as belonging to the territory of Slovakia within the liberal interwar Czechoslovak state and the specific set of opportunities and challenges that reality presented. Building a "Slovak Jewry" was part of the gradual, often arduous process of shifting political loyalties from Hungary to Czechoslovakia.

This social history explores how Jews in Slovakia sought the "right path" in interwar Czechoslovakia and how the Czechoslovak administration and surrounding society understood the range of their efforts from the beginning to the end of the state. The story builds from the ground up, focusing on the interaction of government officials, demographers, police investigators, and the surrounding society with the local Jewish population rather than on elites and intellectuals. It draws on extensive, previously unexamined archival research conducted in Hungarian, Slovak, Czech, and German in Hungary, Slovakia, the Czech Republic, and New York, using the concept of loyalty to investigate fundamental problems of nationality bridging east central European and modern Jewish history.

It does so through "Jewish nationality," a new category of political nationhood created after the First World War based on minority rights protections and a broad range of late nineteenth-century Jewish national movements. The recognition of "Jewish" as a state-recognized nationality classification, where previously it had been officially considered solely a religious matter, illustrates the profound transformation in the meaning and function of nationality overall as it became a state-building tool. Focusing on the little studied yet crucial contested territory of Slovakia, formerly the northern counties of the prewar Kingdom of Hungary, I argue that the Czechoslovak administration made Jewish nationality central to its unique reconceptualization of nationality as an internal conviction in the effort to resolve its nationality questions. Its key tools in the struggle were the basic building blocks of the state: the census and the police. Czechoslovakia stood at the forefront of the change in national dynamics in interwar east central Europe in its voluntary support for Jewish nationality and Jewish national minority rights. This accorded with the national minority status granted to the Jews at the Paris Peace Conference in 1919, an international response to the need for minority protections brought starkly into relief by the massive displacement of peoples during the First World War.

Jewish nationalism emerged in the late nineteenth century in response to anti-Jewish violence and impoverishment in eastern Europe and Russia and to the problem of mainstream modern antisemitism and assimilation in central and Western Europe. Jewish nationalists were inspired by other regional national movements and driven to action by the antisemitism they frequently espoused. Nationalism, Ezra Mendelsohn argues, allowed Jews to be both Jewish and modern with honor and dignity and to seek to win the respect of their neighbors.[95] The Lovers of Zion movement took shape in reaction to the pogroms of 1881–1882 in Russia, organized with the goal of mass emigration to Palestine from Russia and Romania. Leon Pinsker, head of the Lovers of Zion, became well known for creating a theoretical framework for Jewish nationalism with the publication of his German-language manifesto *Autoemanzipation* (*Self-Emancipation*) in 1882. In it he argued that Jewish integration was impossible and undesirable because of antisemitism, an ideology he defined as an incurable psychosis brought on by the abnormal condition of Jewish life in the Diaspora. The only way for the Jews to improve their lot was to seek territorial sovereignty, thus liberating themselves.[96] Concurrently, in Austria students at the University of Vienna organized the Jewish nationalist dueling fraternity Kadimah, outraged by growing antisemitism in the German nationalist fraternities. Their Jewish compatriots in Galicia and Bukovina established Zionist groups similar to the Lovers of Zion.[97] Theodor Herzl ushered the "Jewish Question" onto the world stage with his call for the creation of a Jewish state in 1896, transforming Zionism into a mass movement and political force. Zionism attracted Jews from disparate backgrounds: from modern middle-class Jews forced to "dissimilate" in an increasingly anti-Semitic environment to traditional Jews excited by the prospect of taking the return to the ancient Jewish homeland into their own hands.[98]

In Austria-Hungary, Zionism was strongest in Galicia and Bukovina, with numbers of adherents in Vienna, Bohemia, and Moravia, though very few in Hungary. A distinctive cultural and spiritual form of Zionism blossomed in Prague that was deeply devoted to ethics and humanism, the study of Hebrew language and the Bible, and Jewish history and literature. Members of the Prague "Bar Kochba" Zionist organization in the early twentieth century mostly came from family backgrounds oriented toward German culture. They dedicated themselves to Jewish spiritual and cultural renewal centered on a Jewish national identity, influenced by the cultural Zionists Ahad Ha'am and Martin Buber, and the Czech and German nationalist movements. They felt they were doing *Avodat Am,* the work of the nation, to bring about a Jewish spiritual revival. Prague Zionism became an important "third way" for Jews in Bohemia and Moravia to negotiate the treacherous environment of the Czech-German national conflict.[99]

In contrast, the leading Hungarian Jewish newspaper denounced Zionism as "treason," in reaction to the First Zionist Congress in 1897.[100] Most Jews in Hungary did not even have contact with international Jewish organizations until 1918, when the Central Hungarian Jewish Association appealed to Jews in the Entente countries to save Hungary from imminent territorial loss.[101] They believed that Magyarization, the key element of their "assimilationist social contract,"[102] was the only effective way to stanch and eliminate antisemitism in Hungary. For this reason, modern political Zionism had no notable following in Hungary before the First World War. Hungarian Jewry showed virtually no interest in a movement that would force them to recognize themselves as part of a Jewish nation rather than the Hungarian nation.[103]

Yet this is not the whole story of prewar Zionism in Hungary. Pressburg, close to Vienna and in step with political developments there, was the center of Hungary's small Zionist movement at the turn of the twentieth century. In the 1880s the Lovers of Zion had a small number of followers in Pressburg and in other northwestern Hungarian towns close to Vienna. Seven Hungarian delegates indeed attended the First Zionist Congress in Basel in 1897, including the Pressburg journalist Sámuel (Samu) Bettelheim, the son of an important Orthodox family, and the Transylvanian lawyer József Ronai. Both later organized the establishment of a Hungarian Zionist League in Pressburg in 1902.[104]

In a significant move highlighting the connection of language usage with national orientation, Bettelheim and Ronai switched from Magyar to German with their entry into Jewish national politics. When Bettelheim founded a Hungary-wide Zionist newspaper in Budapest in 1908, he called it—in German—the *Ungarländische jüdische Zeitung.* This linguistic switch, William O. McCagg argues, shows that Zionists seemed to recognize "that their constituency stopped where Magyarization began."[105] The German-language Mizrachi, or Orthodox Zionist organization, was the only branch of the movement to gain an active following and enjoy consistent support. The First Mizrachi Congress also took place in Pressburg, despite the fierce opposition of 121 traditional Hungarian rabbis, who found Orthodox Jewish adoption of the Zionist program in any form unthinkable.[106]

After the war, Magyarization stopped in Czechoslovakia, where German language usage began. The Slovak Jewish press was chiefly a German-language press, and rabbis often gave their sermons in German. Slovak Jewish public life took place in German as Jews gradually made steps toward Slovak language acquisition. In Slovakia, unlike in Bohemia or Moravia, German language usage among Jews was viewed not with suspicion, but as an effort to create distance from Magyarization and the interwar Hungarian irredentist threat. It was still not the best solution in the eyes of the state and surrounding society, which preferred the use of Slovak, the state language, but it was deeply symbolic. It connected the Jews to their pre-Magyarization past, peeling back a layer of secondary acculturation. It also brought Jews closer to Vienna, closer to Orthodox Judaism, closer to Prague (ironically), closer to the international Jewish community, and closer to Jewish nationality.

The movement for Jewish national recognition and national rights dramatically expanded after the Russian Revolution.[107] Lenin's recognition of the Jews as a nationality with distinct cultural and political rights within the newly formed Soviet Union stimulated Zionist efforts throughout east central Europe to achieve the same.[108] Great Britain's issuance of the Balfour Declaration on November 2 of the same year, a carefully worded document supporting "the establishment of a national home in Palestine for the Jewish people," worked to similar effect.[109] In Austria the Zionist conference of July 1917 pushed for the recognition of a Jewish nationality by the Austrian government.[110] In mid-October 1918, in the midst of the collapse of Austria-Hungary, Zionists pressed for the recognition of Jewish nationality and full nationality rights in the proposed federation of national states. Aware that Austria-Hungary was not going to survive to transform into such a federation, however, Jewish political factions formed Jewish National Councils in the newly forming successor states, following the example of other ethno-national groups.

When Austria-Hungary collapsed in October 1918, the Bohemian Zionist organization mobilized to defend Jewish interests in the new Czechoslovak state. The writer, critic, and Bohemian Zionist Max Brod reported to the General Secretariat of the World Zionist Organization in Copenhagen that "the Jewish National Council for the State of Bohemia has just been created."[111] From the start, Jewish national politics in Czechoslovakia were dominated by Bohemian Zionists, mirroring Prague's central position in the broader Czechoslovak political setting.[112] The Jewish National Council established in Prague under the leadership of Karl Fischel, Max Brod, and Czech-speaking Ludvík Singer, representing the Jewish population of emerging Czechoslovakia, requested national minority rights for Jews in the new state.[113]

Marsha Rozenblit argues that of all the Jews of former Austria-Hungary who now needed to construct a new national identity in Czechoslovakia, the Bohemian and Moravian Zionists had the easiest path. Because they were dedicated to the concept of the Jews as a nation within the newly forming multinational state, it seemed obvious and natural to them that the Jews were one of Czechoslovakia's constituent nations. They would simply transfer their old tripartite identity from the monarchy over to Czechoslovakia, she writes, becoming "Czechoslovak politically, German or Czech culturally, and members of the Jewish nation."[114] In addition, they could almost taste the success of their endeavor to win Jewish national rights from the favorably inclined Czechoslovak government. They eagerly awaited drawing Slovakia's large Jewish population to Zionism.[115]

The Bohemian Zionist–led Jewish National Council was savvy. Appearing before the Czech National Council just hours before the proclamation of the Czechoslovak Republic, they presented their smartly constructed argument for recognition of Jewish nationality and Jewish national minority rights in Czechoslovakia in a manner that resonated with their audience. They framed the argument in terms of how the Jews, denied national rights in Austria and Hungary, had been used and exploited as "tools for oppressing the small nationalities." With the recognition of Jewish national rights in Czechoslovakia, not only would such exploitation cease, but also if Jews across the state would declare a "Jewish nationality" rather than German or Hungarian, the statistical weight of the Germans and Hungarians in the state would decrease.[116] The Czech National Council affirmed the demands of the Jewish National Council for the "complete equality of the Jews, [and] national minority rights for the Jewish nation" shortly after the proclamation of the existence of the state from the capital in Prague on October 28, 1918.[117]

Czechoslovakia used Jewish nationality on its finely tuned census to foster relocation of individual Jewish loyalties from defeated Hungary to newly established Czechoslovakia. At the same time the state carried out investigations of Slovak Jews' loyalty based on language usage, communal conflicts, and how they remembered their war dead. Fearing Hungarian irredentist activity, the Czechoslovak state wished to verify that Slovak Jews had indeed severed ties with Hungary and Hungarian Jewry and had renounced their alignment with the Magyar nation. This study traces the ascendancy of national security issues over domestic sociocultural conflict in terms of how the state saw and understood minority loyalty. It shows how loyalty can be used to locate the active meaning and function of nationality and its implications for minority citizenship, especially in relation to minority religious groups, and offers us a deeper understanding of transformations in nationhood and nationality in east central European history.

Political Compass

Vavro Šrobár, minister plenipotentiary for Slovakia, in line with the Czechoslovak administrative position, promoted Jewish nationality as a way for Jews in Slovakia to both demonstrate their transfer of political loyalty and protect their minority rights. Addressing a visiting delegation of Jews from Nitra (Nyitra), Hlohovec (Galgóc), and Piešt'any (Pöstyén), Šrobár declared: "Having been exponents of Magyarization, the Jews would forfeit their reputation for political reliability if they were now to declare themselves as Slovaks. On the other hand, I cannot accept them as Magyars. However, if they were to adopt Jewish nationality, as [their coreligionists] have done in Bohemia and Moravia, we would be ready to grant them full cultural and [linguistic] minority rights."[118] President Masaryk himself admonished the Jews in Slovakia to "return to the worldview of [their] forefathers, be Jews, and abandon [their] role as exponents of the Magyars."[119] Jewish nationality became a compass for Jews in Slovakia to chart the treacherous course ahead.

1 From Hungary to Czechoslovakia

Jewish Transition to the Consolidating
Czechoslovak State

LOCAL RESIDENTS IN the northwestern town of Považská Bystrica, a short distance from Slovakia's provisional capital in Žilina, forced their way into David Büchler's general store.[1] By the time they dispersed, every item in the store was destroyed. All the furniture, the cash register, and display cases lay ruined. The building itself sustained heavy damage. They also broke into his home and made off with bedding, linens, rugs, furnishings, and other belongings. Büchler's store and residence were attacked on November 5, 1918, during the "November Pillages" that accompanied Slovakia's chaotic integration into the newly established Czechoslovak state after the First World War. Hardly a Jewish community in Slovakia was spared.[2]

Eighty years later the youngest member of the Turzikov family, then nine-year-old Pal'ko, still remembered the crash of shattering glass outside as two neighborhood men appeared in their kitchen looking for the innkeeper Arnold Eisler's wife, hidden in the adjoining room. "Nobody's here! Go away!" shouted his grandmother. "Why did you come? We are poor, we don't have men [chlapov]." She shamed them into leaving.[3] Emboldened young men roamed from town to town looking for Jewish shops and inns to "visit."[4] Soldiers celebrated their joy at returning alive from the front by looting Jewish stores—there were no others around, a local history reminds us—and hunting for alcohol. They accused the Jews of bribing their way out of military service in order to remain working as "clever shopkeepers," getting rich on the war economy while Slovaks bled on the battlefield and starved at home.[5]

The Jewish People's Union (JPU) took David Büchler's case to the Czechoslovak administration in Bratislava to request state compensation for his losses.[6] Emil Waldstein, president of the JPU, signed the petition. The damages to Büchler's shop came to a steep 300,000 crowns (US$8,880 in 1920). Büchler was unable to either repair the damages or restock his store for five months after the attack. In spite of this the taxes the new state required on his 1918 profits were twice what he had paid in 1917.[7] The JPU found the tax demand unreasonable and tainted by anti-Jewish bias. The local police chief confirmed the details of the Büchler case on the blank reverse side of a printed Hungarian-language police report form of the kind used in old Hungary. Looting had been so prevalent in November 1918 that it was impossible to pursue the matter on behalf of just one individual, the chief wrote. The National Assembly in Prague had granted amnesty to everyone guilty of plunder during the *Prevrat,* or change of regimes, for this reason. The Slovak people's bias "against everything Jewish" was well known, he added. "David Büchler was robbed like all of the Jews during the *Prevrat,* and so this [grievance] is completely without foundation as a complaint of official discrimination," wrote the county administrator (*župan*) in his assessment of the case.[8] "He cannot be trusted to sell sugar and flour, etc.; furthermore there were even complaints that he abused the authorities' trust during the old regime." The county administrator dismissed the case.[9]

While Czechoslovakia would soon prove to be the most hospitable environment for the Jews of its interwar east central European neighbors, entry into the new state was bitter. Anti-Jewish violence erupted with the regime change across Czechoslovakia. In Prague civilians and demobilizing soldiers together rioted in the streets in early December 1918, attacking Jews and Jewish property.[10] Yet anti-Jewish excesses were especially prevalent in Slovakia because of higher levels of antisemitism there and the widespread desire for revenge against all those who were seen as representatives and proxies of the hated Hungarian regime.

For Jews in Slovakia, reorientation into Czechoslovakia began abruptly with self-defense activity and economic adaptation to the radically transformed geopolitical environment. Immediate Jewish concerns were local. How should they defend themselves against the widespread postwar violence and compensate for damages? How would they best look after their interests, well-being, and communities in a region redefined as the Slovak national space? How would they protect their newly granted rights as Czechoslovak citizens? What would their relationship to the state as a whole be like? The answers to these questions developed from their Jewish religious affiliations and the political leanings those affiliations influenced, their experiences in Hungary and with the surrounding Slovak population, and their expectations of the Czechoslovak administration in Slovakia and in Prague. The first step in their long and often arduous process of reorientation involved creating strategies for postwar protection of their economic, political, and social interests. That process also included the development of Jewish national political practices as well as institution building and territorial reorganization.

At the same time Czechoslovakia was still a nation-state in formation. Successful Czechoslovak state building required incorporating the territory and peoples of Slovakia. This was to be accomplished not by gradually building popular consensus, but through military engagement and diplomatic maneuvering.[11] Drawing the borders in this way would have significant implications for Czechoslovakia's domestic and international nationalities problems. Prague needed the Slovaks, a "state forming nation,"[12] or there would be no independent Czechoslovakia. Without the Slovaks, the Czechs could not form a majority and legitimately create a viable state. The Slovaks likewise needed the Czechs to help them leave Hungary, to help them establish a functioning civil and governmental infrastructure in Slovakia, and to create an educational system for producing Slovak national elites who were ready to take control of that developing infrastructure. The help the Slovaks desired was temporary.[13]

The central Prague government also needed the Jews. Good relations with the Jewish population would help secure the reputation of the new state in the eyes of the international community and supportive international Jewish organizations. Prague sought to positively distinguish the new Czechoslovak state from the old monarchy. Implementing Jewish national rights and securing Jewish well-being tested the state's burgeoning democracy; these rights were themselves part of the state-building process. The wartime plight of Eastern European Jewish refugees had drawn international attention to the need for minority protections. In the aftermath of the war, the new question was how Jewish individual and communal rights would be protected in the new east central European state system.[14] Czechoslovakia was considered the linchpin of that system. The country would attempt to use its handling of the postwar Jewish refugee issue to balance out the damaging anti-Jewish violence of the change of regimes.

The Czechoslovak administration's postwar Jewish refugee management highlights the state's turn from wartime concerns such as public health, scarce resource allocation, and chaos control to state-building concerns like state security and consolidation, currying favor with the international community, population legibility, and fixing the population within the state's borders. State building is a chaotic process. This chapter examines social relations in Slovakia in the immediate aftermath of the war against the backdrop of Slovakia's incorporation into Czechoslovakia. Prague's aim was to bind Slovak and Jewish loyalty to the state while mitigating German and Hungarian resistance to it. To do so, it needed to show both groups that times had changed and that their situation would improve in Czechoslovakia. It was a task beset with complications.

Prevrat

"We have learned to our sad surprise that anti-Jewish riots are occurring even in the new Czechoslovak state," Chaim Weizmann said in a telegram to the first prime minister of Czechoslovakia, Karel Kramář, on December 1, 1918.[15] Weizmann was then president of the World Zionist Organization (wzo), based in Copenhagen, Denmark. Anti-Jewish activity was characteristic of the period immediately after the war across east central Europe, especially in Ukraine, Poland, and Hungary. In contrast to events elsewhere, however, the anti-Jewish activity in Czechoslovakia mainly consisted of looting and attacks on property rather than brutality resulting in scores of fatalities.[16] The American Jewish Joint Distribution Committee (AJDC) estimated the material loss caused by the anti-Jewish outbreaks in Slovakia in November 1918, the worst period of the violence, to be 150 million Czechoslovak crowns (nearly US$4.5 million in 1920).[17] In Bohemia and Moravia it "was not safe for a Jew to be seen in the streets," the AJDC reported. Mobs beat and robbed Jews who had been driven out of cafes and restaurants.[18]

The violence ran counter to President Tomáš Garrigue Masaryk's reputation as a moderate Western-oriented nationalist who opposed antisemitism and supported Jewish national rights. Masaryk had put his university career on the line in 1900 when he took a stand against antisemitism by denouncing the blood libel charges against the Jew Leopold Hilsner and by refusing to alter his position.[19] In exile in England and the United States for most of the war, Masaryk had gained considerable support for the Czechoslovak national state-building project from important figures in the Jewish community, including Bohemian Jews. He later acknowledged Western Jewry's decisive backing of his national work during the war. The Zionist Organization of America congratulated him in September 1918 after President Woodrow Wilson assured him in conversation that the "Czechoslovak nation" would enjoy independence after the war. Masaryk then sent a telegram to the Bohemian Zionist leader Max Brod, with whom he had met at the beginning of the war, guaranteeing that the new Czechoslovak state would respect Jewish rights.[20] The seriousness of the postwar disturbances in Czechoslovakia threatened to upend the important support of international Jewish organizations for the new state.

The WZO office followed developments surrounding the Prevrat in Czechoslovakia carefully, concerned about reports of widespread anti-Jewish disturbances and rhetoric. Although Bohemia and Moravia saw their share of looting and rioting,[21] Slovakia experienced the greatest concentration of serious anti-Jewish activity. The "revolutionary mood" there found more emphatic expression in the chaotic atmosphere produced by the postwar conflict with Hungary. The Hungarian Red Army, under the leadership of Béla Kun during the short-lived Hungarian communist regime, invaded the Slovak territory held by the Czechoslovak regime in spring 1919 in an attempt to reclaim it. The Czechoslovak government called on the aid of the Entente powers to help them, which in the end successfully secured Slovakia.[22] In this atmosphere locals demolished Jewish homes, looted Jewish shops and inns, and stole grain and other food supplies, believing the Jews to have worked as Magyar spies and agitators during the Kun-led invasion.[23]

Two stages to the anti-Jewish disturbances in the aftermath of the war may be distinguished. In the first, soldiers robbed stores and inns as they returned from the front; in the second ideological phase, they joined local Slovaks in seeking revenge against the former Hungarian regime. Soldiers stole in order to feed themselves as they made their way back home on foot after long years in battle or in captivity. They robbed inns and pubs to celebrate their freedom. Once home the soldiers learned how the local population had suffered during the war. They then joined in a brutal campaign of revenge against Hungarian state power and its representatives, often expressed in violence against the Jewish population. "Drunken soldiers vented their rage against people who had remained at home, and their businesses," Yeshayahu Jelínek writes, "because part of those businesses and inns were in Jewish hands, and [because] in Upper Hungary political and social outbursts regularly rained down on Jewish backs, now too the hunger, frustration, and embitterment [of the war] very quickly merged with judeophobia."[24] Armed Slovak soldiers joined in spontaneous uprisings, lashing out against state administrators, notaries, and policemen. They attacked the shopkeepers, innkeepers, and the propertied, all of whom they saw as representatives of the hated war and repressive Hungarian state system.[25] The majority of shopkeepers and innkeepers in many regions of Slovakia were Jewish, while Magyars formed a considerable percentage of the above-mentioned state administrators, notaries, and policemen.[26] When Czechoslovak troops were deployed to defend the Jews, they, too, occasionally took part in the anti-Jewish excesses.[27] In response the Jews in former Upper Hungary armed themselves for the first time in 1918. Like other demobilizing soldiers, they had also returned home carrying their weapons. They formed self-defense units to patrol the Jewish quarters of town and other areas where Jews lived and worked. Demobilizing Jewish soldiers and freed Jewish prisoners of war formed self-defense units wherever possible.[28]

Weizmann's December telegram to Kramář reminded the prime minister that the protection of the Jewish population, "the Jewish nationality group," in Czechoslovakia was essential for continued international Jewish support of the state. "[We are] putting our trust in the message sent by your leader Masaryk to the Zionist Organization of America and in the principles of the freedom of the nations on which the Czechoslovak Republic has been founded," Weizmann wrote. "We and the entire Jewish people are convinced that the government of the State of Czechoslovakia will do everything in its power to ensure the safety of the Jewish nationality group in Czechoslovakia and to assure for it those rights which were requested in the memorandum addressed by the Jewish National Council in Prague to the Národní výbor [National Committee]."[29]

Weizmann again expressed his dismay to Kramář in July 1919, concerned with the significant rise in anti-Jewish activity and press agitation during the summer. Slovaks and Jews were compared to fire and water in a leading Slovak paper, *Slovensko,* which deemed them unable to exist together. One of the two must yield, the paper insisted. The "Czecho-Slovaks" would remain and the Jews would depart. The theme of Jewish departure from the territory of Slovakia appeared frequently in the Slovak press. Another widely circulating paper called for a general boycott of the Jews in trade and industry. Weizmann reminded the minister plenipotentiary of the Republic of Czechoslovakia in London, Dr. Ferdinand Veverka, of the great sympathy shown by worldwide Jewish opinion for Czechoslovakia. He urged the Czechoslovak government to take a strong stand against the current anti-Semitic agitation.[30]

From London, Veverka sent Weizmann's request for an explanation of the violence on to the minister plenipotentiary of Slovakia, Vavro Šrobár. Veverka wrote Weizmann that Šrobár was best qualified to discuss the matter because of his insights into Slovak public opinion based on his forty years' experience as a countryside physician. In his reply Šrobár highlighted the reciprocal prewar relationship between the Hungarian government and the Jews in Slovakia to account for the anti-Jewish excesses that accompanied the Prevrat. Czechoslovak officials were to be commended rather than reproached for their actions, Šrobár informed Weizmann bluntly, since the new regime risked grave unpopularity among the Slovaks "for protecting those who were the cause of such deep grievances." Šrobár went on to say:

> Besides the Magyar nobility and Magyar officials, I am, to my regret, bound to say that it was the Jewish estate-owners and innkeepers who for whole decades did the most serious harm to the Slovak people. . . . The Magyar government was astute enough to make a tool of the Jews in Slovakia to carry out their violent policy of Magyarization, and only too often they found them devoted helpers, informers, agents-provocateurs, spies and agitators against the Entente. . . . During the war this hostile activity towards the Slovak people became more violent. As a result of information lodged by Jews, persons were imprisoned and executed. In return for all this they were rewarded by the Government with various concessions and privileges, to the detriment of the Slovak people. When the revolution occurred, and the Czechoslovak nation threw off the tyrant's yoke, it was the Jews who worked as Magyar agitators against our Republic. During the Bolshevist invasion of June 1919, it was again the Slovak Jews who proved themselves an element hostile to the people and Republic, who led Bolshevist troops, showed them the way, and denounced the loyal Slovaks, so that these were then shot or tortured by the Bolshevists.
>
> The Czechoslovak Government, having espoused the principle of absolute equality and liberty for its subjects, had to exert its whole influence, even at the cost of its own popularity, to prevent the people who had suffered so much injustice from avenging themselves on those who formed a quite essential fac-

tor in the system opposed to them. And it is to the credit of our Republic that, with the exception of a few unimportant cases, which were immediately suppressed by the government at the outset, justice was here dealt out by a legal course. . . . It [would] therefore be a noble task for Jewish organizations to exert a beneficial influence upon those of their coreligionists in the villages of Slovakia who have acted against their own interests.[31]

In his letter to Weizmann, Šrobár defined the Jews in Slovakia as an element entirely at odds with the needs and well-being of the Slovak people. He explained that they had been willing accomplices to Slovak oppression through Magyarization. Now the Jews themselves were expected to take the opportunity to change course. Šrobár placed responsibility with the Jewish communal leadership to enact that change. His remarks indicate a willingness and desire to improve Slovak-Jewish relations within the new circumstances. Šrobár opened the door for greater Slovak-Jewish reciprocity in his correspondence with Weizmann by strategically placing the blame above all on the Hungarians for instigating a collaborative relationship with the Jews in Slovakia. Tensions between Slovaks and Jews had deep social and political roots, which he himself knew well; he even described himself as a "life-long antisemite" in his memoirs.[32]

Unrest and anarchy were characteristic of the prevailing atmosphere in many regions of the collapsing Austro-Hungarian Monarchy in fall 1918. In Slovakia that instability was part of the larger struggle for the future of the newly bounded territory. Unlike other regions of former Hungary being incorporated in the new or transformed successor states, like Croatia (Yugoslavia) or Transylvania (Romania), Slovakia had never been administratively defined on its own, but solely recognized as an area of sixteen counties and four municipalities of northern Hungary. By the end of the war the collapse of the old order without replacement by the new left Slovakia in chaotic condition. Amid the upheaval, looting, and anti-Jewish excesses that typified the period, local national councils formed with the goal of consolidating the new state. But they were too weak to decisively resist regional Hungarian opposition and Budapest's efforts to maintain the territory.[33] While Czechoslovakia's birth was announced in Prague on October 28, 1918, the view from Slovakia was far less definitive. It was not a foregone conclusion that Slovakia would indeed be incorporated into the new state. Slovakia was in a precarious position, loosed from defeated Hungary but not yet officially joined with Bohemia and Moravia.

Slovak historians characterize the unstable Prevrat era as the "Struggle for Slovakia," a view that highlights Slovakia's contested status between the Magyars and the Czechs. Save for a handful of Slovak national leaders, the Slovaks themselves moved through this picture as a frustrated underclass, taking advantage of the volatile, chaotic climate to set upon state administrators, notaries, policemen, shopkeepers, innkeepers, and the propertied. Slovaks found themselves in a moment of great release that offered them a chance to vent their anger and frustration at the war and the Hungarian system. The newly formed local national councils sought to mitigate these widespread outbreaks of violence, yet they had little control or ability to quell Hungarian resistance to the power transfer, which was further impeded by the local power structure of the old state that was still in place. A Hungarian demand for a referendum on the changes surfaced, relying on the fragmentation of the population along regional and social lines, degrees of national consciousness, and lack of information about the political transformation. It was the first time Budapest asked Slovaks for their opinions. The views of ordinary people "varied from enthusiastic welcoming of the new state and the 'liberation' of Slovakia, through apathy and desire for peace, to fear of a new unknown situation, of uncertain permanence and threatening new bloodshed and military solutions."[34]

The Hungarian National Council in Budapest came into being on October 25, 1918, somewhat later than those of the national minorities, and was established by Count Mihály Károlyi, who was widely believed to be the emperor-king's obvious choice for the new prime minister. Oszkár Jászi, the progressive Hungarian social scientist, historian, and politician, wrote up the Hungarian National Council's twelve-point program. It called for Hungarian independence, an immediate and separate peace treaty, universal suffrage with secret ballots, land reform, and recognition of the rights of the national minorities within a federalized Hungary.[35] When the emperor-king appointed Count János Hadik instead, massive antigovernment demonstrations broke out, demanding the appearance of Károlyi.[36] The demonstrations took place on October 28, the same day as the declaration of the new Czechoslovak Republic in Prague. By the night of October 30 crowds of soldiers and civilians demonstrated in the streets. They later occupied public buildings, prevented troops who were loyal to Károlyi from moving out of the city, captured Budapest's military governor, and freed political prisoners as they had done in 1848. Soldiers tore off the emblems on their uniforms and replaced them with asters and rosettes. When Emperor-King Charles retreated, Károlyi formed a new independent Hungarian government. Vanquished Hungary appeared to be on the path to democratization.[37]

Shortly after these events, Slovak national leaders, mostly from central Slovakia, converged in Turčiansky Svätý Martin, the seat of the Slovak national movement, and established the Slovak National Council. Although they had little news of what was happening in Prague, Budapest, or Europe more broadly, they wanted to take a stand on the dramatically unfolding events. The Slovak politician Milan Hodža was still in Budapest in negotiations. He arrived on October 31, one day after the council issued the Martin Declaration announcing the secession of the Slovak territory from Hungary, Slovak self-determination, and its desire for inclusion in the Czechoslovak state, which fulfilled Prague's wishes.[38]

The Slovak National Council did not have military power, so it could neither enforce its program nor maintain order. Individual militias sprung up in towns across Slovakia, engaging in a power struggle with the freshly formed Hungarian National Councils. It was a highly unstable environment. Demobilizing Slovak soldiers formed the mainstay of active Slovak participation in the evolving power struggle. They created paramilitary groups in the forests, especially in western Slovakia, with about four thousand soldiers active around Bratislava. To dispel the threat of anarchy and establish control over the territory, the Czechoslovak National Council brought Slovak representatives into the newly formed National Assembly in Prague in early November 1918.[39]

The Czechoslovak government in Prague set up Slovakia's first provisional "Slovak government" in western Slovakia near the Moravia-Slovak border and began to function on November 6 led by Vavro Šrobár, minister plenipotentiary of Slovakia. On December 12 it was replaced by a Ministry for Slovakia, which Šrobár established in Žilina in the midst of a combined Czech, French, and Italian effort to drive Hungarian troops out of Slovak territory.[40] Less than two weeks later, on December 21, Czechoslovak foreign minister Beneš successfully negotiated French recognition of a demarcation line of the Slovak territory.[41] Entente forces would drive Hungarian troops past the demarcation line on January 20, 1919. That line more or less became the country's official border with the signing of the Treaty of Trianon in 1920.[42] When Šrobár's administration grew too large for Žilina, he deliberated with Samuel Zoch, a clergyman from Modra near Pressburg, who was the principal author of the Martin Declaration of October 30, 1918, on where Slovakia's central government should be moved. They decided in early January 1919 to move it to Pressburg on February 4. Zoch was placed in charge of the Pressburg district administration and orchestrated the Czechoslovak takeover of the city from January 1, 1919. "Bratislava" became the city's standard official name in March 1919.[43]

Hungary would make one more sustained military effort toward maintaining its prewar borders. Under Béla Kun's short-lived Hungarian Soviet Republic, lasting for 133 days beginning March 21, 1919, the Hungarian Red Army made significant inroads into Slovakia. It was driven out only after receiving an ultimatum by the Entente powers at the end of June 1919. The army fully retreated from Slovakia on June 30, 1919, and by July 24 the Czechoslovak government held the entire territory.[44]

On the Czechoslovak state level, the struggle for Slovakia entailed not only the physical, geographic aspect of territorial incorporation but also the more slippery aspect of drawing the multinational population of Slovakia into the mental landscape of the new state. Coming to terms with the World War I Czech argument that the Czechs and Slovaks were two branches of the same Czechoslovak nation and thus together should form the dominant national group within the

Czechoslovak nation-state required a shift in direction. The events of the Prevrat underscore the tense relations between, first and foremost, Hungarians and Slovaks, and Jews and Slovaks, but also, increasingly, between Czechs and Slovaks. These relationships would influence shifts in overall understandings of nationhood and nationality as well as national political programs within the new state.

Jewish Brothers!

In late July 1919 the JPU distributed a manifesto among the Jews in Slovakia, imploring them to join together and face the new Czechoslovak state as a unified Jewish national minority. The JPU included a report on its audience with President Masaryk the month before. That meeting had been intended to alert him to further anti-Jewish activity in Slovakia during the Hungarian Red Army's invasion and occupation of a significant area of Slovakia in the spring. The JPU stamped the union's letterhead with the sage Rabbi Hillel's searching question, "If I am not for myself, who will be for me?" and sent a copy to the American Jewish Committee in New York. "Jewish Brothers!" they cried, "It is the twelfth hour."[45]

> The disastrous consequences of the war and the revolutionary upheavals that accompanied its end have affected no stratum of the population so brutally and so contrary to all humanity as the Jews. A decade-long systematic agitation of the people, playing on the raw instincts of the masses, cultivated the soil out of which a vile state of pillage, plunder and murder grew at the outbreak of the revolution. . . . The damages caused by the destructive rage of a misguided people ran into the hundreds of millions. Hardly a Jewish community of former Hungary and of today's Slovakia was spared; hardly a Jewish family was not a serious victim, unhappily sometimes also mourning life lost.[46]

The first concern of Jews in Slovakia in the immediate postwar period was defense against the anti-Jewish excesses and economic stabilization. In addition to the general impoverishment sustained during the war, Jewish communities had been drained of resources due to their own out-of-pocket care for Galician Jewish refugees who sojourned in their towns. Wartime Hungarian policy toward Galician Jewish refugees who fled before the Russian troops on the Eastern Front was determined by their classification as citizens of the Austrian half of the Dual Monarchy. As such, they received no state aid from the Hungarian treasury while sojourning on Hungarian territory. The Hungarian administration strove to relocate the refugees from Hungarian territory to provinces of western Austria, which primarily meant refugee camps and other accommodations in Bohemia and Moravia. Northern Hungarian Jewish communities that intervened with the Hungarian administration to allow the refugees—primarily the elderly, women, and children—to remain in their towns rather than make the perilous winter's journey to the allotted Austrian accommodations took financial responsibility for them.[47]

In contrast to Austria, where Jewish refugee relief could be framed as "patriotic war work,"[48] and the Austrian administration imagined that providing refugee aid was a demonstration of the "deep and intuitive understanding of the community of fate that binds together all of the empire's peoples,"[49] in Hungary refugee aid led to a conflict with state policy and the state's heightened perception of Jewish goals as conflicting with state goals. Where the goal of Jewish refugee policy was their speedy removal from Hungarian territory, providing and petitioning for their extended stay ran counter to that end. Resentment of the extended refugee sojourn, the scarce resources it required, and the public health risk it potentially posed can also be tied to rising antisemitism within the surrounding society over the course of the war.

Jews collectively and individually suffered from the looting and rioting of the post–World War I upheaval, destruction of housing, and dislocation of prewar channels of trade. Their postwar economic concerns were immediate. Harry Gell, representative of the AJDC for Czechoslovakia based in Košice, explained these postwar economic challenges in terms of territorial division and communal fragmentation. The areas in most dire need of aid were eastern Slovakia and Subcarpathia Ruthenia. The densest areas of Jewish settlement in Czechoslovakia were located in these regions, along with the largest number of Jews and the greatest concentration of Orthodox and Hasidic communities. "The separation of east Slovakia and Subcarpathia from Austria-Hungary has cut Jewry off from its former life-blood centers, Vienna and Budapest," Gell reported.

> It is remarkable that there is not a single Jewish national institution in this entire territory. . . . Jews of these two sections of Czechoslovakia do not hang together. There are those who were the strong Magyar element, interested not at all in things Jewish, and as their direct counterpart the aggressive Zionist group—small in number, but forceful in action. There are large groups of Orthodox and Chassidim. . . .
>   Each faction is exclusive and non-cooperative with the other factions. The Zionists will not sit with the Orthodox. The Orthodox will not sit with the Neolog, etc. It has been an almost impossible task to organize the communities, but, however, it has been done. If the AJDC has done nothing else, it has organized different elements of these communities to work together with and for the [AJDC]. They have a common purpose in helping us carry out our program.[50]

Gell argued that successful adaptation to the new circumstances depended on cooperation between the "strong Magyar element," the "aggressive Zionist group," and the large groups of Orthodox and Hasidim in the east. Religious and political divisions within the Jewish population created stubborn domestic obstacles to the dual AJDC goals of economic relief and vocational training for Jews in eastern Slovakia and Subcarpathian Ruthenia. These two regions had been the most severely affected by the war, with a great deal of postwar looting and economic dislocation. The AJDC provided individual economic aid, loans for rebuilding houses, the organization of credit cooperatives, and the founding of trade schools for artisanal training, in addition to their direct relief programs. Yet, Gell noted, "Progress has been very slow in the organizational work, not only because of the present economic crisis, but also due to the lack of spirit on the part of many communities. Many of them are not socially organized and seem to have little interest or knowledge about the advantages of cooperation."[51] Gell credited the AJDC with forming the necessary bridge between these disparate communities to enable them to work together at all in pursuit of immediate shared goals.[52] American Jewish aid played a critical role in transcending communal factions to stimulate intergroup cooperation.

Gell understood the entire reconstruction process as being bound to the problem of employment. Because the war had destroyed established trading channels, and many Jews found themselves unable to obtain commercial licenses or to compete with newly formed consumer cooperatives, he saw the best employment options in learning a trade. He organized the AJDC establishment of sewing schools in Košice in Slovakia and in Munkačevo and Bilke in Subcarpathian Ruthenia. The AJDC contributed 90,000 crowns (about US$2,700 in 1920 dollars) for building a mechanical workshop in Košice. The Orthodox and Neolog Jewish communities agreed to guarantee the maintenance of the school. Community support in Prešov in Slovakia enabled the AJDC to create a locksmith workshop there. In Michalovce and Bardejov in Slovakia, however, no progress was made toward similar goals. The Jewish communities there could not be convinced to back the projects. Disputes between the Orthodox and Zionist groups in Bardejov made cooperative efforts impossible.[53]

Jewish communities in Košice worked with Gell and the AJDC to keep pace with the needs of the city's rapidly growing postwar Jewish population. They recognized that the charitable associations in place before the war were hopelessly inadequate for coping with the current economic and social crises. They founded new Jewish aid organizations to confront challenges including economic recovery for individuals and families, schooling for children from impoverished families, care for poor and orphaned girls, and accommodations for abandoned and impoverished women.[54] Jewish communities continued to work with the AJDC (often referred to as "the Joint") in establishing economic relief programs for rebuilding houses, organizing credit cooperatives, and founding vocational schools until the Joint ended funding for recovery work in 1923.[55]

The JPU worked jointly with the AJDC to establish an economic and social commission intended to ease the financial hardship of those individuals who had become impoverished as a result of the war or postwar plundering and to provide employment opportunities. The first funding for the commission came from a 100,000 crown (US$2,960 in 1920 dollars) grant from the AJDC. The JPU used the funding to organize Slovak language classes. With Slovak as the official state language and rapidly becoming the language of instruction across the territory, many predominantly Hungarian- and German-speaking Jews were in danger of losing their jobs.[56]

The Central Office of Orthodox Jewish Communities in Slovakia (Central Office) did not participate in the program. The chief Orthodox rabbi of Vrbové, Samuel Reich, strongly criticized the Central Office in the pages of the leading Jewish national mouthpiece in Slovakia, *Jüdische Volkszeitung,* for not support-ing the program.[57] It was clear to him that the Central Office did not wish to participate, since it would require cooperation with the JPU, whose secular and national approach the Orthodox found unacceptable. Rabbi Reich aired his own support of the program in the same paper:

> The significance of this [language] course for Jewry in Slovakia can hardly be [under]estimated. Now he who has witnessed the poverty of the families of the Jewish teachers who have remained without bread since the upheaval, he who has walked with a heavy heart through the deserted Jewish schools in which our youth would be instructed in theology, can fully really understand the blessed significance of this course. . . .
>
> Fortunately, the Jewish People's Union for Slovakia does not hold itself to the narrow boundaries of its program, which only provides for the protection of the political, social and economic interests of the Jews, but instead places itself in the breach and fulfills duties that others neglect.[58]

At the same time questions of national belonging figured prominently in the reorientation process. The east central European successor states of the Habsburg Monarchy had been established on the basis of the national principle, and nation-ality was the primary lens through which the state saw the population. National belonging had economic, social, and political implications and dominated the spectrum of possible types of group awareness and activity. Czechoslovakia since its inception had based its relationship to the Jewish population of the state on the premise that the Jews constituted a nationality and thus included the Jews among the nationalities of Czechoslovakia. Jews who wished to self-identify and self-declare as members of the Jewish nationality would be counted accordingly. This fell in line with the national minority status granted to the Jews at the Paris Peace Conference in 1919 and Czechoslovakia's signing of the Minorities Treaty, an obligation of all the new and enlarged states.[59] International expectations were high for Masaryk's Czechoslovakia, which had affirmed the demands of the Jewish National Council for the "complete equality of the Jews, [and] national minority rights for the Jewish nation,"[60] shortly after the proclamation of the existence of the state from the capital in Prague on October 28, 1918.

The JPU wanted to provide a broadly defined national Jewish platform for the defense of Jewish political, social, and economic rights in the new state as a Jewish national organization, representing the specific needs of the Jews in Slovakia. Under a wide umbrella, the JPU hoped, Jews in Slovakia would be able in good conscience to form a united front to work toward shared goals. The organization deliberately excluded religious questions from their consideration in order to be as inclusive of the diverse Jewish population as possible and to appeal to the Orthodox majority with practical matters of common concern.[61] At its base the Jewish national idea was intended as a binding principle for disparate elements of a diverse Jewish population. Although Jewish national organizations in Czechoslovakia supported the establishment of a Jewish state in Palestine, their immediate postwar ambitions fit more accurately under the rubric of *Gegenwartsarbeit,* work related to the Diaspora rather than to Palestine.

Max Brod, vice president of the Prague-based Jewish National Council, propagated the idea of *Nationaljudentum,* or national Jewry, in the spirit of working toward the domestic well-being of the Jews in Czechoslovakia. Brod wrote about Nationaljudentum as a new concept, distinct from both Orthodoxy and Zionism, through which a common platform could comfortably develop. The "unbelievably simple" program was this: "I am not other than a Jew. I belong (by the full observation of my duties as a citizen) to no other people than the Jewish people."[62] Looking out across the republic from Prague, Brod hoped that a clearer explanation of the concept would attract the Orthodox majority in Slovakia and Subcarpathian Ruthenia to it. But the inclusivity he imagined in a practical national Jewish platform remained unacceptable to the strong Orthodox opposition. It required acknowledgment of the Jews as a national group in a modern political sense, as well as working together with the JPU. The Orthodox opposed it.[63]

President Masaryk's Czechoslovakia held out promises of equality and recognized Jewish national minority rights within the framework of a consolidating parliamentary democracy. Yet establishing the newly dominant position of the Slovaks in Slovakia often meant suppressing Jews' opportunities to exercise their equal rights. The exercise of land reform and problems surrounding Jewish shop closure on Saturday, the Jewish Sabbath, illustrate this issue. While these problems might not be strictly defined as Jewish national issues, the JPU's defense of Jews involved in them clearly reflected its mission to protect and defend all Jewish political, social, and economic rights based on the widely understood principle of belonging to the Jewish nation. When the JPU accused the chief constable of Prievidza in western Slovakia of anti-Jewish bias in administering land reform policy in his district, the constable's response both confirmed the charge and strove to vindicate it. "It's true," he wrote, "that I snatched my oppressed people, Magyarized by the Jews, from Jewish hands and founded fifteen cooperatives in the district, and that not one Jew is selling plots of land in the district of Prievidza."[64]

I consider it my national duty to work against the Jewification of our villages.
. . . There will only be balance if we suppress the Jews a little, so they wouldn't
be higher than the Christian Slovaks. . . . When I took my position in January
of this year [1919], two notaries tried to give plots of land to two Jewish shopkeepers, in defiance of the antisemitic mood of the people. But the citizenry
protested, how can these be new times, if one has to go again to the same Jew
to beg and bow, [to the one] who scorned them throughout the entire war,
threw them out of the store, and only gave them sugar, flour, tobacco when
they came to work for him, brought him butter and hens. . . . I also knew from
personal experience that it was said throughout the war that Jewish merchants
had the entire food supply in their hands. Christian shopkeepers lamented
what would become of them, they couldn't make ends meet, etc. And nobody
stood up for them. . . . That's why we couldn't then, and even now we can't give
the Jews priority. They must suffer punishment for their sins.[65]

Similarly, in a representative case of Saturday rest for Jewish shopkeepers in
Trenčín in western Slovakia, the chief of police argued for Slovak priority. The
Trenčín rabbinate called on the JPU in January 1920 to aid in the shopkeepers'
defense against keeping their shops open on Saturday. According to the complaint, the local chief of police compelled Jews to keep their shops open through
the Christmas holidays. In their defense the JPU petitioned the chief of police,
who, in response, emphasized difficulties faced by the local population in doing
their regular shopping.[66] There were several periods in 1919, he wrote the county
administrator, during which Jewish shops were closed for up to three and a half
days in one week. When the shops opened again, they were quickly sold out,
and then certain items were unavailable afterward. He placed the blame for the
frequent closure of the shops on religious fanaticism and tradition. Slovaks, he
asserted, should not have to suffer the fanaticism of the shopkeepers.[67] In negotiations between the JPU and chief of police, the latter again cited the religious fanaticism of the Orthodox Jews as the cause for conflict, the reason for
the inconvenience and shortages suffered by the Christian population. He recommended that Jewish shops employ several Christians, who would be able to
keep the shops open on Saturday, thus allowing the Orthodox to observe the day.
His suggestion also meant the local shops would no longer be entirely a Jewish
domain. The chief of police met with leaders of the Jewish community to present
his recommendations.[68]

The JPU struggled to implement the promises of the new state in the east. It
quickly became an intermediary body between the Jewish population in Slovakia
and a local administration antagonistic to the Jewish population. The JPU alerted
the state administration in Bratislava of anti-Jewish incidents and advocated for
Jews targeted by violence and boycotts. It kept abreast of the activities of other
Jewish organizations in Slovakia, worked with statewide Jewish national organizations, and kept in contact with international Jewish agencies like the WZO

and the AJDC. It was also involved in refugee aid, along with the Central Office and the AJDC, including citizenship and residency matters. The intervention of the JPU with the Czechoslovak government is important for understanding the development of the Jewish relationship with the state.

Refugees, Residency, and Political Consolidation

The Jewish refugee crisis did not disappear at armistice. It remained a pressing issue for Czechoslovakia even after fixing the state's borders at Trianon. The wartime legacy of mass population displacement demanded continuing attention and new refugee flows were crossing into the state after 1918 as a result of the Polish-Ukrainian War. While precise wartime refugee numbers are difficult to determine because of partial repatriation and their need to flee again with movement of the Eastern Front, available statistics indicate that in 1915 there were 77,090 Jewish refugees in Vienna; 57,159 in Bohemia; 18,429 in Moravia; and roughly 30,000 in Hungary.[69] Post–World War I international Jewish relief organizations in Czechoslovakia recorded 10,000 Jews on the move within three months in mid-1921.[70] Postwar population displacement continued until Ukrainian forces were driven out of Galicia in the summer of 1919.[71] Czechoslovakia gradually brought refugee sojourn on its territory to a close by December 1921, largely through immigration policy.

During the Prevrat the Jewish refugees, too, were robbed and state provisions intended for them were stolen from refugee camp storehouses.[72] The continuing refugee presence and the accompanying strain on scarce resources exacerbated existing Slovak grievances against the local Jewish population. "In Bardejov eighty years ago there were only three poor Jewish families," reported the overwhelmed chief of police on October 26, 1919. "Today there are 2,402 of them. That is 38.5 percent of the whole population, comparatively the greatest [percentage] in the whole republic, with the exception of Užhorod. They are Orthodox, not one family makes a living doing productive work, they are all only *kšeftári* [hawkers], racketeering, smuggling across the border to Poland. The town is in an impoverished state because of them; all business is in their hands. During the war, more than 1,000 of them flooded into the town from surrounding communities."[73] This impoverished refugee population depended on aid from the state and the Jewish community. The Bardejov municipality distributed that aid to eligible recipients in its constituency. Only with the great reluctance did local administrators grant residency, defined as the right to remain in the town and receive aid there.

Jewish refugees who sojourned in Slovakia in the first three years of the republic fell into two overlapping categories. There were wartime refugees from Galicia and the Bukovina who had remained on the territory of Slovakia since their arrival in late 1914 or early 1915, and there were those who were forced to flee Galicia after 1918. Most of the latter group had already been refugees during the world war, repatriated after 1916. This group constituted the majority of postwar Jewish refugees. Wartime Austro-Hungarian refugee policy required Austrian citizens, largely meaning Jews from Galicia and the Bukovina, to be accommodated in Austria and Hungarian citizens in Hungary. As a result, Jewish refugees from Galicia and the Bukovina were transported to refugee camps or similar accommodations in the then Austrian provinces of Moravia and Bohemia. This process fulfilled the policy of clearing the vast majority of refugees from Hungary. There were no refugee camps in Slovakia, but some refugees did settle down in various communities on an individual basis, in small numbers.[74]

The ongoing population displacement in the aftermath of the war pushed the Czechoslovak administration to rapidly define the new state in terms of territory, population, and citizenship. It added urgency to the problem of "fixing" population to territory and building new homelands in the post-imperial successor state.[75] The Jewish refugee presence strained the cohesiveness of state that the administration sought to create. It sharpened already tense ethnic relations, strained already overextended scarce resources, and added to the sense of moral panic and civic crisis.[76] State administrators in the newly created nation-states of east central Europe considered loyalty a factor of "rootedness" and connection to a bounded territory. The bond to territory linked populations with state belonging and entitlements of citizenship.[77]

Bardejov, close to the Polish border, had been the point of entry into Hungary for Galician Jewish refugees during the world war. Now it was their gateway to Czechoslovakia. How would the new administration handle the influx? What wartime lessons would Jewish communities and organizations apply to the current circumstances? How would their activities shape their relationships to each other and to the state? The refugee crisis formed a bridge between former Austria-Hungary and the new Czechoslovak Republic. It offers a useful perspective for examining the evolving orientation of the Jews in Slovakia within the changed circumstances of the new state. How Jews in northern Hungary handled the crisis during the war had been critical to defining their relationship with the Hungarian Jewish leadership in Budapest. Their responses to it after the war acted to differentiate their positions in relation to one another, as well as to formulate methods of interaction with the Czechoslovak state. The JPU and the Central Office dominated refugee aid activities in Slovakia. While the JPU acted on the basis of Jewish national minority protections in Czechoslovakia, the Central Office applied traditional methods of communal self-help and government intervention in their work.

The Bardejov chief of police found himself in a similar position as his predecessor in fall 1914, waiting for orders now from Prague rather than Budapest on how to handle the thousands of Jewish refugees in the border town. Would they be permitted to sojourn in the town, with or without right of residency, or would they be transferred elsewhere? In October 1919 the chief was instructed to update citizenship records for the entire population of Bardejov. Working with a committee of six others he counted fully half of the population—411 families, Jewish and non-Jewish—who did not have the right of residency. Of the 396 Jewish families recorded in Bardejov, the chief of police allowed right of residency for 152 of them, marked 163 for expulsion from the republic, and sent a list of 74 families with ambiguous cases back to the Office of the Minister Plenipotentiary for Slovakia (MPS).[78]

The Bardejov Jewish community asked the JPU in late October to help fifty-five families threatened with expulsion from Czechoslovakia to gain right of residency through intervention with the MPS on their behalf. These fifty-five families were part of the larger group of seventy-four in question in the chief of police's letter. The community told the JPU that a representative of the MPS, a Dr. Markovič, had informed the families that they would either leave the town voluntarily by the end of the month or be escorted to the border militarily. The Jewish community explained to the JPU that these families had come to Bardejov as refugees from Zborov, a town about eight kilometers away on Czechoslovak territory, as a result of the Russian invasion. They were not from Galicia. They had lived on current Czechoslovak territory even before the world war but did not have right of residency in Bardejov.[79]

Defending the families from Zborov led to an important victory for the JPU. The organization was able to prove to the MPS that these families were eligible for right of residency by showing they were rooted in Czechoslovak territory. "[Threatening these fifty-five families with expulsion from Czechoslovakia] contradicts the ministerial order which affirms that citizens of a foreign state who lived in the territory of the Czechoslovak Republic before the war can apply for right of residency to the Ministry through county administrative offices," the JPU argued.[80] The MPS approved their right of residency. The JPU defended the families by demanding the MPS comply with the existing legal framework of the state, where their prewar residency had changed but remained within current borders. Deporting them would be illegal, an act of discrimination.[81] Overall eligibility depended on long-term residency before the war in the territory that would become Czechoslovakia, similar to the requirements for Czechoslovak citizenship.[82]

War refugees who remained on the territory of Czechoslovakia presented a problem to the state administration in questions of residency, citizenship, and the right to economic and material aid. State aid is linked to state belonging. Since wartime refugee relief policy in Austria-Hungary allowed for aid distribution from the Austrian treasury to Austrian citizens on Austrian territory, and likewise for Hungarian citizens, a significant wartime aid strategy among northern Hungarian Jewish communities had been to find ways to connect location and aid. They worked to convince the Hungarian Ministry of the Interior in Budapest to allow Austrian (Galician Jewish) refugees to receive Austrian state aid while sojourning on Hungarian territory (Slovakia) so that they would not have to make the treacherous winter journey to refugee camps on Austrian territory (Moravia and Bohemia).

In a shift from these wartime aid conditions, Czechoslovakia worked in conjunction with Jewish religious communities to provide for the remaining sojourn of the Galician Jewish refugees, who were now Polish citizens, in approved cases. Where their sojourn was permitted, the state granted refugees temporary legal status and the Jewish communities provided for their material needs. Two cases, both from Nitra in western Slovakia, demonstrate how this policy functioned. In the first case the MPS allowed residency to Abraham Widder, though the end of the month, with the proviso that the Jewish community take care of him.[83] In the second, Jozef Weisz was permitted to remain in Czechoslovakia until November 20, 1919, as long as the Jewish community took responsibility for him.[84]

Where refugee sojourn was not permitted, the Czechoslovak administration provided for their transportation by wagon. This was again a shift from the usual though disliked practice of sending refugees off on foot during the war. The county administrator of Gemer-Malohont handled the removal of Galician Jewish refugees and other "unreliable elements" from Rimavská Sobota in central Slovakia in October 1919. The action was postponed because of difficulties in providing wagons for their transport. The county administrator urged the MPS to make the vehicles available quickly so that the refugees could travel before the onset of winter. In addition, he brought the "striking fact" to the attention of the MPS that the majority of landlords in his region were Jews and the factories were in the hands of foreigners, especially those factories that had ceased to work due to a shortage of raw materials. He also wrote that an investigation would soon take place into the citizenship status of inhabitants who were citizens of Hungary but did not have right of residency in Slovakia.[85] All of his concerns were connected to the process of creating Slovak demographic and economic dominance in the region.

From summer 1920 the focus of Jewish refugee aid efforts shifted from the small number of remaining war refugees to the incoming stream fleeing the Polish-Ukrainian War. Overall Czechoslovak policy toward arriving refugees can be characterized by the collaborative efforts between the Jewish community, both locally and internationally, and the Czechoslovak government. Reports from Bratislava show that the Jewish religious community was responsible for refugee care upon arrival. Afterward the state offered them regular material aid as well as the right to apply for asylum in Czechoslovakia. With the agreement of the MPS, the refugees were confined to quarantined refugee camps in order to prevent the spread of contagious diseases. By December 1921 the majority of the refugees had emigrated to Brazil and to Palestine while the remainder left Czechoslovakia for other destinations.[86] Brazil became an increasingly popular destination for Jewish emigrants from east central Europe in the 1920s, with its relatively strong economy, newly formed communal and religious organizations, and its strategic location near well-known Argentina. Perhaps most important, it was one of the few large countries in the Americas without immigration quota restrictions.[87]

From June through August 1920, when the first report explaining the new refugee situation arrived on the MPS's desk from the governmental health adviser, nearly 700 Galician Jewish refugees arrived in Czechoslovakia. Of those 700, only 250 were accommodated in Bratislava. These were the refugees who possessed travel papers. The remaining 450 refugees crossed the border without papers, unsuccessful in their attempts to avoid the border guards.[88] If there were other undocumented refugees who managed to get across the border without detection, they are not recorded, so the precise number of refugees entering Czechoslovakia in 1920 through 1921 is not known.

The 450 refugees without papers were taken into police custody in northern border police stations, primarily in Bardejov and Hummené. The local administration sent the refugees down to Bratislava by train in stages. There is no record that the administration provided for medical exams or considered other refugee health issues. When asked where they were going, the majority of the refugees answered that they were on the way to Palestine. The 250 refugees with papers were sent down to Bratislava immediately. There, local Jewish organizations provided accommodations for them in five locations: (1) the old Pálffy barracks that had been turned into the workers' hostel of the Poale Zion Socialist Zionist organization, (2) the gymnasium of the Orthodox Jewish school on Telocvičná/Torna Street, (3) the elementary school of the Reform Jewish community on Telocvičná/Torna Street, (4) the Hospital of the Merciful Brothers on the Square of the Republic, and (5) dispersed among private homes in and around the Jewish Quarter. Refugees who had not been disinfected upon arrival, a group that included the majority of refugees without travel papers, were to be disinfected in the municipal station on Rastislav Street. The station was open every day except Sunday from five to six in the afternoon and was able to handle about thirty people a day.[89]

The Palestine Office in Bratislava estimated that there were at most twelve hundred to fifteen hundred refugees in Slovakia by the middle of August. The office did not include in that number those refugees who had merely stopped in Bratislava for less than three days to pick up their visas before continuing their journey. They were more concerned with those who would sojourn in Czechoslovakia for a longer period. The Palestine Office acknowledged in their communication with the MPS that the issue put Czechoslovakia in a difficult position. They insisted, however, that a solution be found that would take the concerns of all parties into consideration. They urgently called for a solution to the problem of mass accommodation for reasons of health and hygiene, documentation and safety, and the general housing shortage in Slovakia.[90]

Incoming refugees were required to undergo a health exam and disinfection because of their living conditions in Galicia, malnutrition, the long journey, and exposure to the elements and to contagious diseases. Housing conditions had been deplorable throughout Galicia since the first months of the world war. Hundreds of villages along the Eastern Front were destroyed by the invading Russian troops and in subsequent battles. When the vast majority of world war refugees were repatriated beginning in 1916, they often had no homes left to which to return. In a February 1916 report the AJDC described the desperate housing situation that was prevalent in Galicia: vast portions of the population were "obliged to pass the winter in damp and cold earth-holes, with foul straw for their beds and bare of all clothing. Cholera, spotted typhus and dysentery daily cause[d] large gaps among them."[91]

The housing situation was critical in Slovakia after the war. The shortage of suitable accommodations made the refugees' position all the more precarious. The Palestine Office urged the Czechoslovak government to find a solution quickly. It promised that the greater part of the cost of caring for the refugees, especially the provision of foodstuffs, would be taken up by the AJDC. The Palestine Office added that it was necessary to comment on the poor handling of refugee accommodation during the war and demanded greater humanity now in the refugee camps organized by Czechoslovakia than had been the case in the "infamous concentration camps of the old Monarchy."[92]

"Why not house the refugees in the Mikolov barracks?" wrote Rabbi Koloman Wéber to the Bratislava chief of police a week later. Rabbi Wéber headed the Central Office of Orthodox Jewish Communities in Slovakia.[93] The barracks in Mikolov had been constructed for refugee accommodation in Moravia in 1914 and 1915. The largest compound in Moravia lay in Uherské Hradiště, which had held nearly ninety thousand refugees in the winter of 1916 before their repatriation. Eight thousand refugees had been housed in Mikolov.[94] Rabbi Wéber wrote that it made sense to take advantage of already extant barracks. The Central Office urged the MPS to allow the refugees housed throughout the Jewish Quarter in Bratislava to be moved to the Mikolov barracks as soon as possible. They recommended a combined effort of the state and the Jewish communities in providing for the refugees. The state would provide foodstuffs to the Central Office, which would then prepare it according the rules of kashrut, the Jewish dietary laws.[95]

The Bratislava chief of police agreed to the plan. He wrote to the MPS explaining Rabbi Wéber's proposal. The accommodations would indeed be suitable, he concurred, but the state would have to arrange the paperwork and decide how to handle questions of health and hygiene.[96] After some consideration the MPS forwarded the proposal, with both his approval and that of the Bratislava chief of police, to the Ministry of National Defense in Prague.[97] By the end of September the paperwork and details of accommodating the Jewish refugees in the camp at Slámený boudy/Strohhütte, located in the Koliba section of Bratislava, were completed. It appeared that although the government found the proposal of the Central Office workable, the available barracks in Koliba were more convenient for the present need.

Each refugee would be required to undergo a health exam and disinfection before being given permission to intern at the refugee camp. None would be allowed to leave the camp, and their freedom of movement within it was to be limited. However, the refugees would be accommodated there in functional facilities and provided with kosher meals. There was room for more than five hundred people at the Slámený boudy/Strohhütte camp. The AJDC headquarters in Košice, in conjunction with local Jewish organizations, agreed to take full responsibility for the refugees and for carrying out the rules governing their accommodation laid out by the authorities.[98]

Not all proposals for refugee accommodation worked out so successfully and rapidly. Not all unoccupied barracks would be made available for refugee housing. In August 1920 the AJDC in Košice wrote to the chief medical officer in Bratislava proposing that Polish Jewish refugees be accommodated in the military barracks there that were no longer in use. There were many barracks available, and other types of housing were nearly impossible to secure. They requested two barracks, promising again that the AJDC would take full responsibility for the refugees for the duration of their sojourn on the territory of Czechoslovakia. The suggestion was rejected. The Polish Jewish refugees would not be allowed to intern at the military barracks on Raktár Street, as the buildings had to be left available as a quarantine station.[99]

Despite the fact that this proposal was not realized, the method, form, and tone of communication shows a willingness to find workable, mutually agreeable solutions. The AJDC and the Central Office sought to better the lot of the Jewish refugees by linking their resources with those of the Czechoslovak state. They submitted proposals that they hoped took into account state concerns for the health of the general population and the overall housing shortage. They took responsibility for the refugees, assuring that state protocols would be followed, and thus acted as an intermediary between the refugees and the state administration. The state authorities in Bratislava and Prague listened to the proposals of the Jewish organizations and responded in keeping with their main priority of protecting the health and well-being of the general population. When the state authorities felt it was no longer possible to care for the refugees without putting the general population in jeopardy, it would cease cooperation with local and international Jewish organizations for refugee provision in Czechoslovakia.

The case of Róza Reizer marked a turning point in the evolution of postwar refugee aid in Czechoslovakia. It convinced the Czechoslovak administration to close the borders to further refugee influx for the health of the general public and for state consolidation. The Bratislava Administrative Council presented Róza Reizer's case in a summary report toward the end of February 1921 in order to support the request that no further Jewish refugees from Poland be allowed into Czechoslovakia. The bilingual Hungarian and Slovak report gave an overview of developments in the contemporary refugees' situation. After reviewing refugee accommodations in Bratislava, the report came to the main area of complaint concerning continued refugee movement on the territory: the refugees had come from regions "swimming in epidemics," many in need of immediate medical care. Before the beginning of the school year they were housed at the former military barracks at Koliba, Slámený boudy/Strohhütte, where after disinfection they were placed under continual medical supervision. While a good part of the refugees emigrated to Palestine and to other places after receiving their travel papers, more refugees entered the state, replacing them, so their number remained close to four hundred. Even in February 1921 approximately four hundred refugees remained in the city, although their extended residency expired in mid-December. As a result of permanent medical control, careful disinfection, and removal of lice, the medical supervisors reported that they had successfully managed to rid the new refugees of disease and epidemics.[100]

Róza Reizer was a textbook example of an unwitting disease carrier. She was barred from the refugee camp at Koliba after undergoing a medical examination by the camp doctor in January. The camp doctor sent her on to the state hospital, where she was diagnosed with typhus. The origin of her infection, the Bratislava Administrative Council asserted, was to be found on the road from Stanislav in Galicia to Bratislava. Róza arrived in Bratislava in January after fleeing her home in December 1920. She spent eight to ten days in Lwów (Lvov), two days in Tešín, and eight days in Prague. She had about thirty traveling companions, none of whom had fallen ill. According to the calculations of the hospital, she probably became infected in Prague. She had exhibited the first symptoms of the disease in early January, and fever appeared ten days later. The incubation period for the disease was twenty-one days. According to the report's conclusion, Róza's case demonstrated that "all of the efforts to secure the health of the refugees and the general population could be in vain if just one or two refugees from Poland wandered into the city carrying an infectious disease." That disease could easily become a dangerous epidemic; therefore, they asked the MPS to dissolve the camp. The Bratislava Administrative Council reminded the MPS that the extended residency permission for the refugees had expired on December 15, 1920, and the refugees should be sent elsewhere.[101]

Emigration then became the primary means by which the Czechoslovak state dealt with the Jewish refugee situation. By December 1921 the majority of refugees who had sojourned on the territory of Czechoslovakia had emigrated to Brazil, Palestine, or other destinations.[102] Propertyless Jewish refugees from Poland who sojourned on the territory of Slovakia in the Koliba refugee camp close to Bratislava, where they were provided for by the AJDC, were sent gradually to Prague, where the Jewish community handled their emigration. Refugees underwent a medical examination before leaving Bratislava. They were examined once again at an immigration station in Libeň on the outskirts of Prague before continuing on to the Jewish town hall.[103] The first group of twenty refugees from the Koliba camp in Bratislava left Prague for Brazil on February 28, 1921.[104]

Less than two weeks before the refugees' departure for Brazil, Czechoslovakia conducted its first statewide census. The state was moving from flux to consolidation. The postwar upheavals had come to a close; the struggle for Slovakia was over. The ongoing refugee presence represented the last tie to the war and upheaval in its aftermath. Prague was eager to proceed with the business of state building. It was imperative to complete the transition from Austria-Hungary through the war to the Czechoslovak-dominated nation-state. Prague needed to define and connect the state's population to the newly bounded territory and to fully incorporate Slovakia into a centralized, stable political system. Jews and Slovaks in Slovakia had begun their reorientation toward Prague in relation to each other. For each, their feeling of rootedness in the state would depend on the extent they could live freely, work toward their economic betterment, and separate themselves from their past Hungarian experience. Vavro Šrobár had expressed confidence that "our Jews" would be clever enough to seek the "right path." Jews in Slovakia would prove his confidence well-founded yet the "right path" elusive.

2 Nationality Is an Internal Conviction

Jewish Nationality and Czechoslovak
State Building

JOSEF MRÁZ OF the Czechoslovak State Statistical Office set off from Prague for Žilina,[1] the provisional capital of Slovakia, in mid-January 1919 to propose his ideas for the upcoming Slovak census to Vavro Šrobár, the minister plenipotentiary of Slovakia. His talks with Šrobár lasted an exhausting four days, during which time they debated how the structure, method, and concept of the census could best meet its chief goal: to find out how many Slovaks were living in Slovakia. Upon his arrival in Prague, he wrote up a report of the Žilina proceedings and the census instructions upon which they had agreed. He sent the instructions off to be translated into Slovak, Hungarian, and German.[2] Mráz included in his report a new, subjective definition of "nationality" that would challenge prewar methods of counting and classifying the population based on language. This definition would be the point of departure for fresh debates and reevaluations of nationhood in the evolving circumstances of the interwar Czechoslovak state. He argued that "in contrast to [mother tongue], the concept 'nationality' means confession to a certain *internal conviction,* which cannot be explained in an ambiguous way, similar to religious conviction," and that it follows from this conclusion that Jews should have the option of declaring either their own Jewish nationality or the nationality of others, without regard for religious affiliation.[3]

Debates over "Jewish nationality" formed the centerpiece of the overall reevaluation of nationality and nationhood in Czechoslovakia. Jewish nationality came to be used as an exceptional example in formulating opposing positions on the meaning, classification, and function of nationality in the new state. Through it, Czechoslovakia shifted the concept of nationality closer to an ethnic or racial understanding of the term rather than a linguistic or cultural one. The Czechoslovak government together with the multinational population of the state took part in actualizing theoretical concepts of nationality and nationhood through three significant events in the formative years of the new state: the 1919 census in Slovakia, the 1920 parliamentary elections, and the 1921 census in Czechoslovakia. Responses to these events gave nationality meaning in the postwar environment, in the context of new states created on the principle of national self-determination. In order to understand the postwar evolution of nationality in Czechoslovakia and the place of Jewish nationality in it, the present study overall focuses on points of intersection between state and society and their implications. It treats the nationality question from the perspective of the central government in Prague, local conditions in Slovakia, statewide Jewish considerations, and the specific position of the Jewish population in Slovakia.

Mapping Slovakia

In the introduction to his memoir of the formative years 1918 through 1920, *Osvobodené Slovensko* (Liberated Slovakia), Vavro Šrobár recounted his first meeting with R. W. Seton-Watson, the influential English historian and political activist who brought nationality questions in Austria-Hungary to the world's attention. In 1907 Seton-Watson came to Rózsahegy (Ružomberok) in the central Slovak Low Tatra region, where Šrobár was then working, while researching the national question for what would be Seton-Watson's first major work, *Racial Problems in Hungary*.[4] Because of the objectivity and calm with which Seton-Watson discussed Magyarization, Šrobár found himself unable to discern where his visitor stood on the issue. Before they parted, Seton-Watson surprised Šrobár with a question: "And what is your state program?" he asked. After a moment's hesitation, Šrobár replied, "Great Moravia, with Bohemia, Moravia, Silesia, Slovakia, and Pannonia," which Seton-Watson "accepted without commentary."[5] "That [conversation] took place seven years before the outbreak of the world war," Šrobár said, "and eleven years afterward 'Great Moravia' received the name the 'Czechoslovak State.'"[6]

In his memoir Šrobár professed that language was the connection between the "Czechoslovak tribes" from their ancient roots to the present. Even the establishment of a new literary language in Slovakia, thanks to Ľudovit Štúr's nineteenth-century codification of the central Slovak dialect, "did not for a moment disturb the consciousness of Czechoslovak tribal unity," he asserted.[7] "The longing for close cultural, economic, and political unity increased yearly in proportion to the growing pressure of brutal Magyarization," he added.[8] In his celebratory and didactic jubilee-year volume Šrobár underscored a romantic one-thousand-year story of the unitary Czechoslovak nation/tribe—focusing on shared language, history, interests, and ancestral ties—that had been greatly successful in garnering international support for the Czechoslovak state-building project during the war.

Although the idea of a unitary Czechoslovak nation prevailed internationally, the most compelling connection between the Czechs and Slovaks for the prospects of independent statehood was demographic. Czechs constituted a majority in Bohemia and Moravia, but they feared the collapse of Austria-Hungary would spell their incorporation into a Greater Germany due to the existence of a substantial German minority in these lands. In the beginning of the war, Czech leaders first sought a reorganization of the monarchy along federal lines with a large degree of autonomy for the Czechs, though they soon discarded the plan as unfeasible.[9] In working toward the ultimate goal of independence, the idea of incorporating the three-million-strong Slovak population became an increasingly attractive solution to counterbalancing the significant German minority in Bohemia and Moravia.[10] By the end of the war Masaryk and Beneš had the commitment of the Entente powers to an independent Czechoslovakia. The Slovak population in Slovakia became the key to the Czechoslovak nation's demographic legitimacy in its new multinational national state. The Paris Peace Conference called upon the Czechoslovak delegation to statistically demonstrate the dominance of the Slovaks in the multinational territory of Slovakia. The viability of the Czechoslovak state depended on it.

In order to collect the necessary data, the Czechoslovak government organized a provisional census for Slovakia. Such a census could not be carried out until the borders of the territory were defined and secured and military upheavals had ceased. This meant waiting until the ultimatum given by the Entente powers had driven Béla Kun's Red Army troops out of Slovakia at the end of June 1919, and until the Czechoslovak government had control over the territory at the end of July. While the change of regimes was not officially over, and the borders were not fixed by law until Hungary signed the Treaty of Trianon on June 4, 1920, Czechoslovakia held the de facto borders securely enough by August 1919 that it was feasible to set the census in motion. The primary goal of the census was "[to gather] the necessary information for the Peace Conference concerning how many Slovaks there [were] in the occupied territory of the former Kingdom of Hungary, so that it would be possible to correct and prove false the Hungarian census of 1910, as well as to ascertain other general national proportions in Slovak communities, namely the [extent of] the Magyarization of these communities, the Magyarization of schools and churches."[11]

The 1919 census was the first attempt by the Czechoslovak government to nationally map the territory of Slovakia for state-building purposes. Mapping Slovakia meant reframing the national ratios of multinational/ethnic/linguistic Slovakia in terms of Slovak, and thus Czechoslovak, dominance. The Czechoslovak government had to prove that the former government sought to create Magyar demographic superiority in the same lands through forced assimilation and manipulation of statistics. In other words, the aim of the census was to find the ethnic Slovaks whose numbers would prove that a "falsification" or deliberate Magyarization of the nationalities had taken place in the decades before the war.

In the process of creating the 1919 Slovak census, Czechoslovak demographers also came to a preliminary decision regarding how Czechoslovakia would "see" and count Jewish nationality.[12] The Jewish case was especially problematic because Czechoslovakia did not consider the Jewish population in Czechoslovakia to possess its own national language, even in Slovakia and Subcarpathian Ruthenia, where Yiddish language usage was more widespread, but nevertheless did not dispute Jewish national status within the state. An influential work on national questions published in Prague in early 1919 declared: "Language forms the distinguishing characteristic of the nation: a nation must have its own language, otherwise it is not a nation."[13]

How would the Czechoslovak state square its recognition of Jewish national status with the alleged lack of a distinctive national language among the Jews of Czechoslovakia? Debates surrounding Jewish nationality and its codification for census purposes lay at the core of a Czechoslovak reevaluation of the overall meaning of nationality in the postwar period. Decisions regarding the meaning and function of Jewish nationality within the Czechoslovak context went hand in hand with the process of integrating Slovakia into the Czechoslovak state.

The Jewish case illuminates how the process of Czechoslovak state building—including the interrelated efforts to arrive at the true number of Slovaks and Czechs and to reconcile the dissonant linguistic-national circumstances of the Jewish population so as to codify Jewish nationality within Czechoslovakia—led to an increased unbundling of language from nationality as an absolute indicator of national belonging and to a movement toward a definition of nationality as an internal conviction. To understand how the Czechoslovak state saw Jewish nationality, therefore, it will be examined side by side with questions of the integration of Slovakia and the reconceptualization of nationality in the larger context of Czechoslovak state building.

To begin, it is helpful to take a step back to look at the relationship between language, nationalism, and nationhood and then to consider their relationship as applied to the institutionalized collection of data for census purposes. First of all, for the peoples of east central Europe, including the Jews, the nation-building process was a fundamental component of modern politics. Nation building required raising the national consciousness of the members of the group as well as making a convincing case to the world that the group was indeed a real nationality. The most important proof of national existence was language: a special, unique language belonging to the national group alone.[14]

Nineteenth-century nationalism deemed language the most important characteristic marking one nation from another; language was the primary determinant of nationhood.[15] Nationalism assumes that people naturally group themselves into nations, that these nations have identifiable characteristics, and that their only legitimate form of government is self-government.[16] Making language central to nationalism, argues Elie Kedourie, erases the distinction between linguistic and racial nationalism, because then the conception of nationalism itself contains all linguistic, racial, religious, and other features. The connection between language and ethnicity is also heightened.[17]

Nation—"one of the most puzzling and tendentious items in the political lexicon"[18]—has been variously defined as dependent more on "objective" factors such as language, religion and customs, territory, and institutions than as coalescing from "subjective" factors like attitudes, perceptions, and sentiments.[19] The features deemed "objective" have been conceived to mark the boundaries of nation, and features deemed "subjective" to give it internal cohesion and solidarity. "Objective" criteria like language are not enough in and of themselves to establish whether a group is a nation or not. Rather, suggests Walker Connor, "the essence of the nation is a psychological bond that joins a people and differentiates it, in the subconscious conviction of its members, from all nonmembers in a most vital way."[20] His conception closely agrees with Ernest Gellner's, in which a common language does not bind a group of people into a nation without mutual recognition of each other: "A mere category of persons (say, occupants of a given territory or speakers of a given language, for example) becomes a nation if and when the members of the category firmly recognize certain mutual rights and duties to each other in virtue of their shared membership in it."[21] A people must feel its nationhood. That feeling of nationhood, the condition of being a nation, has been theorized in two main ways in its European context. The first is considered to derive more from a sense of mutual belonging to a political community in which equal citizens participate in a common culture; the second is regarded as more related to a sense of mutual belonging to an ethnocultural community of descent with political ambitions.[22] Neither is exclusive nor analogous to the state. States can be defined by their autonomous institutional activity and by their "legitimate monopoly of coercion and extraction in a given territory," but the state itself is not the national political community.[23]

Anthony Smith's paired conceptions of nation and *ethnie* highlight the group's internal cohesion, solidarity, and mutual loyalty. Smith defines "nation" as "a named human community occupying a homeland, and having common myths and a shared history, a common public culture, a single economy and common rights and duties for all members," as distinguished from "ethnie," "a named human community connected to a homeland, possessing common myths of ancestry, shared memories, one or more elements of shared culture, and a measure of solidarity, at least among the elites."[24] Smith's concept of the ethnie is especially important in the Jewish case for understanding the coherence of the group without territory and without a special, unique, shared vernacular. Late nineteenth-century Jewish nationalism relied on "subjective" characteristics for modern Jewish nation building, above all a common heritage and shared historical experience. Language was conspicuously absent from the short list. "Who amongst us has a sufficient acquaintance with Hebrew to ask for a railway ticket in that language?" Theodor Herzl famously asked in 1896.[25]

How, then, do you count "nationality" on the census? What, in fact, is being counted? Census-creating demographers differ from theorists in their need to count and quantify, classify and categorize state populations. Definitions of "nation" push and pull against the institutional demands of the state. The real question here is how the complex and fluctuating "nation" is tagged and boxed and bureaucratized for use by the state. What does it mean and how is it used? Nation indeed becomes, as Rogers Brubaker explains, "practical category, institutionalized form, contingent event, and category of practice."[26] "We should not ask 'what is a nation,'" he writes, "but rather: how is nationhood as a political and cultural form institutionalized within and among states? How does nation work as a practical category, as classificatory scheme, as cognitive frame?"[27] The crystallization of Jewish nationality in Czechoslovakia exemplifies the process by which nation is bureaucratized and given institutional form in interwar east central Europe. Jewish nationality became an exceptional category of practice within the borders of interwar Czechoslovakia; it was the only nationality in east central Europe unbound from language.

Demographers began to answer the question of how to count nationality on the census at the meeting of the International Statistical Congress in St. Petersburg in 1872. There they agreed that language was the primary marker of nationality and that counting nationality according to language was the most effective means of capturing and recording nationality for the interests of the state. The question of how to codify nationality in a state census had first been debated at the demographers' 1857 congress in Vienna, but without conclusive results. The St. Petersburg congress decided that language was the best objective indicator of nationality, the most reliable one, and the least confusing, as "each perfectly knows the language used since childhood to think and express oneself."[28] But how should the census ask about language? The conclusions of the St. Petersburg conference point to an acceptance of mother tongue as the most valid language situation type to use in codifying nationality for the census. Other language situation types include, but are not limited to, language most commonly used, language of daily use, family language, language in which one prays, and the language that one speaks with one's children.[29]

Language was first counted on the Austrian and the Hungarian census in 1880. In Austria language was counted according to "language of daily use" (*Umgangssprache*), while in the Kingdom of Hungary language was counted according to "mother tongue" (*Anyanyelv*). When Czechoslovakia came into existence after the First World War, it brought together two traditions of national codification through language proxy. In discussing the relationship of language to nationality for the development of the census, Czechoslovak demographers favored "mother tongue" over "language of daily use." They argued that counting according to language of daily use had led to an underrepresentation of Czechs on the Austrian census and inherently underestimated the numbers of minority national groups in which the official language was that of the dominant national group. The dependent position of the Czechs had resulted in more Czechs declaring themselves as Germans when counted this way, they asserted, because a Czech in a German language environment would indeed have used that language on a daily basis. Counting according to mother tongue had led to even greater statistical manipulations in the Kingdom of Hungary.

Czechoslovak demographers contended that corruption of the census process in Hungary for the purpose of statistically increasing the number of Magyars had resulted in a gross underestimation of the number of ethnic Slovaks. Consequently, Slovaks as a people suffered more greatly in Hungary than the Czechs in Austria. Yet they agreed that if the census were carried out properly, counting nationality by mother tongue would yield the most accurate and objective picture of the demographic composition of the state.[30] Czechoslovak demographers accepted the definition of "mother tongue" as "the language which is most familiar to a person since childhood and with which they think, or simply the language which their parents taught them in their earliest youth."[31]

Josef Mráz worked with the definition of "mother tongue" as well as its caveat, which was used on the 1910 census of the Kingdom of Hungary to make the mother tongue category as broad as possible, in reformulating the conception of nationality for the 1919 Slovak census. He did not dispute the Hungarian definition's core: mother tongue is the language "to which one confesses as one's own and with which one best and most gladly speaks."[32] It was the caveat that troubled him: "Although mother tongue is identical with the language which everyone learned in their childhood in the majority of cases, usually from their mother, it can nevertheless happen that a child has another mother tongue than the mother, especially when the child acquired it in child-care (!), in school (!), or as a result of circumstances by which the parents have different mother tongues, another language than the language of the child's mother."[33] By broadening the definition of "mother tongue" so that it became disengaged from the language one's mother actually spoke, Hungarian demographers allowed for a greater number of people to declare Magyar as their mother tongue than would have otherwise been possible. While this definition may have obtained in a number of cases due to widespread linguistic assimilation in the Kingdom of Hungary, it left the door open for abuses.

Table 2.1. Mother Tongue of the Hungarian Population According to Religion in 1910

ACCORDING TO ABSOLUTE NUMBER

	TOTAL	HUNGARIAN	GERMAN	SLOVAK	ROMANIAN	RUSYN	CROATIAN	SERBIAN	OTHER
Roman Catholic	10,888,138	5,924,665	1,372,103	1,406,207	8,531	5,109	1,810,302	3,892	357,329
Greek Catholic	2,025,508	304,570	1,785	79,338	1,133,671	463,604	9,511	1,908	31,121
Calvinist	2,621,329	2,573,683	26,964	10,645	1,412	57	1,028	49	7,491
Lutheran	1,340,143	418,449	429,687	463,912	1,592	56	791	128	25,528
Greek Orthodox	2,987,163	40,851	2,494	706	1,799,255	1,031	860	1,099,386	42,580
Unitarian	74,296	73,267	168	64	559	4	7	21	206
Jewish	932,458	705,488	203,230	5,830	991	2,702	10,387	91	3,739
Other	17,452	9,602	1,004	1,268	3,021	24	276	996	3,739
Total	20,886,487	10,050,575	2,037,435	1,967,970	2,949,032	472,587	1,833,162	1,106,471	469,255

ACCORDING TO PERCENTAGE

	TOTAL	HUNGARIAN	GERMAN	SLOVAK	ROMANIAN	RUSYN	CROATIAN	SERBIAN	OTHER
Roman Catholic	52.1	54.4	12.6	12.9	0.1	0.1	16.6	0.0	3.3
Greek Catholic	9.7	15.0	0.1	3.9	56.0	22.9	0.5	0.1	1.5
Calvinist	12.6	98.2	1.0	0.4	0.1	0.0	0.0	0.0	0.3
Lutheran	6.4	31.2	32.1	34.6	0.1	0.0	0.1	0.0	1.9
Greek Orthodox	14.3	1.4	0.1	0.0	60.3	0.0	0.0	36.8	1.4
Unitarian	0.3	98.6	0.2	0.1	0.8	0.0	0.0	0.0	0.3
Jewish	4.5	75.7	21.8	0.6	0.1	0.3	1.1	0.0	0.4
Other	0.1	55.0	5.8	7.3	17.3	0.1	1.6	5.7	7.2
Total	100								

Source: *Magyar Statisztikai Évkönyv. Új Folyam XXIII. 1915* (Budapest, 1918), 20, chart 13, "A népesség anyanyelve vallások szerint 1910-ben."

Table 2.2. Mother Tongue of the Hungarian Population in 1900 and 1910

	TOTAL POPULATION			
MOTHER TONGUE OF THE POPULATION	1900		1910	
	ABSOLUTE NUMBER	PERCENTAGE	ABSOLUTE NUMBER	PERCENTAGE
Hungary				
Hungarian	8,651,520	51.4	9,944,627	54.4
German	1,999,060	11.9	1,903,357	10.4
Slovak	2,002,165	11.9	1,946,357	10.7
Romanian	2,798,559	16.6	2,948,186	16.1
Rusyn	424,774	2.5	464,270	2.5
Croatian	191,432	1.1	194,808	1.1
Serbian	437,737	2.6	461,516	2.5
Other	333,008	2.0	401,412	2.9
Total non-Hungarian	8,186,735	48.6	8,319,906	45.5
Total	16,838,255	100	18,264,533	100
Croatia-Slavonia				
Hungarian	90,781	3.8	105,948	4.1
German	136,121	5.6	134,078	5.1
Slovak	17,476	0.7	21,613	0.8
Romanian	920	0.0	846	0.0
Rusyn	4,673	0.2	8,317	0.3
Croatian	1,490,672	61.7	1,638,354	62.5
Serbian	610,908	25.3	644,955	24.6
Other	64,753	2.7	67,843	2.6
Total non-Hungarian	2,325,523	96.2	2,516,006	95.9
Total	2,416,304	100	2,621,954	100
Hungarian Kingdom				
Hungarian	8,742,301	45.4	10,050,575	48.1
German	2,135,181	11.1	2,037,435	9.8
Slovak	2,019.641	10.5	1,967,970	9.4
Romanian	2,799,479	14.5	2,949,032	14.1
Rusyn	429,447	2.2	472,587	2.3
Croatian	1,682,104	8.7	1,833,162	8.8
Serbian	1,048,645	5.5	1,106,471	5.3
Other	397,761	2.1	469,255	2.2
Total non-Hungarian	10,512,258	54.6	10,835,912	51.9
Total	19,254,559	100	20,886,487	100

Source: *Magyar Statisztikai Évkönyv. Új Folyam XXIII. 1915* (Budapest, 1918), 15, chart 11, "A népesség anyanyelve és magyarul tudása 1900-ban és 1910-ben."

In their analysis, and in their own efforts to bolster Slovak numbers, Czecho-slovak demographers were uninterested in linguistic assimilation, seeking instead to strip the inhabitants of Slovakia down to their national skins. Their efforts illustrate what Dominique Arel has explained as a backward-looking orientation toward language categories in censuses. Arel argues that even though nationalists portray linguistic assimilation as "forced, unnatural, and fundamentally illegitimate, the result of destructive policies by an 'imperialist' state," it is in reality a normal and expected occurrence. Among speakers of a less prestigious language, there are individuals who will choose to linguistically assimilate for social advancement.[34] In those cases declaration of one's mother tongue as the "language one best and most gladly speaks" may well differ from the language of one's mother. According to this reasoning, Czechoslovak demographers were backward-looking because they sought to discover the "real" nationality of the inhabitants of Slovakia, their "true group belonging" based on their ancestral origins rather than linguistic assimilation, whether coerced, statistically falsified, or voluntary.

Czechoslovak demographers sought to demonstrate the unreliability of the 1910 census of the Kingdom of Hungary through critical comparative examination of the data collected within the language categories of "mother tongue" and "language knowledge."[35] In a typical example, Jan Auerhan pointed to the 301,694 Magyars with knowledge of Slovak who were counted on the 1910 census within the sixteen counties and four municipalities of the Kingdom of Hungary that in whole or part became Slovakia.[36] Two-thirds of these people were likely to be ethnic Slovaks, he concluded. Counting them as Slovaks, instead of as Magyars with Slovak language knowledge, would raise the ethnic Slovak number from 1,708,592 to 1,900,000.[37] The likelihood that a Slovak would be proficient in the Magyar language in an environment where Magyar was the official language—the language of instruction in schools, the language used in government offices and the court system—was incomparably greater than that of a Magyar speaker's being proficient in Slovak.

Mother tongue was not a perfect indicator of nationality, but what could be offered in its stead to collect national data? Mráz, in his Žilina report, strikingly concluded that people's nationality alone be used for data purposes. Rather than employ language proxy, the census should ask the population directly for their nationality. This was a controversial method because of its high level of subjectivity. Nationality declaration would not be linked to language as an external marker. Considering how Czechoslovak demographers regarded mother tongue to have been manipulated on the censuses of the Kingdom of Hungary, Mráz wrote:

> In contrast to [mother tongue], the concept "nationality" means confession to a certain *internal conviction*, which cannot be explained in an ambiguous

way, similar to religious conviction. That confession to a certain nationality is the only correct one for ascertaining national ratios. "Mother tongue" has for this reason been eliminated from the demographic markers and as a surrogate question for "nationality."

In connection with this is the question at hand, whether a separate "Jewish nationality" should be accepted without regard to religious affiliation. It follows from the concept of nationality described that it is not possible to force someone to declare a separate Jewish nationality, if [that declaration] is to express their *internal conviction;* because the Jews indeed form a separate race, there will, however, be no recommendation in the instructions for this procedure, except that Jewish nationality shall be left to the rubric of "Other nationality." The Jews should be left the option of declaring themselves either for their own separate nationality or for the nationality of others, which with the influence of environment and education or the like they have accepted as their own. For the stating of the Jewish race the remaining rules of the statement of affiliation to the Jewish confession shall suffice.[38]

Mráz's interpretation of nationality as an "internal conviction" was most closely related to the definition advanced by Károly Keleti at the International Statistical Congress meeting in St. Petersburg in 1872. Keleti was the first director of the Hungarian Statistical Bureau, founded one year earlier, and helped create the 1867 and the 1880 censuses for the Kingdom of Hungary.[39]

The 1872 St. Petersburg congress debated not only nationality enumeration on the census but also the meaning of "nationality" itself. Three conceptions of nationality emerged from the deliberations: (1) *political,* in which nationality is equivalent to state belonging; (2) *physical,* in which nationality is defined racially; and (3) *psychical,* in which nationality is understood as a psychological community penetrating individual feeling and collective endeavors.[40] Keleti took the position that nationality cannot be equivalent to state belonging, as that is so-called political nationality, common in Western Europe but not in the multinational states of central and Eastern Europe. Nor does ethnic (*Stamm*) belonging answer to nationality, even if its main marker is language. "Nationality" was best defined, according to Keleti, as a "subjective state internal to the individual, a feeling analogous to religion that depends on origin and the environment in which a person lives and grows."[41]

Keleti's definition was based on social-psychological criteria for which it is difficult to secure an objective external marker. It moved away from language as a definite indicator of nationality, leaving room for one to profess a nationality whose language one may not use daily or is not considered a viable national language (like Hebrew or Yiddish in the view of the Czechoslovak state). This was a big plus for Mráz and his colleagues but also ambiguous enough to allow for pressures and falsifications, like those they presumed were embedded in the last Hungarian census before the war. Yet Keleti's definition was attractive to

the Czechoslovak demographers preparing the 1919 Slovak census. This definition would enable the individual to confess nationality as directly as religion, as
an expression of their internal conviction and self-understanding. Czechoslovak
demographers hoped it would bring out the numbers of ethnic Slovaks who had
previously been hidden from view because they had been counted as Magyar
speakers. They would now be recorded under the banner of their "real" nationality, free to directly profess their "true" group belonging. Jews, too, would be able
to declare their "true" group belonging for the first time—not only as a religion
but also as a distinct nationality.

Antonín Boháč found that Keleti's definition coincided with concepts of
ethno-racial group belonging.[42] "Since the means for expressing psychological
states is language," Boháč wrote, "as Keleti [elsewhere] has stated, the concept
of nationality in this sense is quite close to the concept of nationality as ethnic/
racial belonging (*kmenová příslušnost*), for which language is the main connecting bond and main external marker."[43] Boháč is correct to observe that Keleti's
definition bore a strong resemblance to a physical understanding of nationality,
which gave race or ethnicity an expanded role. Language remained the main
outward indicator of nationality but was no longer considered identical to nationality itself. Espousing this conception moved nationality closer to ethnicity
and elevated ethnic understandings of the self and the group.

The final formulation of the 1919 census shows that the Czechoslovak administration and its demographers accepted Mráz's definition of "nationality"
based on Keleti's: "an individual national-political conviction according to ethnic belonging to a certain national unit or nation."[44] Five subheadings were
placed under "Nationality" on the census form: "Slovaks and Czechs," "Rusyns,"
"Magyars," "Germans," and "Others."[45] Czechoslovak demographers understood Jewish nationality to be included under the subheading "Others." While
"Jewish nationality" was an available option, though not a requirement, for the
Jewish population, the category was not included on the actual census form in
1919. The 1919 census asked directly for nationality without the intermediary of
language.

In the late August heat of 1919, census takers dispersed across the territory
of Slovakia to ask the population about nationality. Many complained that the
whole endeavor was disorganized and insufficiently thought through. Census
takers expressed frustration that they had received the census forms with not
enough time to look them over nor to fill one out to use as an example. Lacking
funds and with inadequate organization, many found themselves forced to sleep
in train stations and on park benches during the census period, which surely
affected their ability to fulfill their duties. One census taker reported that his
census materials were stolen from him while he slept! The population and often
even local community officials had not been informed about the purpose of the

census nor when it would take place.[46] If these complaints are accurate, they undermine the seriousness with which the Czechoslovak administration prepared the foundation of the 1919 census, as well as the importance they placed upon it as a means of accurately proving national ratios in Slovakia.

Yet last-minute pre-census agitation to prepare the Slovak population did take place. The prominent Slovak national newspaper *Národnie noviny* called on Slovaks "to consciously and openly confess their Slovak stock . . . to let the beautiful words: 'I am Slovak' consciously and boldly sound from the mouths of loyal citizens."[47] This example is atypical, however, as the agitation took place in the western Slovak town of Turčiansky Svätý Martin, the seat of the Slovak national movement and home to the Matica Slovenska Slovak cultural society. *Národnie noviny* explained that the purpose of the census was to prove that Slovakia was Slovak and that taking part in the census was essential for building their own independent country. Every citizen could participate in building that independent state through the census, the article stressed, an idea meant to reinforce the democratic spirit of the new era.[48] "You have no reason to be ashamed of [declaring Slovak nationality]," counseled the leading newspaper in Šariš county, a region of eastern Slovakia where national consciousness remained minimal. "The Czechoslovak name has the best reputation not only in Europe but also in America and Asia." The paper ran boldface announcements at the foot of its pages urging all Slovaks to proudly declare to the census taker that they were Slovak.[49]

Yet these reassurances did little to assuage prevalent Slovak fears about the real purpose of the census. This terribly urgent appeal itself may have caused anxiety for a population with a low level of national consciousness. Suspicions ranged from the belief that the goal was to raise or introduce new taxes, undertake military recruitment, or carry out a plebiscite to divide the territory. The military rumor was the most widespread. Many Slovaks worried that a war would soon break out between the Poles and Magyars and that the job of the census takers was to find able-bodied men to fight. Any man who declared he was of Slovak nationality would be conscripted to fight once again, while other nationalities would be freed of that duty. Although it was later revealed that the rumor began in Magyar circles, many people in the border counties still held back from declaring themselves as Slovak. Others believed the census to be connected to imminent requisitioning of cattle and grain. Some, more optimistically, believed more satisfactory food and fuel distribution would follow, and possibly a more advantageous land distribution. Still others imagined the census to be an exercise in identifying foreigners (especially Magyars, Poles, and Magyarone Slovaks) and expelling them from Czechoslovakia.[50]

Widespread fears and suspicions about the real intentions of the 1919 Slovak census not only underscored the atmosphere of uncertainty and insecurity in Slovakia at the beginning of the Czechoslovak state-building project but also contributed to a certain level of inaccuracy in the results. Of the four national groups that were the most interesting to the state—Slovaks, Magyars, Germans, and Jews—the greatest difficulties arose in recording nationality for Slovaks and Jews. Magyars and Germans were by and large ready for the census and decisive in their declarations of nationality. Within the ethnic Magyar population, only state and municipal employees exhibited uncertainty in their declarations.[51]

Magyar language use, national uncertainty, fear, and mistrust accounted for the greatest difficulties in recording the highest possible number of Slovaks on the 1919 census. Magyar or Magyarone Slovak census takers were known to record entire ethnic Slovak or mixed nationality villages as being Magyar or to count individuals as Magyar because they were able to communicate with Magyar-speaking census takers without the help of an interpreter.[52] The latter illustrates precisely what Mráz and his colleagues had hoped to avoid in bypassing language as identical with or as a surrogate for nationality. They did not want ethnic Slovaks counted as Magyars based on their Magyar language proficiency. Other problems stemmed from uncertainty surrounding the meaning of "nationality" (primarily in eastern Slovakia). Many Slovaks feared what might happen to them if they did not declare themselves Magyars. They distrusted the "godless Czechs" and "false prophets from Prague" who came to their doors.[53] The Slovak population tended to be quite a bit more religious than the highly secularized Czech one, and Slovak national leaders expressed wariness about the "agnostic progressivism" of the Czech intelligentsia.[54] Common answers among Slovaks when asked about their nationality included "Slovak and Magyar" (*aji Slovák, aji Maďar*), "it doesn't matter" (*to všetko jedno*), and "Hungarian Slovak" (*Uhorský Slovák*).[55] In eastern Slovakia other answers included "I speak Slovak and Magyar" (*hutorím po slovensky i po maďarsky*), "I pray in Slovak" (*modlím sa po slovensky*), and "Catholic" (*katolík*).[56] Mráz noted in his analysis of the results that Slovaks often confused religion with nationality.[57]

Interestingly, this observation recalls the proximity of religious and national feeling within Czechoslovakia's reconceptualization of nationality, as well as the fine distinction made between them in recognizing "Jewish nationality." Nationality was something to be understood and felt as an "internal conviction, similar to religious confession," but consciously separated and given a higher position than religion in the hierarchy of self and group values of definition. One's nationality, not one's religion, was of the greatest interest to the state. One's nationality, not one's religion, was the primary indicator of one's most strongly held inner values and loyalties.

For the Jewish population, answers to the question of nationality were most striking for their variety. Census takers disparaged the eclecticism of the Jewish response, attributing it to opportunism. In some cases, they remarked, national declarations among Jews reached comical proportions: the head of one household declared as a Slovak, his wife as a German, and the children as Hungarians. They noted, however, that often Jews stuck to Jewish nationality so that they would not have to affiliate with any of the other nationality choices.[58] The majority of Jews in Slovakia chose the Jewish nationality option on the 1919 census, which was officially recorded as "Other." Census takers recommended that a separate "Jewish" column be made available on the next census because so many Jews had expressly asked for it.[59] In the uncertain environment that prevailed in Slovakia in August 1919, shortly after the rollback of Béla Kun's Hungarian Red Army forces but before the de jure securing of the Czechoslovak borders, Jews in Slovakia wanted to avoid a difficult and possibly treacherous national affiliation decision through declaring Jewish nationality. Many Jews viewed Jewish nationality as an escape from the nationality conflict. Choosing Jewish nationality appeared to be a good way to opt out, to take a neutral position, to make the safest bet on an unpredictable future. Basing the decision to declare oneself as Jewish under these criteria made it more a strategic and less a heartfelt choice. For the time being, at least, it had less to do with deep-seated feelings of belonging to a Jewish national group and more to do with trying to make the best possible choice in a high-stakes gamble.

The popularity of the Jewish nationality declaration on the 1919 Slovak census (as "Other"), combined with a majority ethnic Slovaks declaration as "Slovak," led to a significant decrease in the number of Magyars recorded in Slovakia compared with the previous, prewar census.[60] This decline heightened the Czechoslovak administration's awareness of further potential benefits rendered to the state by Jewish nationality. If the Jews, who traditionally affiliated with German speakers in Bohemia and Moravia and Magyar speakers in Slovakia, declared "Jewish" nationality, then the statistical legitimacy of the Czechoslovak nation-state would rise as the numbers of Germans and Hungarians fell. "Jewish" nationality would work to the advantage of the dominant "Czechoslovak" nationality and national state.

If Jewish nationality favored the Czechoslovak nationality in solving the state's nationalities problems, as this argument goes, then declaring Jewish nationality was not really a way of opting out. It was not a neutral position. It could not be an escape from the nationality conflict if it meant—once again—casting one's lot with the dominant state nationality. Jewish nationality may have seemed like an exit, but this was an illusion. One could not avoid taking sides in the interwar nationality conflicts.

It is a valid and important point that the Czechoslovak government would favor Jewish nationality for its ability to statistically reduce the number of Germans and Magyars in the state. But that conclusion neglects the deeper meaning of its inclusion beyond the statistical benefits it could render. Creating a "Jewish nationality" category manifested how the meaning of national affiliation had transformed through the cataclysm of the First World War and the establishment of east central European successor states based on the national principle. Josef Mráz elegantly and succinctly summed up these changes when he said that a person's declaring a certain nationality was an expression of *internal conviction*. Because the very meaning of national affiliation had changed, "Jewish" emerged as a recognized nationality category. Nationality had taken on the problematic role of the manifestation of one's personal convictions, inner values, and ultimate loyalty. Nationality moved ever closer to an essential ethnic or racial understandings of "true" group belonging.

The 1920 Elections and the "Associated Jewish Parties"

The same transformations in the meaning of nationality and nationhood in the state that gave rise to "Jewish nationality" also opened the door for Jewish participation in Czechoslovakia's political life. Czechoslovakia acknowledged the Jewish population as a national minority and nationality, which was important to the state in its attempt to solve its nationality problems. But Jews also sought political representation to secure their rights and interests. While Jewish nationality was largely the province of Czechoslovak demographers, who made it available as a category of national affiliation, Jewish national politics in Czechoslovakia was predominantly a Zionist enterprise. By the time of the first parliamentary elections in 1920, a statewide Jewish political party was ready to present its list of candidates. Despite their similarity in origins, "Jewish" as a category of national affiliation and Jewish national politics were not equivalent. Their relationship is distinguished primarily by the influence of Zionists in Bohemia on shaping the outlook and program of Jewish national politics in Czechoslovakia. "A Jew cannot be a Zionist without national consciousness, but a nationally conscious Jew does not have to be a Zionist," remarked Yeshayahu Jelínek.[61]

The Prague-based Jewish Party struggled throughout the twenty years of the republic to gain the votes of the majority Orthodox Jews in Slovakia and Subcarpathian Ruthenia, whose numbers were needed to achieve a parliamentary mandate.[62] Though a majority of the Jews in these two provinces would declare Jewish nationality on the interwar censuses, their Jewish nationality affiliations usually did not tally with votes for the Jewish Party. The reverse held true in Bohemia, where Jews declared Jewish nationality in lower proportions in 1921 and 1930 than they turned out for the Jewish Party.[63] Through the process of Czechoslovakia's first parliamentary elections in 1920, the Jewish national political leadership in Slovakia established its relationship to the Jewish Party. The Jewish People's Union for Slovakia (JPU; Ľudový zväz židov pre Slovensko/Volksverband der Juden für die Slovakei) would join together with the Jewish National Council (Jewish Party) of Bohemia and Moravia-Silesia for the sake of the elections but would otherwise pursue its own path. At the same time the Orthodox clarified their oppositional strategies and Slovak discontent with the interwar Jewish anti-assimilationist position grew.

Jews in Slovakia organized a Jewish Committee of their own on November 3, 1918, in Piešťany, on the heels of the Slovak National Council's creation in Turčiansky Svätý Martin, the seat of the Slovak national movement. Delegates from the Jewish Committee in Slovakia joined members of other Jewish groups in Slovakia at the congress of the Jewish National Council in Prague in January, where Jewish leaders from Bohemia, Moravia, and Slovakia met for the first time, establishing contacts and sharing ideas for future cooperation. When the delegates returned to Slovakia from Prague, they held a convention in Piešťany, where they established the JPU. The JPU became the Slovak section of the Associated Jewish Parties in February 1920 when it resolved to affiliate with the Jewish National Council in preparation for the first Czechoslovak parliamentary elections scheduled for April.[64] The Associated Jewish Parties functioned as the organizational coalition for statewide elections. In all of its endeavors, this coalition sought to defend newly gained Jewish national rights in Czechoslovakia and to detach the Jewish population from its prewar cultural alliances and assimilationist trends.[65] The upcoming elections offered the opportunity to institute those changes.

The JPU concentrated on the everyday challenges confronted by Jews in Slovakia while maintaining its position in the Associated Jewish Parties' electoral coalition. The common Czechoslovak Jewish national platform appealed to them, but implications of the social, economic, and cultural legacies of Hungary for their current position in Slovakia were foremost among their concerns. The JPU faced the task of balancing the broader Czechoslovak program with their specific local Jewish needs. But although it valued the statewide Jewish alliance that had already been concluded, it wished to maintain its autonomy within that coalition, which had been formed only, as it understood, because of the difficulties involved in securing a parliamentary mandate for their small minority party.[66] "It is evident from the outline of the [Associated Jewish Parties] program," explained Leopold Ringwald, the JPU delegate from Trenčín in his remarks to the Piešťany congress, "that the alliance of the Jewish groups in Slovakia with the other Jewish parties in Bohemia, Moravia and Silesia has taken place exclusively for the goal of the election and with consideration for the technical necessities of electoral law. For all other intents and purposes, the position of Jewry in Slovakia shall be differentiated from that of the Jews in Bohemia, Moravia and Silesia."[67]

Minority political parties faced special difficulties in achieving parliamentary representation due to obstacles built into the state's electoral system. Election law required that each party presenting a list of candidates must have twenty thousand votes in at least one electoral constituency, or all votes for that party throughout the state would be lost.[68] This law challenged smaller parties, like the newly formed Associated Jewish Parties, to create electoral strategies designed to achieve the required level of district representation in order to participate in statewide elections. A further barrier to electing Jewish representatives in Slovakia was Czechoslovakia's maintenance of the old Hungarian administrative system for the region until 1923. Under that system Slovakia was divided into seven districts (*župy*), in none of which did the Jews constitute 20 percent of the population.[69]

The Czechoslovak electoral system was adapted from its Austrian predecessor. Suffrage was universal and compulsory for the adult voting population in parliamentary elections. The system maintained a large number of parties of limited size, an outcome of its basis in proportional representation. In spite of this, it was remarkably stable and its coalition cabinets cohesive. This was because a great deal of power was concentrated in the hands of a small number of party leaderships.[70] Czechoslovak politics took shape around "ideological" parties and was chiefly split along economic and ethnic fault lines. Class-oriented parties were a distinctive presence, but even these found ethno-national replication. Czech and German parties roughly mirrored each other's political alignments. Slovaks and Hungarians did not follow the same patterns as the Czechs and Germans. Instead, Slovak and Hungarian parties lacked the range of class-based parties, favoring ethno-national and religious organization. Their most important parties were Andrej Hlinka's Slovak People's Party and the Hungarian Christian Socialists. Ethno-national communities tended to vote for the ideological party affiliated with their nationalities (i.e., Czechoslovak Social Democratic Party, German Social Democratic Party, and the Hungarian Social Democratic Party).[71] It was because of the national character of the electoral system in Czechoslovakia that Jewish national leaders believed it was essential to form a Jewish Party to represent Jewish national interests. With the exception of the communists, national parties of all ideological stripes existed. A candidate of another nationality could not run on the ticket of another nationality's party.[72]

In the lead-up to the elections, the Bratislava-based organ of the Associated Jewish Parties in Slovakia, the *Jüdische Volkszeitung*, fleshed out the central concepts of the shared program that drove the overall party platform: defense, unity, and neutrality. Beyond serving as a means to defend common Jewish political, social, and economic interests, voting for the Associated Jewish Parties ostensibly offered a way out of the nationalities' conflict at the ballot box. The *Jüdische Volkszeitung* lauded this opportunity as a way to avoid taking sides. The Jews could free themselves from the consequences of national affiliations that they knew so well through voting for the Associated Jewish Parties.

Not so, argued Rabbi Koloman Wéber. The chief Orthodox rabbi of Piešt'any staked out his position as primary oppositional figure to Zionism and Jewish national politics in the republic. Rabbi Wéber contended in early 1920 that the Jews would do better by casting their votes for a number of supportive non-Jewish candidates for parliament.[73] This sort of argument, the Associated Jewish Parties countered, split Jewish voters, making it all the more difficult to achieve parliamentary representation.[74] In his address to the February Piešt'any meeting, Angelo Goldstein, the cofounder and president of the Jewish Party (Jewish National Council of Bohemia and Moravia), charged Rabbi Wéber with promoting what he called a destructive pattern of Jewish alignment with the dominant state nationality. Changed times demanded different tactics, he contended.[75]

In contrast to Rabbi Wéber, the chief Orthodox rabbi of Vrbové, Rabbi Reich, supported Jewish national political activity in Czechoslovakia. "Every Jew in Slovakia who does not close his eyes to obvious facts must surely realize that the Jewish Party offers the only possibility of avoiding conflict with every party, every religion and every nationality, of eliminating all misunderstandings," he wrote.[76] Rabbi Reich disagreed with Rabbi Wéber on both political matters and transitional aid strategies. He supported the Slovak-language training program for Jewish educators that took place in 1919 in Bratislava, for instance, a program to which the Central Office of Orthodox Jewish Communities did not contribute because it was organized by the Jewish People's Union. Rabbi Reich was an important ally for the Associated Jewish Parties to have. The Jewish national political parties hoped his support might convince the majority Orthodox Jewish population of Slovakia and Subcarpathian Ruthenia to cast their votes for the Jewish national parties.

Preparation for the 1920 parliamentary elections activated and located Jewish national politics in Czechoslovakia. Debates within the Jewish community over political strategies and alliances for the upcoming election clarified each faction's position within the Czechoslovak political system. This was an important step in the larger process of political orientation as citizens of the new state. The Associated Jewish Parties aimed to create a Jewish minority voting bloc to achieve the distant goal of representation by keeping the Jewish voting public from voting for other parties. Rabbi Wéber, on the other hand, urged Jewish voters to seek representation and protection through the dominant, non-Jewish parties and not engage in minority politics. The JPU concentrated on major local economic and social issues in drawing voters to the Associated Jewish Parties' list: reimbursement for damages sustained during the Prevrat plundering, the right to keep Jewish stores closed on Saturday (the Jewish Sabbath), the right to establish Jewish schools, and the establishment of a Jewish hospital in Bratislava.[77]

Just three days before the parliamentary elections, the Czechoslovak administration in Bratislava granted Orthodox Jewish communities in Slovakia full autonomy over their affairs. The Orthodox communities established a Central Autonomous Orthodox Office in Bratislava, which would be responsible for administering all Orthodox Jewish communities in Slovakia. The Central Autonomous Orthodox Office had the authority to approve or veto election results within Jewish communities, hire and dismiss rabbis, and play an active role in Orthodox Jewish community affairs across Slovakia. The JPU and the Jewish Party opposed this action as the government privileging the Orthodox; however, they could do nothing to mitigate the elevated status of the Orthodox. Since they saw the Bratislava government as bowing to Orthodox demands and turning a blind eye to antisemitism in Slovakia, Jewish national organizations lacked trust in local authorities. The newly formed Central Autonomous Orthodox Office showed its gratitude for government favor by agitating for government parties within Orthodox communities before the elections.[78] The Czechoslovak government continued to favor the Orthodox throughout the interwar period. The state repeatedly referred to the 1920 separation of the Orthodox Jewish community in Slovakia from Budapest as proof of their superior state loyalty when compared with the Neolog Jewish community, which would not separate from Budapest until 1926.

Czechoslovak governmental favoritism of the Orthodox reflected its understanding of the political underpinnings and aspects of collective identification connected to the Jewish religious division in Old Hungary. Favoring the Orthodox served not only to more tightly bind the majority Jewish population in Slovakia to the state but also to demonstrate the advantages of renouncing the historical alliance with the Magyars among the Neolog, along with giving up their deeper social and cultural Magyarization. The Orthodox were also more legible to the state than the Jewish national JPU or supporters of the Jewish Party. The state preferred the clear, traditionally framed Orthodox state loyalty.

The results of the April 1920 elections signaled success for the Associated Jewish Parties. Although the coalition did not receive a single mandate in parliament, 79,714 people across the republic voted in favor of the Associated Jewish Parties. Nevertheless, this raised concerns about the Jewish position and led to a reconsideration of how the Piešt'any program for the protection of the political, social, and economic rights of the Jewish in Slovakia could be fulfilled. The sense of urgency that characterized the initial calls for national Jewish politics in Czechoslovakia was fed by increased agitation and activity as the Jewish leadership sought other means of self-help and defense. Yet even without gaining a parliamentary mandate, voter turnout on behalf of the Associated Jewish Parties was significant. Close to 80,000 of the statewide Jewish voting-age population cast ballots for the Jewish Party. In Slovakia 45,000 of the Jewish voting-age population,[79] or nearly 70 percent, voted for the Associated Jewish Parties[80]—that is, 45,000 votes out of approximately 65,000 among the Jews in Slovakia. That left 34,714 votes cast for the Jewish Party in Bohemia, Moravia, and Silesia.

For Emil Waldstein, president of the JPU, the opportunity to vote for a Jewish party for the first time had been nothing less than a national plebiscite. As such, the election results were highly gratifying, he cheered, proving "We are a People" (*Wir sind ein Volk*).[81] Garnering close to eighty thousand votes for a political party that had been formed just shortly before the elections was no mean feat. Despite the lack of success in achieving a parliamentary mandate, the election gave Jewish politics a wide base of support. The Associated Jewish Parties met in Brno, Moravia, in June to create an extra parliamentary forum for Jewish national representation in Czechoslovakia. "The [Brno] Congress unanimously, clearly, and distinctly gave the understanding that the Jewish People no longer want to be treated as second-class citizens, and demand their rightful place in political life," wrote the *Jüdische Volkszeitung*.[82]

The Associated Jewish Parties' failure to win a parliamentary mandate in 1920 heightened tensions between the Jewish national political leadership and the Orthodox. Jewish national circles provoked the Orthodox, asking if their Bratislava office could defend the rights and interests of Jews in Slovakia as well as Jewish national political representation could.[83] Political fragmentation and conflict within the Jewish community had strongly contributed to the inability of the Associated Jewish Parties to enter parliament, in addition to the demanding 20 percent election law and Czechoslovakia's maintenance of Slovakia's seven Hungarian electoral districts. The Orthodox Conservative Jewish Party and Jewish Economic Party, the latter headed by Rabbis Wéber and Simon Hirschler, split the vote by each presenting their own separate lists. Many Jews also voted for the Social Democratic Party, the Hungarian National Party, and the Communist Party. The assimilationist Union of Slovak Jews (*Sväz Slovenských Židov*) also opposed the Associated Jewish Parties.[84] Tensions came to a head between Jewish national and Orthodox Jews in 1926. The 1925 elections had been a great disappointment, and Emil Margulies, president of the Jewish Party, suspected foul play. He took the Orthodox to court that year for allegedly accepting 100,000 crowns (US$2,960) in bribes from the Agrarian Party to divert votes to their Jewish Economic Party during the 1925 parliamentary elections. Rabbis Wéber and Hirschler lost this highly publicized, two-year-long case, in which Margulies assembled a set of well-documented evidence against them.[85]

The statutes of the "Conservative Jewish Party" reveal what more of substance was behind the formation of the party than divisive electoral strategy. Above all, party leadership emphasized its dedication to the Czechoslovak state and to Jewish tradition. "The 'Conservative Jewish Party' wants to be a leading and state-forming party," Rabbi Wéber declared in the party's statutes, "and it will seek to align itself and cooperate only with such groups which have taken it as their highest and overarching goal to exert their efforts to protect the state and its development."[86] The Conservative Jewish Party sought to build on the equal rights guaranteed for every citizen of the state rather than secure Jewish rights as a recognized national minority.[87] Five points defined the Conservative Jewish Party program, beginning with the dedication to a Torah-true Jewish lifestyle. The party favored Jewish religious community autonomy, refused to associate with elements that were subversive to the state, worked toward the well-being and betterment of all social classes, and observed "the strongest neutrality" in the nationalities question, refusing to mix into the debates of the various national parties.[88] For the Orthodox the commitment to neutrality meant unconditional loyalty to the state in a fulfillment of the injunction for Jews living in the Diaspora to "seek the peace of the city," to dedicate themselves to the well-being of the state and its leadership, and to recognize that "the law of the land is the law."[89]

Neither the Orthodox nor the national Jews wished to be caught up in the national fray. But their strategies differed sharply and invited mutual confrontation. Both positions were non-integrationist and sought "the right path" by working for what they saw as the best interests of the Jews without taking the side of one nationality against the other. Both worked under the assumption that neutrality in the nationalities conflict was in fact an achievable goal and that it was in agreement with the desires of the Czechoslovak state. The primary difference between them lay in the contrast between the traditional strategies of national accommodation of the Orthodox versus the Jewish Party's embrace of modern Jewish national politics.

The Jewish national position was attractive for its newness and for its seeming ability to help the Jewish population break with old habits and patterns of national accommodation that had turned against them so bitterly in the aftermath of the First World War. It had strong appeal in the multinational east central European successor states as a way for Jews to avoid national conflicts. According to Oscar Janowsky, "In the mixed population of east-central Europe the association of the Jews with a nationality other than their own would be exceedingly dangerous for themselves and troublesome for others. . . . [Precedents show that] wherever two or more nationalities shared the same territory the Jews were under suspicion as an agent of denationalization, unless they declared themselves of Jewish nationality."[90]

Janowsky saw Jewish nationality as the best escape from fateful questions of national affiliation in the multinational state. In his view, aligning solely with a separate Jewish national group for the purposes of voting, census declaration, and social interactions would establish an equal Jewish position between the nationalities and provide a beneficial working strategy. Many Jews agreed that there were national answers to long-standing social and political Jewish questions. Ezra Mendelsohn points to multinational interwar in east central Europe as an "ideal environment" for modern Jewish national politics. Jewish nationalism tends to fare well in multinational regions where, in particular, the surrounding nationalities have a low acculturational attraction, long-standing patterns of Jewish acculturation and integration have been suddenly disrupted, and antisemitism discourages Jews from attempts to join the dominant nationality.[91]

The assimilationist or accommodationist answers of the past became object lessons for the present. The *Jüdische Volkszeitung* took this angle in fashioning its response to a provocative article by the publicist Karel Kálal in which he speculated on the benefits of Jewish assimilation for the Slovak nation. "There are 140,000 of them in Slovakia and 80,000 in Subcarpathian Ruthenia," he wrote, "in total nearly a quarter million educated and well-to-do people. If they were to go with the [Slovak] nation, for example through voting and through fundraising for the national cause, the decision would mean a strengthening of the Slovak nation. If they were to go with the Magyars or the Germans, though, this would surely damage us."[92]

The *Jüdische Volkszeitung* dismissed Kálal's proposal as a destructive remnant of a bygone world. Times had changed. The paper presented its narrative on past patterns of national accommodation and its consequences in prewar Hungary. "We do not wish to deny that the position of much of the Jewish intelligentsia in former Hungary, so also in the territory of Slovakia, was unfortunate and blameworthy, not only from the standpoint of the Slovaks and the remaining non-Magyar nationalities, but chiefly from the Jewish perspective," read the article:

> Even though the Jews did in no way participate in the oppression of the other nationalities, and lived mostly on the best terms with their Slovak, German, Romanian, and Serbian neighbors, the chauvinistic behavior of the Jewish intelligentsia incurred the hatred of the non-Magyar ethnicities against the Jews. Should the Jews in Czechoslovakia now fall into the same errors, as Mr. Kálal seems to wish, and assimilate culturally and nationally to the Slovaks? With that they would surely incite the enmity of the Germans, Magyars, Poles and Ruthenes upon them.[93]

The *Jüdische Volkszeitung* chose to scapegoat the Jewish intelligentsia in acknowledging the predicament of the non-Magyar nationalities in Hungary before the war. It separated out the circle of Jewish intelligentsia from the Jewish population as a whole and laid the blame at its feet. But it would not advocate a new policy of assimilation to the Slovaks to repent for past errors. Assimilation policy had done more damage to the Jews themselves than to anyone else, the paper reminded its readership, and should not be repeated. It was time to start anew.

For Jews in Slovakia the presumed ability to rid themselves of associations with the Magyar government and its Dualist-era Magyarization policy through Jewish nationality and Jewish national politics appeared as a great strength of the Jewish national argument. It also served as a general defense against assimilation. The steadily clarifying Jewish national position in Slovakia is evident in the period following the 1920 elections. Jewish national political work became more firmly grounded by the end of the year. It became localized in the Slovak environment and its characteristics defined less by broader international conceptions. As the mouthpiece of the Associated Jewish Parties and the organ of the Jewish national minority cause, the German-language *Jüdische Volkszeitung* was central to filling the Jewish national position with meaning for the Jews in Slovakia. Since the emergence of Jewish national associations in the territory of Slovakia, German was the language of the movement. Assimilation, and especially Magyarization, ceased at the Jewish national border. German language usage was a way to show separation from Hungary and Magyarization while underscoring a feeling of Jewish national belonging. Tensions with the Orthodox, rejection of any assimilationist position, distancing from the "chauvinistic Jewish intelligentsia" of the Dualist period, and reaffirmation of the neutrality principle were the key components of the postelection Jewish national position.

Counting the Nationalities

Preparations for the first statewide Czechoslovak census reopened debate over how the state would view and count nationality after analysis of the 1919 results in Slovakia and the parliamentary elections were complete. Decisions that Josef Mráz had made for the 1919 Slovak census again came under close scrutiny. The understanding of nationality as an internal conviction he advocated, which became formalized as "an individual national-political conviction according to ethnic belonging to a certain national unit or nation,"[94] could now be more carefully considered in an atmosphere of lesser haste. The census had to be designed to fit a structured legal framework reflecting the newly ratified Czechoslovak constitution.[95] Now the debate centered on the question of how to count nationality. Should the statewide census ask the population directly for nationality as had the Slovak census? Or should language again be used as an objective external marker, a surrogate for nationality, as it had been on the censuses of the Habsburg Monarchy? The answer to this question had important implications for the practical application of minority rights protections in multinational Czechoslovakia.

The Czechoslovak constitution guaranteed minority protection on both individual and corporate levels. Individually, members of national, religious, or ethnic/racial minority groups were to be treated no differently than members of the Czechoslovak national majority; all were to be equal before the law. Members of minority groups had the same civil and political rights as members of the majority, as well as the same right of entry to public service and offices, to attain any promotion or dignity; to practice any trade or calling; and to use any language in any private and business relations, in all religious affairs, in the press, in publications of any kind, and in public assembly.[96] These rights were constitutionally guaranteed without regard to the numerical strength of the minority group.[97]

Numerical strength became an issue as it pertained to guarantees of corporate minority rights. In contrast to the rights that individuals were entitled to enjoy automatically, corporate minority rights required proof that the national, religious, or linguistic group in question comprised a considerable fraction (*značný zlomek*) of the population of a town or district, where a considerable fraction was defined as 20 percent. That proof was to be furnished by the state census.[98] For example, in towns or districts where a national, religious, or linguistic minority consisted of at least 20 percent of the population, and where public funds had been set aside for educational, religious, or philanthropic usage, that minority was entitled to a share of those public funds.[99] Where the allocation of public funds was involved, the state was obliged to clearly and objectively ascertain national, religious, and linguistic ratios within the population.

The Czechoslovak state most fully elaborated its minority protection guarantees with respect to language. An additional language law, found at the end of the constitution, delineated language usage in Czechoslovakia, defining precisely what was meant by establishing the Czechoslovak language as the official language of the state, as well as where and how minority languages would be officially employed.[100] By the principles of minority language rights established by the constitution and the language law, in towns and districts where there lived a national minority comprising a considerable fraction (20 percent) of the population the language of that national minority was to be used simultaneously with Czechoslovak for all official notices of the courts, offices, and organs of the state; the instruction in and administration of schools for members of the national minority was to be given in their language; and all educational and cultural institutions set up for that national minority were to be administered in their language.[101]

The emphasis placed upon numerical strength for the exercise of corporate linguistic rights of national minorities made it imperative for the state to correctly assess linguistic ratios to ensure fair application of the law. In addition, the wording of the language law set up "language" and "nationality" as parallel terms, indicating that the framers of the law viewed the two as identical. As such, the language law stood in contradiction to the method used for the 1919 Slovak census, which asked the population directly for their nationality, disengaging language as an absolute marker of national belonging to get at "real" national ratios beyond linguistic assimilation. In order to make the 1921 census methodology accord with corporate minority language rights guarantees, the 1919 basis of how the state defined and counted nationality would have to be rethought.

Antonín Boháč, in an article for the *Czechoslovak Statistical Bulletin* weighing the pros and cons of counting nationality directly or using mother tongue as a surrogate, argued the case for mother tongue. In doing so, he cited the law of February 29, 1920, regarding the rights of linguistic minority protection. "The law demands the determination of linguistic ratios in the census," he simply stated.[102] The answer to the question of how nationality should be counted on the 1921 census seemed clear to him: it had already been decided in the ratification of the Czechoslovak constitution and accompanying language laws.

Even so, Boháč did not wholly dispute the arguments made in favor of direct national declaration. There are nations, he agreed, that may have lost their national language but still had not ceased to live their own peculiar national life. The Jews were the prime example of this atypical case within the Czechoslovak context, he explained. The Jews in Czechoslovakia, he continued, had lost Hebrew, their mother tongue, and did not even speak the so-called jargon (Yiddish), and yet they remained a nation. However, Boháč felt that while the Jewish case provided sufficient proof that linguistic statistics were not identical to national statistics, it was more important for the state to count mother tongue as an objective external marker for the purposes of the census rather than to slip into the morass of subjectivity by asking everyone to directly declare his or her nationality.[103]

When he later reflected on the debate surrounding nationality in the preparation of the 1921 census, Boháč came to the following conclusion: "In actuality, the dispute between the advocates of mother tongue and nationality was in fact led by whether Jewish nationality should be recognized or not."[104] The case of the Jewish national minority held a central position in the overall reevaluation of nationality within the context of Czechoslovak state building. The preparers of the 1921 census used Jewish nationality as an exceptional example with which to compose their arguments both for and against direct national declaration, with both sides having nearly equal representation.[105] At its base the recognition of Jewish nationality meant foregoing counting the population according to one's mother tongue and keeping with direct national declaration as it had been done in Slovakia in 1919. The primary objective at that time had been proving the inaccuracies of the census of the Kingdom of Hungary in order to show the Paris Peace Conference how many Slovaks there actually were. Direct national declaration facilitated that goal and indeed would also work in favor of a clearer overall assessment of the numbers of ethnic Czechs and Slovaks in the state.

Now, however, there were additional issues to be taken into consideration. Foremost among these was making good on pledges of minority protections. The dilemma here was that recognizing an independent Jewish nationality, and therefore fulfilling Zionist demands by allowing for corporate Jewish minority protections, aroused the fear of the German minority that their corporate protections, based on language, would be compromised. They feared that the overall number of German speakers in the state would be reduced by Jews' declaring "Jewish" instead of "German" nationality.[106] While the Jewish minority bore a relatively light statistical weight within the state,[107] Jews had the potential to tip the scales of linguistic ratios in a given town or district. If this were to happen, the much more numerous German minority could lose its 20 percent (or considerable fraction) of a district population necessary for securing German-language schooling, cultural institutions, and official administrative usage.[108] Czechoslovakia contended with the problem of fulfilling its obligations to the two types of recognized national minorities within the state: kin-state linguistic national minorities such as the Germans, whose corporate protections were based on linguistic criteria; as well as non-kin-state nonlinguistic national minorities such as the Jews, whose corporate protections were based on subjective recognition of national minority status that allowed them political representation.[109]

The Ministry of the Interior called for a subcommittee to convene and offer its proposal on this contentious issue. That subcommittee met in early fall 1920, composed of seven members, including the notable Bohemian-German statistician Heinrich Rauchberg, professor of statistics at the University of Vienna before the war and later in Prague. The subcommittee agreed, albeit following a four to three vote, that nationality should be determined on the basis of mother tongue.[110] Alongside their decision the subcommittee offered a compromise that, in their words, could satisfy the national feelings of the Jews. The compromise entailed offering the opportunity to indicate their nationality in addition to mother tongue to individuals for whom these categories differed. The subcommittee, however, had this comment to add to the proposed compromise: "Admittedly, declaring Jewish nationality would have neither statistical nor scientific value, because it would be done arbitrarily, and would not express the cultural affiliation of the Jewish minority, but only its efforts to declare neither for the Czechs nor for the Germans."[111] Thus the subcommittee saw the Jewish nationality category as a means for the Jews to opt out, to declare neither for the Czechs nor the Germans, to take the third road. Based on this interpretation, it appears that the subcommittee would have looked more favorably upon Jewish nationality had it been a more obvious expression of Jewish cultural affiliation.

But what would have satisfied committee members as proof that the Jews were declaring Jewish nationality as an expression of their cultural affiliation? Since the subcommittee as well as the central census preparation committee took the parameters of national relations in Bohemia as their focus point, and not those in Slovakia or Subcarpathian Ruthenia, where the number of Jews was substantially higher and their communities more strongly bound by Jewish cultural and religious affiliations, it was indeed difficult for them to see Jewish nationality as more than an escape from declaring Czech or German. The wording of the comment also indicates that the subcommittee understood nationality chiefly in terms of cultural affiliation rather than ethnic belonging, where language would be the obvious indicator of nationality.

The main census preparation committee took the decision of the subcommittee into account in reaching an official definition of nationality. The definition that the committee narrowly accepted was a compromise in favor of direct national declaration, a move that was intended to reconcile the proponents of mother tongue: "Nationality is understood as ethnic belonging, whose main external marker is as a rule mother tongue."[112] Although this definition recognized mother tongue as the primary indicator of nationality, it maintained the three key points upon which the 1919 Slovak census had been based: (1) nationality is an expression of ethnic/racial belonging; (2) mother tongue is usually but not always identical to nationality; and, most important, (3) nationality should be counted directly. This formulation allowed for linguistic national minorities, such as the Germans, to be guaranteed corporate rights based on their direct national declaration, which was understood as a simultaneous declaration of mother tongue. Jews were able, but not required, to declare "Jewish" as their nationality regardless of mother tongue. To further clarify the basis of direct national declaration, the Czechoslovak government signed a statute requiring that nationality be registered according to mother tongue as a rule. The statute allowed exceptions only for individuals who did not speak their mother tongue in their family or at home and had completely mastered the tongue of another nationality and for Jews. Jews could declare Jewish nationality or any of the other nationality choices as they deemed appropriate to their individual situation.[113]

The constitutional provisions, extent of the debate, and legislative decisions that followed suggest the seriousness with which the Czechoslovak state regarded minority rights protections and its mandate to fulfill them. It appears that Czechoslovakia was sincere in its intention to secure the rights of all of its citizens within a democratic framework. The focus of the debates indicates that Czechoslovakia was most concerned with the position of its German minority and took criticisms of that minority's representatives the most seriously of any national minority within the state. The debates also indicate that questions of national relations between Czechs and Germans took precedence over others. This study, therefore, faces the challenge of assessing how decisions driven by the central Czech/German question affected Slovakia.

A deciding factor in the census committee's ultimate decision for direct national declaration was undoubtedly the fact that it advantaged the dominant Czechoslovak nationality. No matter what language Czechs and Slovaks used daily or in which they maintained some level of proficiency, regardless of whether it had been acquired voluntarily or by force, their numbers would no longer be added to another national group to which they did not feel they belonged simply on account of language. Czechoslovakia was their state, they were the dominant nationality, and it made sense to declare nationality in the way they believed most accurately represented their numbers, as long as in doing so they had made every effort to secure the rights of others. In reflecting on the changes Czechoslovakia had made in its census methodology, Cyril Horáček cited the repression of the Czechs and especially the Slovaks under the Habsburgs. He explained that in a state whose basis was the Czechoslovak nation, it was necessary to make legislative modifications to reflect current conditions.[114]

That these modifications allowed for state recognition of Jewish nationality on the individual and corporate levels benefited Czechoslovakia alone. First, Czechoslovakia's willing compliance with the Minorities Treaties, with the provisions for minority protections in the Treaty of St. Germain, and with the demands of the Jewish Council of Czechoslovakia reinforced its democratic standing in the eyes of the international community. Second, it cannot be denied that if Jews who had previously declared German or Magyar in the previous, prewar Austrian and Hungarian censuses would now confess to the nonlinguistically bound Jewish nationality, the numbers of German and Magyar citizens of Czechoslovakia would shrink, thereby enhancing the statistical legitimacy of Czechoslovakia as a nation-state. The "Jewish" nationality category also worked symbiotically with the "Czechoslovak" one in arguing for and reaching the ethnic/racial definition of "nationality" that would be used throughout the interwar period in Czechoslovakia. Jewish nationality worked in favor of the centralized Czechoslovak state idea. As such, a declaration for Jewish nationality was in this context an indirect vote for the Czechoslovak nation, a way of casting one's lot with the dominant state nationality.

It is in fact no great stretch to regard national declaration on the census as a vote. Both the census and the elections gave individuals the opportunity to assert their political relationship to the state, based on their personal sense of national belonging. While earlier the state had been interested in counting the population for the purposes of conscription and taxation, the creation of states based on the national principle after the First World War pushed the nation into the dominant position of state legitimacy and made it imperative for the state to classify its population nationally. National belonging simultaneously moved to the top of the hierarchy of possible individual identities. Both the census and elections were politically important ways for the state to understand, map, and shape the collective national identities of the population.[115]

The census process itself has been compared to a political campaign.[116] As in a political campaign, groups desiring a specific outcome seek to influence the population to vote in a way that will be advantageous for their cause. In the case of the Czechoslovak census of 1921, national groups actively sought to sway the most unpredictable segments of the population: Slovaks, Jews, and Rusyns. In their monitoring of pre-census agitation among the nationalities of the state, therefore, the authorities paid special attention to Slovakia. National consciousness and certainty of national belonging were at the highest levels in Bohemia and Moravia and at much lower levels in Slovakia and Subcarpathian Ruthenia. The authorities collected newspaper clippings, pamphlets, and flyers, and submitted reports to the minister plenipotentiary of Slovakia that documented national declaration persuasion efforts.[117]

Agitation from the Magyar side relied on arguments advocating Magyar declarations based on language usage. This was a good tactic. It agreed with statute 86/30, which required that nationality be recorded according to mother tongue as a rule. The statute stressed the importance of Magyar declarations for Magyars who may have been tempted to declare for another nationality in the changed circumstances, and had the potential to influence Slovaks and Jews who spoke Magyar proficiently or as their mother tongue. For example, a Magyar-language flyer circulated in the beginning of February in Nové Zámky in southern Slovakia by the Magyar Christian Socialists and the Magyar Smallholders, Agriculturalists, and Artisans Party called on local citizens to stand by their Magyar mother tongue. "Whoever abandons Hungariandom now destroys the future of their children," the flyer warned. It also offered instructions on how to fill out the census forms in order to avoid confusion or misrepresentation: enter "Czechoslovak" as your citizenship in column ten, the flyer coached, but enter "Magyar" as your nationality in column eleven.[118]

An article in the daily *Magyar Ujság* dealt directly with the question of how Jews should fill in the same controversial column eleven, arguing that declarations of Jewish nationality would put the Jews in a delicate position regarding the Magyar national minority. If the Jews would not declare themselves as Magyars, the article stressed, the Magyars in numerous towns and districts would lose their 20 percent of the population and along with that their minority rights. Would the Jews now want to sacrifice the cultural and economic fellowship they had shared with the Magyars for centuries? If the Jews were to declare Jewish nationality, it would not affect the Czechs or Slovaks, the article asserted, but it would greatly affect the minorities, as it would deprive them of their linguistic and cultural rights. The article suggested that the Jews would be better off forgetting about Jewish nationality until they used Hebrew as their vernacular, privately and professionally.[119] With its emphasis on how Jewish national declarations might negatively impact Magyar-Jewish relations in Czechoslovakia, the *Magyar Ujság* made an emotional appeal to the Magyar-speaking Jewish population of Slovakia to maintain their traditional national affiliations. The implication was implicit: if the Magyars lost their 20 percent, they would know who to blame.

Jewish national circles attempted to brace the Jewish population of Slovakia against arguments like those of the *Magyar Ujság*. Pre-census articles in the *Jüdische Volkszeitung* emphasized the Jewish national position as the only honest one for Jews to take and underlined the protection of Jewish nationality within the Czechoslovak legislative framework. This contrasted with what the paper called the falsity of the assimilationist position, the shamefulness and cowardice of aligning with other nationalities than one's own. Special bitterness was reserved for the former Jewish position in relation to the Magyars, the bankruptcy of which, the paper pronounced, had by now become evident.[120] Contributions to the *Jüdische Volkszeitung* recalled sentiments from the 1920 parliamentary elections. Now, however, the discussion moved forward with a greater sense of confidence and purpose, built on the 79,714 votes won by the Jewish Party, 45,000 of them in Slovakia alone. "The great mass of Slovak Jewry with [their votes] documented that they stand behind us," a lead pre-census article proclaimed. "They acknowledge and approve of the objectives of our developing Jewish politics."[121]

More than half of the Jewish population in Slovakia did indeed declare Jewish nationality in 1921. Out of a total number of 130,843 Czechoslovak citizens of the Jewish religion in Slovakia, 71,018 of them, or 54.28 percent, chose "Jewish" as their nationality on the census. Of the remaining Jews by religion in Slovakia, the largest percentage chose "Czechoslovak" nationality (22.27 percent), followed by "Magyar" (16.49 percent), "German" (6.68 percent), "Russian" (.14 percent) and "Other" (.14 percent).[122] The results in Slovakia were the most diverse in the state. While a clear 54 percent majority professed Jewish nationality, the overall responses point to the continuing internal diversity of the Jewish population. Jewish national politics had a strong following but did not totally counter the appeal of other nationality choices, even if there was a 32-point drop between "Jewish" and "Czechoslovak," the option receiving the second largest number of declarations. Declarations of both "Jewish" and "Czechoslovak" by Jews in Slovakia marked a significant break with prewar national affiliations.[123]

Results in Slovakia contrasted with the overwhelming majority of Jews by religion who opted for "Jewish" nationality in Subcarpathian Ruthenia, a full 86.81 percent in the region with the densest Jewish population in the state (15.39 percent of the total population). They also stood out against the small number of Jewish national declarations in Bohemia (14.6 percent), where the real contest was between "Czechoslovak" (49.49 percent) and "German" (34.63 percent) nationality. Jewish declarations in Moravia evidenced a three-way division of national affiliation choices. There, close to half of the Jewish population by religion (47.8 percent) chose "Jewish" nationality, followed by "German" (34.85 percent), at a 13-point drop from the leading "Jewish" nationality category, and "Czechoslovak" (15.71 percent).

In his overview of the 1921 census Antonín Boháč wrote that Jews in Slovakia formed an important national minority within the multinational region. Not only were Jews about four times more numerous in Slovakia than in Bohemia or Moravia, he said, but also, unlike the Jews in the historic lands, they lived in both urban centers and the countryside, and more than half considered themselves Jewish by both religion and nationality. Considering the geographic spread of

Table 2.3. Comparison of Jews by Religion and Jews by Nationality for Czechoslovak Citizens and Foreigners in Czechoslovakia, 1921, in Absolute Numbers and Percentages

DISTRICT	JEWS BY RELIGION/ ABSOLUTE NUMBERS	JEWS BY RELIGION/ PERCENTAGES	JEWS BY NATIONALITY/ ABSOLUTE NUMBERS	JEWS BY NATIONALITY/ PERCENTAGES	JEWS BY RELIGION DECLARING JEWISH NATIONALITY/ PERCENTAGES
Bohemia					
City of Prague	31,751	4.69	6,534	.9	20.58
District around Prague	8,894	.83	530	.05	5.96
Pardubice	2,313	.48	205	.04	8.86
Hradec Králové	2,621	.52	309	.06	11.79
Mladá Boleslav	4,300	.58	536	.05	12.47
Česká Lípa	3,507	.62	680	.11	19.39
Louny	9,561	1.22	1,416	.16	14.81
Karlovy Vary	5,358	1.0	604	.09	11.27
Plzeň	7,762	1.03	1,244	.15	16.03
České Budějovice	3,710	.66	520	.09	14.02
Jihlava	4,909	1.13	2,168	.47	44.16
Moravia					
Brno	13,761	1.82	5,309	.58	38.58
Olomouc	6,237	.78	2,780	.31	44.57
Uherské Hradiště	4,977	1.31	3,408	.88	68.47
Moravská Ostrava	10,407	1.59	5,892	.67	56.62
Těšín	5,015	1.62	3,564	.99	71.07

Table 2.3. *(cont.)* Comparison of Jews by Religion and Jews by Nationality for Czechoslovak Citizens and Foreigners in Czechoslovakia, 1921, in Absolute Numbers and Percentages

DISTRICT	JEWS BY RELIGION/ ABSOLUTE NUMBERS	JEWS BY RELIGION/ PERCENTAGES	JEWS BY NATIONALITY/ ABSOLUTE NUMBERS	JEWS BY NATIONALITY/ PERCENTAGES	JEWS BY RELIGION DECLARING JEWISH NATIONALITY/ PERCENTAGES
Slovakia					
Bratislava	36,454	5.07	16,607	2.25	45.56
Nitra	16,460	3.7	8,543	1.9	51.90
Turčiansky Svätý Martin	11,664	2.77	5,903	1.36	50.61
Zvolen	11,746	2.38	4,400	.87	37.46
Liptovský Svätý Mikuláš	11,712	3.66	5,525	1.66	47.17
Košice	47,882	7.93	32,650	5.28	68.19
Subcarpathian Ruthenia	93,341	15.39	81,529	13.35	87.35
Provincial Totals					
Bohemia	79,777	1.19	12,578	.17	15.77
Moravia	37,989	1.43	18,440	.58	48.54
Silesia	7,317	1.09	4,681	.59	63.97
Slovakia	135,918	4.53	73,628	2.38	54.17
Subcarpathian Ruthenia	93,341	15.39	81,529	13.35	87.35
Czechoslovakia Total	354,342	2.6	190,856	1.35	53.86

Source: Úřad statistický, *Sčítání lidu v republice československé ze dne 15. února 1921* (Praha, 1924), 65* část textová, Table 57.

Table 2.4. Czechoslovak State Citizens of the Jewish Religion in Bohemia, Moravia, Silesia, Slovakia, and Subcarpathian Ruthenia According to Nationality in Percentages, 1921

PROVINCE	CZECHOSLOVAK	GERMAN	MAGYAR	JEWISH	OTHER	TOTAL
Bohemia	49.49	34.63	-	14.60	1.28	100
Moravia and Silesia	15.71	34.85	-	47.84	1.60	100
Slovakia	22.27	6.68	16.49	54.28	.14	100
Subcarpathian Ruthenia	.78	.29	7.49	86.81	.78	100

Source: Úřad statistický, *Sčítání lidu 1921 v republice československé ze dne 15. února 1921* (Praha, 1924), 90 čast textová, Tables 104 and 105 combined.

Jewish national declarations in Slovakia, Boháč noted that Jews in eastern Slovakia formed a nearly continuous population block and that declarations of Jewish religion and nationality were nearly the same. He also made the important observation that Jews who lived in more densely Slovak regions were more likely to declare Jewish nationality than Jews who lived in more densely Magyar regions (such as in the southern counties bordering Hungary).[124]

The continuing attraction of traditional affiliation to the Magyars among Jews who lived in southern Slovakia, where the Jewish population tended to more strongly identify with the Magyar nation more deeply than in external linguistic forms, is indicative of the impact of relations with the surrounding population to national declarations. Where the Jews lived primarily among Slovaks, the tendency to affiliate or identify with them was much more unusual. The two most popular choices among Jews in Slovakia on the 1921 census, "Jewish" and "Czechoslovak," reflected both a heightened Jewish national political consciousness as compared to prewar levels and adjustment to changed geopolitical circumstances, whatever the motivation for that adjustment: traditional alignment with and show of loyalty to the state, fear, reasons of livelihood, belief in the centralized Czechoslovak state, or, in the most unusual case, affiliation with the surrounding Slovak national majority.

A central question in the preparation of the 1921 census for the linguistic national minorities in the state (Germans and Magyars) had been whether and to what extent their numbers would be reduced by counting nationality according to ethnic belonging rather than according to mother tongue alone. When the census results became public, the German minority learned that their numbers had fallen by 626,757 from 1910 levels. The total number of Magyars had dropped

Table 2.5. Czechoslovak Citizens by Nationality in Percentages, 1921

DISTRICT	CZECHOSLOVAK	GERMAN	MAGYAR	JEWISH	TOTAL IN ABSOLUTE NUMBERS
Bohemia					
City of Prague	94.18	4.58	.14	.89	663,295
District around Prague	98.80	1.05	.05	.04	1,058,404
Pardubice	87.48	12.29	.12	.03	475,119
Hradec Králové	71.60	28.20	.08	.05	502,823
Mladá Boleslav	68.89	30.91	.07	.05	726,784
Česká Lípa	10.81	88.89	.15	.11	550,217
Louny	59.87	39.86	.05	.15	773,564
Karlovy Vary	2.96	96.87	.03	.09	521,992
Plzeň	66.48	59.86	.09	.15	750,631
České Budějovice	71.94	27.82	.09	.08	553,996
Jihlava	69.36	29.86	.009	.46	424,526
Moravia					
Brno	81.07	18.22	.04	.58	745,687
Olomouc	62.39	37.19	.01	.31	794,101
Uherské Hradiště	98.35	1.22	.01	.88	375,534
Moravská Ostrava	64.68	34.20	.01	.67	626,354
Těšín	65.07	8.42	.01	.99	272,972
Slovakia					
Bratislava	60.40	5.98	31.12	2.25	706,633
Nitra	64.32	4.72	28.88	1.89	442,254
Turčiansky Svätý Martin	93.79	4.04	.64	1.36	418,186
Zvolen	67.54	2.05	29.14	.87	488,486
Liptovský Svätý Mikuláš	72.27	10.01	14.37	1.66	313,820
Košice	60.50	3.10	16.85	5.27	589,178
Subcarpathian Ruthenia	3.29	1.74	17.02	13.34	599,808

Source: Úřad statistický, *Sčítání lidu v republice československé ze dne 15.*
února 1921 (Praha, 1924), 29, Table IV.

**Table 2.6. Czechoslovak, German, Magyar, and Jewish (1921)
National Declarations 1910 and 1921 in Percentages**

| DISTRICT | LANGUAGE OF DAILY USE OR MOTHER TONGUE, 1910 | | | NATIONALITY, 1921 | | | |
	CZECH OR SLOVAK	GERMAN	MAGYAR	CZECHOSLOVAK	GERMAN	MAGYAR	JEWISH
Bohemia							
City of Prague	93.76	6.12	-	94.19	4.59	0.14	0.90
District around Prague	98.62	1.35	-	98.81	1.05	0.05	0.05
Pardubice	86.48	13.47	-	87.48	12.29	0.13	0.04
Hradec Králové	68.90	31.02	-	71.60	28.20	0.09	0.06
Mladá Boleslav	60.33	35.61	-	68.90	30.92	0.08	0.05
Česká Lípa	4.27	95.69	-	10.82	88.90	0.1	0.11
Louny	53.68	46.27	-	59.87	39.87	0.05	0.16
Karlovy Vary	0.73	92.26	-	2.97	96.88	0.03	0.09
Plzeň	64.38	35.60	-	66.49	33.22	0.1	0.15
České Budějovice	66.61	33.36	-	71.95	27.83	0.09	0.09
Jihlava	61.53	38.29	-	69.36	29.87	0.01	0.47
Moravia							
Brno	73.89	26.06	-	81.08	18.22	0.04	0.58
Olomouc	57.52	42.28	-	62.39	37.20	0.01	0.31
Uherské Hradiště	90.64	4.29	-	97.82	1.23	0.01	0.88
Moravská Ostrava	55.68	41.64	-	64.68	34.21	0.02	0.67
Těšín	39.95	11.23	-	65.07	8.43	0.01	0.99
Slovakia							
Bratislava	51.45	9.21	37.89	60.40	5.99	31.13	2.25
Nitra	53.12	6.12	40.17	64.33	4.72	28.88	1.90
Turčiansky Svätý Martin	87.33	6.38	5.16	93.79	4.05	0.65	1.36
Zvolen	57.25	2.30	39.23	67.54	2.06	29.14	0.87
Liptovský Svätý Mikuláš	61.93	10.35	21.51	70.66	10.01	14.38	1.66
Košice	45.49	6.26	30.88	60.84	3.11	16.86	5.28
Subcarpathian Ruthenia	1.29	10.66	29.22	3.29	1.74	17.03	13.35

Source: Úřad statistický, *Sčítání lidu v republice československé ze dne 15.*
února 1921 (Praha, 1924), 46–54, Table VI.

by 325,423.[125] What factors caused the decline in German and Magyar numbers and the great rise in Czechoslovak ones? To what extent was it a result of the inclusion of the "Jewish" nationality category?

The analytical section of the census gave five explanations for the dramatic decline in German numbers: (1) many Bohemian Germans had become Austrian citizens and, as foreigners, no longer counted as part of Czechoslovakia's domestic population; (2) prewar districts with a German majority had lost 152,357 residents while districts with a Czechoslovak majority had decreased by only 7,440; (3) a segment of the German-speaking Jewish population declared "Jewish" as their nationality; (4) many Czechs had been registered as Germans on the 1910 Austrian census due to national unawareness and social and professional dependence, which artificially enhanced German numbers, an inaccuracy that was corrected with the 1921 Czechoslovak census; and (5) immigrants to Slovakia and Subcarpathian Ruthenia who had since acquired citizenship identified themselves as Czechoslovak. The analysis indicated that the fourth reason was the most significant in accounting for the great change.[126]

Three reasons were given for the decline in declarations of Magyar nationality: (1) after the Prevrat many Magyars left Slovakia and Subcarpathian Ruthenia for the postwar Hungarian Republic; (2) many Jews who had given their mother tongue as "Magyar" ceased to declare Hungarian nationality; in Slovakia the number of Jews who designated "Magyar" as their nationality declined from 106,552 in 1910 (in the sixteen counties and four municipalities that fully or in part became Slovakia) to only 21,584 in 1921; in Subcarpathian Ruthenia, the number of Jews professing "Magyar" nationality declined from 36,236 in 1910 to 6863 in 1921; and (3) after the Prevrat the majority of Slovaks and Russians, who had been recorded as Magyars during the Dualist period, returned to their original nationality. The analysis gave the third reason as the most important for the drop in Magyar numbers in Slovakia and Subcarpathian Ruthenia. The Magyars lost their absolute majority in fifteen towns and districts in Slovakia and Subcarpathian Ruthenia and sank below the 20 percent mark in twenty-three others.[127]

Proportionately, the inclusion of "Jewish" as a category of national declaration on the census had a greater impact in Slovakia and Subcarpathian Ruthenia than in Bohemia and Moravia. This was partly because of the greater number of Jews in Slovakia and Subcarpathian Ruthenia and partly because of the greater overlap of Jewish religious and national profession among them. The overlap grew progressively stronger in eastern Slovakia and farther eastward, where declarations of Jewish religion and nationality were nearly congruent. Whereas Jewish nationality counted as only one of five factors in the decline of German national declarations, it counted as one out of three in the Magyar case. The German national question was naturally of greater consequence in Bohemia and

Table 2.7. Nationality in Slovakia According to the Censuses of 1919 and 1921

NATIONALITY	ABSOLUTE FIGURES 1919	1921	CHANGE FROM 1919 TO 1921 ABSOLUTE CHANGE	% CHANGE	% OF POP. DECLARING 1919	1921
Czechoslovak	1,954,446	2,025,003	+70,557	+3.61	66.86	67.48
Russian*	81,332	88,970	+7,638	+9.39	2.78	2.97
Magyar	689,565	650,597	-38,968	-5.65	23.59	21.68
German	143,466	145,844	+2,378	+1.66	4.91	4.86
Other	54,405	90,456	+36,051	+66.26	1.86	3.01
Total	2,923,214	3,000,870	+77,656	+2.66	100	100

Source: Úřad statistický, *Sčítání lidu v republice československé ze dne 15. února 1921*
(Praha, 1924), Table 74: Národnosti na Slovensku podle sčítání lidu z roku 1919 a 1921.
*Great Russian, Ukrainian, Rusyn

Moravia, and the Magyar one was more important in Slovakia and Subcarpathian Ruthenia. In both cases the most important reason for the respective drop in German and Magyar numbers was not the inclusion of Jewish nationality, but the counting of Czechs and Slovaks along ethnic lines, instead of linguistic ones, as it had been done in 1910.

The most significant changes between the results of the 1919 and 1921 censuses were in the "Magyar," "Czechoslovak," and "Other" nationality categories. (Table 2.7 illustrates those changes.) The authors of the census attributed the substantial decrease in the number of Magyar declarations to two factors: that many Jews who still chose Magyar nationality in 1919 opted instead for Jewish nationality in 1921, and that increasing numbers of formerly Magyarized Slovaks now declared themselves as Czechoslovak.[128] The results for Slovaks and Jews had been more unpredictable in 1919. Members of these two groups, along with the Rusyns, had again been considered the most likely to change declarations in 1921.

The fact that more Jews and Slovaks opted for "Jewish" and "Czechoslovak" nationality, respectively, in both cases reflects greater confidence in and acceptance of the viability of Czechoslovakia. It also indicates a growth in national self-awareness. Slovaks may have felt greater trust in Prague than they did in 1919, less fear of not declaring as "Magyar," and greater distance from an *Uhorský* (Hungarian; Kingdom of Hungary) self-understanding. Jews may have believed "Jewish" to be their most honest nationality declaration, they may have sought to "opt out" of the nationality conflict by choosing a seemingly neutral position, or they may have been supporters of Jewish politics who also voted for the Associated Jewish Parties in 1920. For whatever reasons they chose to declare "Jewish" and "Czechoslovak" nationality, these were both positive votes for Czechoslovakia and worked in favor of the centralized Czechoslovak state.

The 1921 census consolidated a centralized Czechoslovak state view of nationality. Preparations for the census brought together considerations of the correlation of language to nationality, what that meant in terms of building a Czechoslovak nation-state, and the obligation to fulfill pledges of minority rights, especially as regarded corporate minority rights based on constitutional and other legislative provisions. It gave practical form to carefully deliberated decisions on the above issues, based primarily on questions of the Czech/German relationship in the historic lands.

The methods and results of the 1919 special census in Slovakia were useful in providing a tested model of nationality investigation based on subjective, internal, ethnic/racial criteria that were already approved before an international body (the Paris Peace Conference). The 1919 census had been an experiment in bringing methods of counting and recording the population into line with the new postwar vision of the national state. The 1921 census built on 1919 methods in circumstances that required more than securing the new borders; they required filling the demarcated territory with meaning and answered the dual questions of what Czechoslovakia was and how nationality and nationhood would function in this state.

Overall, examining the 1919 Slovak census, the 1920 parliamentary elections, and the 1921 census together furnishes a picture of major events of national political self-determination in the formative years of Czechoslovakia. It offers insight into how the new republic understood itself as the manifestation of Czechoslovak self-determination and the place of the rights of the other nationalities to their own self-determination within this framework. It allows us to see how the Jewish population in Slovakia advanced their understanding of and relationship to a Jewish nationality and political program. A powerful point of the Jewish national program stressed that declaring Jewish and voting Jewish was a neutral stand in the endemic nationalities conflict. The Jewish national movement promoted Jewish nationality and politics as an escape, a means of demonstrating separation from the destructive assimilationist practices of the Dualist period. This was especially important with regard to Prague, which wanted to see proof that the Jews in Slovakia had "abandoned their role as exponents of the Magyars."[129] How the Jewish population in Slovakia dealt with the burden of that proof is the subject of the next chapter.

3 Contested Loyalty

Proving Slovak Jewish Loyalty
to Czechoslovakia

THE CZECHOSLOVAK ADMINISTRATION warned local police authorities across Slovakia in early 1925 of the "Magyar-nation orientation" of Neolog Jewish communities, which were allegedly administered by "Magyar rabbis who spread propaganda for Hungary." These communities were seats of Hungarian revisionist activity, cautioned the influential Prague daily *Lidové listy,* the mouthpiece of the Christian Czechoslovak People's Party (Československá strána lidová). Most Jews in Slovakia, however, were "completely loyal" to Czechoslovakia, the paper allowed. As proof it cited the fact that the majority Orthodox Jewish community had separated from the Central Office in Budapest shortly after the founding of Czechoslovakia and established a new headquarters in Bratislava.[1] The administration copied *Lidové listy*'s article into its Slovakia-wide memo.

Of the three branches of Jewish religious affiliation in Slovakia—Orthodox, Neolog, and Status Quo Ante—the regime was most suspicious of the Neolog. All three branches carried over to the successor states in regions that had been part of the pre–World War I Kingdom of Hungary, not only in Slovakia but also in Transylvania (Romania), and Vojvodina (Yugoslavia). Czechoslovakia found Neolog Judaism's distinctive connection to the process of Jewish emancipation in Hungary, and more so its particular alliance with the Dualist-era Hungarian regime, a cause for vigilance. Neolog Jews tended to have "Magyarized" more deeply before the First World War, even undergoing a process of social assimilation and collective identification with the Magyars rather than the linguistic acculturation and political allegiance to the Hungarian government that was more common among the Orthodox and Status Quo.[2]

The Czechoslovak state watched Neolog Jews more closely than the Orthodox or Status Quo; Hungary and Hungarian Jewry courted them more strongly for the revisionist cause. Jews in all three branches faced the considerable challenge of adapting their existing religious-communal organizations to the redrawn borders. While the Orthodox majority did indeed open a new Central Office in 1920, the Neolog Jewish community would only do so in 1926. And not until two years later, the tenth-anniversary jubilee celebration of the founding of the republic, did the Neolog and Status Quo communities join together to form a separate organization under the name Ješurun.[3]

Yet Jews in Slovakia, no matter their religious affiliation, acknowledged that life was better for them in Czechoslovakia than it was for their coreligionists and former compatriots in neighboring Hungary. The collapse of Austria-Hungary and the subsequent peace settlement devastated Hungary and Hungarian Jewry. The Treaty of Trianon dissolved the old multinational Kingdom of Hungary and left in its place a largely nationally homogenous, bitter pariah state that was hostile to its Jews. The series of political upheavals the state experienced in the aftermath of World War I further damaged the relationship of the Jewish population to the new postwar Hungarian state.

The disastrous and short-lived Hungarian Soviet Republic of 1919, which counted many communists of Jewish origin among its leadership, was most significant in this respect. The new government of Admiral Miklós Horthy came to power riding a crest of legitimacy stemming from its reaction against the 133-day Soviet Republic. Defeat and collapse, the significantly reduced territorial holdings of postwar Hungary, and polarizing postwar revolutionary chaos shaped the course of interwar Hungarian politics. Many Hungarians held "Jewish traitors" responsible for the humiliation of the country and considered "anti-Jewish politics [to be] justice for a nation wronged."[4] The Hungarian parliament passed the *numerus clausus* law—the first anti-Jewish legislation in interwar Europe—in 1920, limiting the number of students of each racial and national group admitted to institutions of higher learning to their proportion of the population.[5] The exclusionist law marked the end of the Hungarian government's tolerant, liberal prewar policy toward the Jewish minority.[6] The memory of the Soviet Republic cast a long shadow of suspicion over Hungary's postwar Jewish population, while the numerus clausus underscored the new regime's understanding that the Jews were racially distinct from the Magyars.

Jews in Slovakia understood that revising the postwar borders to place themselves under the Horthy regime's control was not in their best interest. They recognized the opportunities available to them as citizens of Czechoslovakia under the benevolent leadership of President Masaryk and turned toward him. The Weiss family of Košice, a city that was both a Hungarian national and Neolog center in the interwar period, took advantage of their Czechoslovak citizenship to bring up relatives from Sátoraljaújhely, a Hungarian town close to the border with Slovakia. Becoming the second largest city in Slovakia after the war, Košice grew dramatically in importance as a regional center and immigration magnet.[7] Its Jewish population swelled by twelve thousand in the aftermath of the war to reach an unofficial total of seventy-two thousand.[8] Erzsébet Weiss recalled, "My father brought up [my mother's three younger sisters] to Košice because the standard of living was higher than in Hungary. It was a civic democracy; we lived on an incomparably higher standard than our relatives in Hungary." Her father arranged for more relatives to come up from Hungary as well.[9]

But acknowledging and enjoying the advantages of Czechoslovak citizenship, despite its challenges, was not compelling evidence of political loyalty. Slovakia was the object of the interwar Hungarian regime's revisionist ambitions, so the government paid special attention to feared accomplices of Hungarian irredentism threatening the existence of the Czechoslovak state. Individual cases like the Weiss family, the Jewish community's public expressions of loyalty, and the praise for President Masaryk were not enough to soothe Czechoslovakia's territorial insecurity, nor was a thorough remapping of collective Jewish belonging to the territory: economically, socially, politically, and materially. The government watched closely while Jews in Slovakia transformed the built Jewish communal landscape and became "Slovak Jews." It inspected Jewish communal and political activity in Slovakia as well as contacts between Jews in Slovakia and their coreligionists in Hungary for irredentist content. It investigated Slovak Jews' loyalty based on language usage, communal conflicts, and especially how they remembered their war dead. The Czechoslovak state wanted to see proof of Slovak Jewish loyalty in very practical terms: by cutting their ties to the Magyars.

Building Slovak Jewry

In October 1928 the *Jüdisches Familienblatt,* the leading Jewish newspaper in Slovakia, published in Bratislava (Pressburg, Pozsony), issued a special jubilee edition highlighting Jewish communal achievements in Slovakia since the founding of the Czechoslovak state. Following praise that likened the Czechoslovak nation to a "pearl in the diadem of the human race" and exalted President Masaryk for guarding the welfare of the liberated nation with his spirit and soul[10]—pervasive sentiments expressed in tenth-anniversary publications throughout the state—it went on to feature particular homage. The retrospective photo spread of newly constructed synagogues across Slovakia; register of all standing Jewish religious, social, educational, philanthropic, political institutions, and territory-wide Jewish organizations based in Bratislava; and article celebrating the establishment of the long-awaited Jewish hospital emphasized the successes of the gradual and often arduous process of economic, social, and political reorientation among Jews in Slovakia that accounted for their well-being in the state.[11]

Building communal institutions was an important way Jews in the territory of Slovakia accompanied and facilitated their overall reorientation from defeated

Hungary to the newly established state of Czechoslovakia after the First World War. As Slovakia itself became a bounded territorial unit for the first time, so too did a distinctive "Slovak Jewry" emerge from the radically transformed geopolitical environment of postwar east central Europe. This entirely new collective self-understanding as "Slovak Jews" was tied to the conditions created by the movement from empire to national state. Reorientation was a tripartite process. It consisted above all of practical strategies for postwar economic adaptation to the new environment, the development of Jewish national political practices for negotiating the Jewish relationship to the state and surrounding population, and transformations in their understanding of the place of Jewish communities within the Slovak space. Changes in the built Jewish landscape reflected the postwar creation of a Slovak national space.[12] By remapping their belonging to that space, Slovak Jews detached themselves from Hungary and Hungarian Jewry, buttressed their distinctiveness from Czech Jewry, and affirmed the relocation of their political loyalty to Czechoslovakia.

Jewish communities across the territory of Slovakia, though especially in its two largest cities, Bratislava and Košice, embarked on a building boom during the 1920s, constructing new synagogues of all sizes and resonant architectural styles for their Orthodox, Neolog, Status Quo, and Hasidic congregations. They built schools from the elementary level to Talmud Torahs and yeshivas, matzah bakeries, and kosher slaughterhouses. They refurbished ritual bathhouses (*mikvaot*) and installed modern heating systems in communal buildings. The Bratislava Jewish community enthusiastically reconstructed the prayer hall used by the Hatam Sofer, which had been destroyed in the fire of 1913. The *Jüdisches Familienblatt* included in its jubilee register social welfare institutions like the Burial Society (Chevra Kaddisha) and the Sisterhood, the Jewish secondary-school students' cafeteria, the well-respected Jewish hospital in Bratislava, and organs of the Jewish press.[13]

Jewish communities built a total of thirty new synagogues and prayer halls across the territory of Slovakia between the world wars. With few exceptions, construction took place in the latter half of the 1920s, between the economic stabilization of Czechoslovakia in 1923 and the onset of the Great Depression in 1929. Most communities completed their projects before the tenth-anniversary celebrations in 1928, the rest only after sufficient economic recovery in the mid-1930s.[14] In Jewish communal celebrations of the anniversary, speeches typically stressed the favorable comparison of Czechoslovakia with Hungary, the loyalty and orientation of Jews in Slovakia to Czechoslovakia, and their deep admiration for President Masaryk as benefactor of the Jewish people. "We in this state freely and frankly may say what we, as Jews, think and feel," declared Dr. Viktor Stein in his anniversary address as president of the Neolog Jewish Community of Bratislava.

In happy contrast to so many other countries, we no longer need to wear the yellow mark on our backs; here no temples have been destroyed nor burial sites disgraced . . . here we have no numerus clausus, which not so long ago led to deeply regrettable and shameful excesses against Jewish students in our immediate vicinity.

From the moment of the existence [of this state] we were, and I emphasize this, good and honest citizens. However, because we were and still are honest, I can also openly confess that which no man of character would find remarkable, namely that after the Prevrat we based our loyalty more on sober considerations than on our hearts. The human heart is not a radio receiver that from one moment to another can be tuned to a new wavelength. . . .

During the past decade we have learned to prize the liberal and democratic basis on which the Czechoslovak Republic is founded and which has had great consequences for us. We have learned to esteem and treasure the state itself. Today we no longer feel and view ourselves—and hopefully neither do others—as foreign bodies in the state, and with our entire hearts take part in the jubilee festival as equals, like-minded and equally loyal.[15]

Social factors in Hungary, especially popular antisemitism and exclusionary legislation, contributed to Jewish reorientation in Czechoslovakia. Beyond their appreciation of the higher standard of living and civic democracy, the ability to think, feel, and live freely as Jews steadily drew Jews in Slovakia into the Czechoslovak mental landscape. Hungary's enactment of the numerus clausus pushed Jews to acquire the state language in order to fulfill their educational strategies. With the Hungarian universities closed to them, entry to institutions of higher learning in Czechoslovakia, especially the prestigious Charles University in Prague, became the goal. János Vass recounted his education:

I began attending first grade in the Jewish elementary school [in Košice] in the Magyar language, but from the second on I was registered for Slovak. Obviously, while ours was a Magyar family, we took on the Magyar fate for our Jewish survival. Because by 1929 it was clear that Czechoslovakia was a stable system, and because in Hungary there was still numerus clauses at the universities, [we looked to] the university here, the Prague Charles University. . . .

In the Slovak language class at the Jewish elementary school with me, all told, there was one native speaker of Slovak. By that time, Jewish parents [wanted] us to master the state language to the extent that we would pass our state exams; that we could gain admittance to the academy and university in Brno, Bratislava, or Prague without batting an eye.[16]

Jewish enrollments in Czechoslovak gymnasia in Slovakia rose precipitously in the 1920s. Their numbers increased from 33.5 percent of all Jewish gymnasia students at the outset of the state in 1919, to 55.3 percent in the school year 1925–1926, and 61.9 percent in 1930–1931. As early as 1925, a clear majority of Jewish students attended Czechoslovak, rather than Magyar or German, gymnasia in Slovakia.[17]

Yet acquiring the state language did not mean, or require, abandonment of Magyar. Czechoslovak law allowed for the preservation of Magyar linguistic and cultural affiliations. State protections existed for minority language rights on the individual level as well as on the corporate level in towns or districts where members of the minority language group numbered 20 percent or more, known as a "considerable fraction" of the population.[18] Magyar-speaking Jews in Košice tended to maintain their Magyar language and culture as Czechoslovak citizens. Gábor Sarlós was one of them. When Sarlós recalled his interwar youth, he spoke of the linguistic toleration of the state with special fondness. "The First Republic was magnificent," he effused.

> Believe me, it cannot be equaled, those twenty years were glorious, it was a beautiful republic. I know, for example, that in Beregszáz [now Berehovo, Ukraine], which was purely Magyar, the president of the republic declared that even the tobacconist could only be a Magyar. Such a splendid state it was. And they actually nominated a Magyar war invalid! In Beregszáz, where there was a qualified Magyar minority, it was possible to conduct business in Magyar everywhere, in the court of law, in the district court. All petitions could even be written in Magyar. I am not saying that the Czechs were very happy about it, but that's the way it was. . . . When the Magyars came here [1938], they brought with them such a world that was absolutely unfamiliar to us.[19]

Jenő Silber concurred with Sarlós in his own recollections:

> Notwithstanding Zionism, we were very Magyar. . . . There was a Slovak theater here, for example. It was not very well attended, but during the summer recess the Magyars always came and appeared as guest performers, and then it was packed! It was impossible to get a ticket. In Slovakia the Jews maintained the Magyar culture; even in the [Neolog] Jewish community we only spoke Magyar.[20]

Silber's Magyar cultural orientation coexisted with his Jewish national affiliation and activity in the youth movement. He belonged to the Ha-shomer Ha-tsair (the Young Guard) youth organization, for which his older brother was the regional secretary.[21] The group organized outings every Sunday, had an orchestra, and met every Sunday evening at the Zionist club. They learned Hebrew. The Sunday evening meetings were regularly packed, Silber recalled, and there were a lot of girls. More often than not there was not enough room for everybody in the large event hall.[22]

Julius Reisz, head of the Jewish Party representing Slovakia and Subcarpathian Ruthenia,[23] reflected on the separation between Magyar's linguistic-cultural orientation and Hungarian politics in a 1928 interview with *Kassai Napló*, the Košice-based Magyar newspaper. "I am the last one who would renounce Magyar culture," he said. "I was raised on Magyar culture, the majority of what I read is in the Magyar language, and even now I openly speak Magyar, but to mix Magyar culture with Hungarian politics is none other than dilettantism."[24]

Jews in Slovakia so steadily reoriented themselves to the contours of the new state that by 1928 it was already possible to recognize the existence of distinctive Slovak Jewry. The *Jüdisches Familienblatt* did so in an eponymous lead article in February of that year. "Today, just a short nine years since the historic act of the founding of the Czechoslovak state, we can speak of a 'Slovak Jewry,'"[25] the paper asserted, placing quotation marks around the term. For the *Jüdisches Familienblatt* did not intend to suggest that Jews in Slovakia had taken the improbable step of assimilating into the Slovak cultural nation. Rather, this was "a Jewry embraced by the borders of Slovakia, which has the opportunity to develop here securely and peacefully."[26] "Slovak Jewry" was a communal category binding loyalty to Czechoslovakia with Slovak territoriality rather than an expression of emotional attachment to or identification with the Slovak nation. The article pointed to no other integrative commonalities among the Jewish population in Slovakia than the borders and the advantages of Czechoslovak citizenship. Its point was to the contrary. The separate paths of Jewish religious practice born in old Hungary—Orthodox, Neolog, and Status Quo—reached full development in Slovakia, it argued. The pressure felt by the majority Orthodox Jewish population of Slovakia to adhere to the unified Neolog model favored by the prewar Hungarian government disappeared after the war. The very ability to freely pursue autonomous religious communal development, the *Jüdisches Familienblatt* explained, was an outcome of being Jewish citizens in the liberal Czechoslovak state.[27]

These were not isolated sentiments. The great majority of Slovak Jews defined themselves geographically, as belonging to the territory of Slovakia and the specific set of challenges and opportunities that reality presented. Slovak Jews anchored themselves locally, becoming more intensely aware of their relationship to the towns and villages in which they lived and expressing their presence in a transformed communal landscape.

The Union of Slovak Jews (Sväz Slovenských Židov) used this heightened sense of territoriality among Jews in Slovakia as the foundation stone of their assimilationist program. The group, representing only a negligible slice of Slovak Jewish opinion, consisted of Jewish intellectuals and secondary school students (*vysokoškolákov*) led by the Bratislava physician Hugo Roth.[28] Roth contended that while Slovak Jews were not part of the Slovak tribe in the sense maintained by Ľudovít Štur in *Hlas k rodákom* [A Word to My Countrymen],[29] and they were not Svätopluk's descendants,[30] Jews had made their home on Slovak soil longer than many families of today's "good and ardent patriots."[31] "Slovak Jews have lived for centuries in Slovakia together with the Slovaks," Roth argued, "and were oppressed in the same way." [32] As a result of their common experience, he concluded, Slovak Jews and Slovaks shared the same fate and interests. Roth therefore urged Slovak Jews to identify themselves not only with the territory but also with the Slovak nation, and to do everything in their power to work toward its advantage. Based on the successes of the Czech Jewish example, Roth argued that Jewish children in Slovakia be raised in the spirit of the Slovak nation, its language and culture.[33]

Roth and the Union of Slovak Jews made every effort to distance themselves from the Zionists and other national Jews in Slovakia,[34] whom they perceived to "obstruct peaceful coexistence" between Jews and Slovaks. "National solidarity connects us with the Slovaks, religion connects us with the Jews," Roth wrote. He espoused a position consistent with Reform and Neolog post-emancipation thought that considered Judaism solely a religion.[35] Accordingly, the Jewish religion itself would not interfere with the ability of Jews rooted in Slovakia to bind themselves to the Slovak nation. The Union of Slovak Jews offered a reinterpretation of Jewish history in Slovakia that was meant to utterly reshape Slovak-Jewish relations in the postwar era. It intended to draw the Jewish population of Slovakia into long-standing practices of state accommodation and acculturation that were familiar in the German, Hungarian, and even Czech cases, but still foreign in the Slovak case. Heightened territoriality without Slovak national assimilation, however, proved to be of much greater consequence for the emergence of Slovak Jewry.

Jewish nationality and national politics, rather than traditional strategies of accommodation with the surrounding population, marked the fault line between Jews in Slovakia and their coreligionists and former compatriots in Hungary. The article "The Jews of Slovakia" published in Budapest in 1929 in the prominent and widely read *Magyar Zsidó Lexikon* (Hungarian Jewish Lexicon) gave special attention to Jewish nationality and national politics as a defining feature of Slovak Jewry. Jewish national developments, organizations, political parties, and press in Slovakia constituted the lion's share of the article, as the author detailed the divergence of Slovak Jews from those in Hungary since the end of the war.[36] In contrast to Jews in Slovakia, Jews in postwar Hungary vehemently renounced Jewish national politics. Affiliation with a Jewish nation, they argued, would exclude them from the Magyar one. Jews in postwar Hungary considered their growing exclusion from the Magyar nation to be the most alarming political development of postwar period. The numerus clausus law enacted in Hungary in 1920 evidenced the separation. Under these circumstances of increasing discrimination, Hungarian Jews found the pursuit of modern Jewish national politics unwise.[37]

Despite allotting the majority of the *Magyar Zsidó Lexikon* entry to Jewish national politics in Slovakia, the author of the article concluded that the most striking development since the founding of the new state was the construction of new grandiose (*pompás*) synagogues in Lučenec (Losonc) and Košice. He noted that the growing Hasidic population in eastern Slovakia, who had arrived primarily from Galicia during the First World War, had built prayer halls for themselves in Košice, Michalovce (Nagymihály, Gross Michl), and Medzilaborce. A Slovak Jewish Museum opened its doors in the eastern Slovak town of Prešov in 1928, founded and funded by the local Jewish population.[38]

The first communal building mentioned in the *Magyar Zsidó Lexikon* to be completed was the Hasidic prayer hall on Krmanova Street in Košice in 1920. It still stands today, used as a metals testing laboratory.[39] The growing Hasidic community in the town formed a prayer association immediately following the war, where they raised the funds to establish a meeting place. Similar to Hasidic communities elsewhere, they maintained their own separate community, a de facto separate division within Košice's Orthodox Jewish community. Their prayer hall is a simple, undecorated building, closed off from the street by a stone wall.[40] The original unaltered structure was built around two eastward-facing prayer rooms. This hall is a typical example of the traditional rural synagogue structure. What makes it unusual is its location in the middle of Košice. It is a rural transplant, an indicator of the rapid in-migration of rural eastern Jews to Košice as the border shifted and this provincial town became the second largest city in the territory of Slovakia.

Following chronologically we arrive at the monumental domed synagogue at 66 Moyzesová Street, completed by Košice's Neolog Jewish community in 1925. The building lies just a short walk due southeast from the centerpiece of Košice's elegant elongated main square, Saint Elizabeth's Cathedral, Europe's easternmost Gothic cathedral. Its unusual elliptical dome reaches over 120 feet (37 meters) in height, topped today by a lute, denoting it as the current home of the State Philharmonic. The original Star of David the lute replaced is now part of the Holocaust memorial dedicated by the postwar Jewish community in the Jewish section of the Rastislavová Street cemetery in April 1969, when the first concert took place under the cupola. Residents of Košice refer to the State Harmonic Hall as the *bužna,* the synagogue.[41] While exterior elements of its Baroque revival design have been largely well-preserved, the building's interior was completely altered during its transformation into a concert hall, an appropriate use of its excellent acoustics and two-tiered eleven-hundred-person seating capacity. The enormous, richly decorative interior space was originally intended to accommodate six hundred men on the ground level and five hundred women in the semicircular upper gallery, according to Neolog practice and the demands of a rapidly expanding community.[42]

A contemporary described the building as "Slovakia's most beautiful, most ornamental, and most artistically executed synagogue."[43] The opening ceremony for the new Neolog synagogue upon its completion in 1925 took place at three in the afternoon. It began with a stirring processional down Moyzesová Street holding the Torah scroll aloft, accompanied by the singing of psalms. Mólnár Jenő, president of the Neolog Jewish community of Košice, emphasized the generosity of individual contributions to the project in his inaugural speech. While the municipality donated a sum of 50,000 crowns (US$1,480) toward its completion, the remainder of the funds needed to finance the 4.5 million-crown building costs—including the synagogue, cultural center, and the ten-classroom elementary school with additional rooms for teachers, a gymnasium, laboratory, and an office—came from private donations, the usual source of funding for Jewish communal building projects. Construction of the synagogue complex took place according to the plans of the distinguished Budapest-based Hungarian Jewish architect Lajos Kozma, winner of the international competition sponsored by the Neolog Jewish community.[44] Kozma's drawings, furniture design, and architecture drew on Hungarian folk motifs while placing them in an overall modernist conception.[45] Kozma designed the Moyzesová synagogue to feature the Baroque motifs favored in interwar Hungarian architecture.[46]

The Lučenec synagogue, completed in 1926, is a colossus, still standing today although abandoned, decaying, and looted of all items of any possible value. The Neolog Jewish community in the southern Slovak town of Lučenec close to the Hungarian border commissioned the prominent Budapest-based Hungarian Jewish architect Lipót Baumhorn for the work. It is considered one of Baumhorn's most impressive structures. He authored more than two dozen Neolog Jewish synagogues throughout Hungary, as well as in regions that carried over the Neolog tradition to today's Slovakia, Romania, and Serbia. The synagogue's grandiose size, highly ornate exterior and interior detailing, and huge domed roof are characteristic of Baumhorn designs.[47] Baumhorn's eclectic style combined Moorish, Byzantine, and Art Nouveau elements for the Lučenec project, built on his favored Greek cross ground plan.[48]

The two grandiose Neolog synagogues marked a prominent presence in Lučenec and Košice. The communities had become prosperous, and their enormous size and expense called attention to the local Jewish community. They were proud that they had made a successful economic transition to Czechoslovakia. The Jewish communities in Lučenec and Košice, like others across the territory of Slovakia during the 1920s building boom, staked their claim to the towns and villages in which they lived through communal institution building. They anchored themselves locally and expressed their belonging through their usage of the public space. For in a way that was similar, though not analogous, to how Slovaks transformed urban spaces after 1918 to reflect the symbols, personalities, and events that were central to their newly dominant national narrative,[49] Jews, too, expressed their emerging Slovak Jewish identity through shaping the local public space and their own territoriality. Hillel Kieval remarks of the monumental Moyzesová synagogue in Košice that he cannot help but imagine that [it] was intended both to evoke and replace the great Dohány Street Synagogue in Budapest, until then the architectural jewel in the Neolog crown. Oversized, perhaps, for its location in a city of only 72,000 and allegedly constructed in a Magyar idiom, this edifice constituted the new "address" of liberal Judaism in Slovakia and signaled the desire of the Neolog community to attain rootedness in the Czechoslovak environment.[50]

Kieval's observation illuminates an essential point: despite ostensible Hungarian architectural style in some, though not all cases, synagogue building was crucial to broader Jewish communal reorganization reflecting Jewish communal needs, networks, and orientation within Slovakia itself, not across the border. The grand, magnificent synagogues built in the 1920s in Slovakia replaced those of Budapest. Perhaps Hungarian in architectural style, they were Slovak Jewish in context. Jews in Slovakia had become Slovak Jews: loyal citizens of Czechoslovakia belonging to the territory of Slovakia. Their loyalty to the state was their greatest expression of a "Czechoslovak" identity. Deeply devoted to President Masaryk, theirs was a broad dedication to the centralized Czechoslovak Republic and its civic political culture from their home beneath the Tatra Mountains.

This point is borne out in the founding of the Slovak Jewish Museum. From its conceptualization the museum was an act of creating a distinctive Slovak Jewish identity that belonged to the separate territory of Slovakia. It served as a physical structure—a ritual space—for building Slovak Jewish collective identity.[51] A contemporary observed that the Jews of Berlin, Budapest, and Prague all had their museums, and this one would be "our own independent Jewish museum."[52] Eugen Bárkány and Teodor Austerlitz traversed eastern Slovakia in Bárkány's car in the mid-1920s seeking financial support and local Judaica for the project. They succeeded in collecting representative objects from larger Jewish communities as well as in raising the necessary funds.[53] The museum moved from its original site to a larger building in 1931 in order to exhibit the growing collection more effectively. After 1945, state authorities moved the Bárkány collection to the Jewish Museum in Prague, where it remained until the dissolution of Czechoslovakia in 1993. The Slovak Jewish Museum is now again located in Prešov, housed in the women's gallery of the painstakingly restored Orthodox synagogue in the center of town.

For Slovak Jews the "right path" appeared to be a separate one, independent from Hungary and Hungarian Jewry, bound to the territory of Slovakia, and to the opportunities of Czechoslovakia under Tomáš G. Masaryk. Slovak Jews built their new collective identity around three dominant elements connected to their experience of geopolitical reorientation from Hungary to Czechoslovakia. The first was refugee aid, welfare work, and self-help programs during the war and after, which fostered a rising bond of solidarity among Jews and Jewish communities in the territory in a range of ways, both religious and secular. The second element, Jewish nationality and national politics, was a position espoused by the majority of Jews in Slovakia. It promised to be an "authentic" and "neutral" route of remaining "true to ourselves" in the nationalities conflict, which also seemed to demonstrate political separation from the Hungarians while supporting Czechoslovak national dominance in the state. Both Hungarians and Czechoslovaks recognized that Jewish nationality was a significant point of divergence between Hungarian and Slovak Jews. Finally, the third element of reorientation involved the transformation of Jewish territoriality through building communal institutions designed to meet the needs of Jewish communities within the new borders, shaping the development of the public space, and anchoring themselves locally. Through it all it is important to remember the influence of continuing tensions with the Slovak population, caught up in its own crucial and long-deferred process of national development. Czechoslovakia wrote and reconstructed their national story in the streets, squares, institutions, and monuments, and took "linguistic possession" of the territory.[54]

The emergence of a Slovak Jewish identity is a phenomenon that is inseparable from the larger story of interwar state building in east central Europe. While the behavior, customs, and habits of Jews in the northern counties of the Kingdom of Hungary were indeed discernibly different from those of their coreligionists in the central plain,[55] there was no force binding them together as a separate group that would overcome their persistent regional distinctions and discrete communal and cultural networks until the creation of Slovakia and its incorporation into Czechoslovakia.

The Investigation of Rabbi Doctor Samuel Funk

On October 28, 1926, the eighth anniversary of the founding of Czechoslovakia, the Neolog Jewish Community of Bratislava gathered in the grand Moorish-style synagogue on Rybné Square adjacent to St. Martin's Cathedral for a commemorative service led by their chief rabbi, Dr. Samuel Funk. They were joined by representatives of the government administration and other religious confessions. Toward the end of his sermon, from his position behind the lectern an increasingly agitated Rabbi Funk turned and pointed with an angry finger at the members of the assimilationist Union of Slovak Jews in attendance. He publicly accused them of destroying Jewish unity and making it impossible for the Jewish Party to win a parliamentary mandate.[56] He reproached them for serving their own personal interests rather than those of the community. Rabbi Funk concluded his sermon by recalling a meeting he had recently enjoyed with President Masaryk. The president, he related, regarded it as very embarrassing that in spite of the one hundred thousand votes the Jewish Party had received in 1925,[57] it was not able to obtain even one parliamentary mandate. Rabbi Funk reported that Masaryk respected only those Jews who declared Jewish as their nationality.[58]

The Union of Slovak Jews recounted this narrative of events in the grievance they lodged against Rabbi Funk with the Bratislava police on February 17, 1927. Their action marked the opening of a six-year investigation of Bratislava's Neolog Jewish community centered on the personality of Rabbi Funk. The state took a keen interest in the complaint, as the dispute was a window through which it could view the swiftly evolving world of modern Jewish politics and attempt to understand the implications of the conflict between Jewish nationalist and assimilationist positions within Slovak parameters. The first report of the Bratislava police correspondingly framed the utility of the incident: "Recently, the Zionist movement in Slovakia has significantly expanded—much greater attention needs to be paid to Jewish movements in Slovakia generally, and from this standpoint the public outburst of Rabbi Dr. Samuel Funk should be evaluated."[59]

During the course of the investigation, the state made a dramatic turnaround in its evaluation of Rabbi Funk. From an initial assessment of him as a "magyarophile element" working under the cover of Zionism, the state concluded in 1932 that Rabbi Funk was a "loyal Czechoslovak citizen" and even an advocate of the Jewish lower classes. How and why did this astonishing change occur? The state's final assessment reflected the changing set of indicators it used to form its perception of Rabbi Funk and to draw conclusions about Jewish political loyalty in the interwar Slovak context more broadly. In the end the state showed greater interest in the ongoing dispute between Rabbi Funk and the leadership of the Neolog Jewish community in Bratislava than it showed in the Union of Slovak Jews. The state found the former conflict to be "not without a certain flavor"—that is, a result of the Neolog Jewish community's allegedly problematic relationship to Czechoslovakia.[60] The shift in the state's attention from Rabbi Funk to the Neolog Jewish community marks the growing ascendancy of transnational security issues over domestic sociocultural affairs.

It was useful for the state to follow Rabbi Funk. He was a well-known eccentric and choleric character whose outspoken opinions often exposed the fault lines in Jewish community politics. By all accounts Funk used his position as chief Neolog rabbi to proclaim his political judgments and hurl insults from behind the lectern. He was a great admirer of Masaryk, whom he habitually quoted and referred to as the "Benefactor of the Jews" (*dobrodinca židov*). Rabbi Funk also included passages from well-known Czech authors in his sermons, which was said to make members of the congregation who had been raised as Hungarians uncomfortable. In general Rabbi Funk's unpleasant temperament earned him a remarkably small following. Many members of the Neolog community allegedly avoided him at all costs.[61] The Bratislava police investigating the case of the grievance of the Union of Slovak Jews against Rabbi Funk viewed it as characteristic of the local Zionists to allow an irresponsible person like Funk to act as the mouthpiece of the movement in their struggle against the Jewish union.[62] This observation was typical of the investigation's generally unflattering evaluation of Funk's personality and behavior.

Rabbi Funk's attack on the Union of Slovak Jews put him in an awkward position. Now he had to prove that he was a loyal citizen who did not harbor anti-Slovak feelings. The situation was made more disagreeable by the fact that since his meeting with Masaryk, Funk had trumpeted himself as a confidant with whom the president consulted in serious political and cultural matters.[63] Things did not look good for Rabbi Funk. He attempted to clear his name by airing his side of the story in a leading Slovak daily (*Slovenský denník*), but the editorial board refused his request. He tried to become a member of the Slovak League (Slovenská líga), a prominent Slovak national organization, but found no success. At the consecration ceremony of the new synagogue in Parkaň (Hungarian: Parkány, later renamed Štúrovo), close to the border with Hungary, Funk gave his address in the state language, Slovak, instead of his usual German.[64]

To Rabbi Funk's dismay the investigation turned up an article published during the war in the leading Hungarian Jewish newspaper (*Egyenlőség*) in which he sharply criticized Czech national ambitions as treasonous to Austria-Hungary. The investigation understood this as evidence of how deeply Funk subscribed to Hungarian political opinion in spite of the article's wartime publication in a staunchly patriotic paper. Rabbi Funk argued that *Egyenlőség* was hardly a reliable source on such matters; he was not prepared to have his current state loyalty evaluated in terms of a 1917 Hungarian publication. Although he attempted to convince the investigation that even during the war he always spoke of Masaryk with admiration, the police remained unswayed.[65]

Leo Sipos, a Bratislava lawyer and leading figure in the Zionist movement in Slovakia, was the only source interviewed in the early phase of the investigation who spoke in support of Rabbi Funk. Sipos confidentially testified in 1927 that Funk's attack on the Union of Slovak Jews derived from the rabbi's belief that the founding of a Slovak Jewish political party would harm Jewish interests and undermine the wishes of President Masaryk, who admonished the Jews in Slovakia to "return to the worldview of [their] forefathers, be Jews, and abandon [their] role as exponents of the Magyars."[66] Sipos stressed that Rabbi Funk condemned Jewish assimilation and believed it essential for Jews to achieve national independence.[67]

Sipos's argument articulated the perceptions of Jewish nationality held by the Jewish national movement. The Jewish national leadership advanced Jewish nationality and Jewish national politics as an inherently anti-assimilationist position, considering it an honest way of remaining "true to ourselves." By declaring

Jewish nationality and pursuing Jewish national politics, they argued, Jews could simply be Jews and avoid the dangers and misunderstandings of national affiliations in the multinational state. As such, it also seemed to be a good means of demonstrating separation from the prewar practice of affiliating with the dominant Magyar nation. Understood in this way, Jewish nationality was an elegant fulfillment of Masaryk's appeal.

In the eyes of the state, however, the embrace of Jewish national politics was not compelling evidence of abandoning one's "role as an exponent of the Magyars." The state suspected a Magyar subtext to Jewish national politics in Slovakia, revealed in the same anti-assimilationist stance of the Jewish national program that Jews thought cleared them of that suspicion. "Zionism here in the republic has a political background," concluded the 1927 report, "which means that Jews who were brought up in the German or Magyar spirit and who still sympathize with Magyar thinking—they are against any kind of assimilation." The state believed that Jews in Slovakia who maintained a Magyar orientation found defense against pressures to assimilate to the new Slovak environment under the banner of Jewish national politics.[68]

In the case of Bohemia, the most closely analogous suspicion stemmed not from the state, but from the Czech Jews (*Čechožidé*). Before the 1920 parliamentary elections, the Czech Jewish leadership suggested to the Czech National Council that the Jewish national candidate from the Associated Jewish Parties may not be loyal to the Czech nation if elected to parliament. They argued that Zionists with a German or Hungarian past and upbringing may be beholden to the interests of another party that would be representatives of the Czech nation, which could work against Czech interests. Masaryk, Beneš, and other leading governmental figures did not take the advice of the Czech Jews to reject the candidate from the Associated Jewish Parties, but instead supported the Jewish national movement, its leadership, and its candidates. The Jewish national movement in Bohemia and Moravia reciprocated the continuing support of the government with efforts to make Czech the language of the movement, especially in Moravia, and promoting the use of Czech in Zionist meetings and periodicals. As a protest against Nazism, the German language was not used at all at the Zionist Congress in Prague in 1933. It is worth noting that across Czechoslovakia it was the Jewish assimilationist movements that stressed the potential disloyalty of the Jewish nationalists to the state.

The Czechoslovak administration concluded its first report on the Funk affair in 1927, a year that, not accidentally, marked a turning point in the history of the Hungarian movement to revise the borders established by the Treaty of Trianon. In that year the English baron Harold Harmsworth, Lord Rothermere, began his "Justice for Hungary" campaign in his newspaper the *Daily Mail*; the Hungarian Revisionist League was founded; international financial and military monitors left Hungary; and the Horthy government signed a treaty of friendship and cooperation with Mussolini's Italy. In addition, the intensification of the Hungarian revisionist campaign coincided with the beginning of the Tuka affair in Czechoslovakia, in which Vojtěch Tuka was found guilty in 1929 of working for the restoration of the prewar Kingdom of Hungary as an agent of the interwar Hungarian government under the guise of struggling for the creation of an independent Slovakia. Together these events generally heightened Czechoslovak state suspicion of Jews in Slovakia as potential accomplices to Hungarian ambitions and colored its interpretations of Jewish politics.

Hungarian Jews staked their claim on the Jews in Slovakia for the interwar Hungarian government's revisionist cause with renewed vigor that same year, framing it as their own territorial restoration. "The Treaty of Trianon cut Hungarian Jewry off from the territory where it was most strongly represented," wrote Mór Schick in the prominent Budapest Jewish newspaper *Zsidó Ujság* in 1927. "If the borders should be drawn according to the wishes of the English newspaper king [Lord Rothermere], in which the Magyars are in the majority, then one should not forget about the Jews who live there, who have so frequently expressed their desire to belong to Hungary."[69] Since the end of the war Jews in Hungary had asserted to the world that the Jews in Slovakia and Transylvania desired to be a part of Hungary, as they were "one and all Hungarian, in heart and soul."[70]

Slovak Jewish papers as a rule refrained from dealing with the revisionist issue. But in this case the editorial board of the *Jüdische Familienblatt* decided it was their duty and in the interests of the Jews in Slovakia (*im Interese der hierländischen Juden*) to respond. In doing so, they wrote, they hoped they might avert harm from befalling Slovak Jewry (*slovakische Judentum*).[71] "The absurdity of [Schick's] words is so obvious that one must be astonished that an editor of a Jewish paper could print such a thing," ran their response.

> The author of the article demands that not only the number of ethnic Magyars, but also the number of Jews be taken into consideration in a potential redrawing of the borders, so that [the Jews] would also count toward the Magyar population. . . .
>
> The mad idea that the borders of a European state should be drawn according to the number of Jewish inhabitants of the region can only spring from the politically debased head of a Hungarian Jew. We must energetically protest against this slander from the Czechoslovak Jewish position, as it exposes the Jews who live in the [ethnic] Hungarian territory of the Czechoslovak state to a danger that they do not deserve.[72]

The *Jüdische Familienblatt* expressed astonishment and resentment that Slovak Jews would be so calculatingly instrumentalized by Schick, the *Zsidó Ujság*, and their Hungarian Jewish brethren. The board was saddened to consider the circumstances that would push Hungarian Jews to make such assertions. Their paths had fundamentally diverged. The *Jüdische Familienblatt* vigorously disputed the implications of Schick's argument in defense of the local Jewish population. Connecting them to the revisionist argument placed them in the threefold danger of being treated as a treasonous element by the Czechoslovak state and surrounding population, of being manipulated as pawns by the Hungarian government, and subjecting them to the same anti-Semitic legislation and hostilities as the Jews in Hungary if the borders were to be redrawn.

The Funk affair raised awareness of the variety of Jewish opinion on the question of national affiliation within the Jewish community and within the population at large. Until then, noted the prominent Slovak daily *Národný denník*, little was generally known about the activities of the Union of Slovak Jews. Jews were Jews, and that was that. Now, the paper continued, the differences between the Jewish national and Slovak assimilationist camps were becoming visible.[73] Jewish intellectuals and Jewish secondary-school students comprised the tiny membership of the Union of Slovak Jews. Although the organization was established prior to the 1920 elections and there had even been minor Jewish support for the Slovak national movement before the First World War,[74] it was not until the late 1920s that a movement dedicated to Jewish integration into the Slovak nation could grow. Its growth reflected the belated emergence of a mature Slovak nation through the development of its own intellectual and political elite.[75] In the 1925–1926 school year the number of graduates from Czechoslovak gymnasia in Slovakia surpassed the number of graduates from Hungarian gymnasia for the first time.[76] Czechoslovak gymnasium education was a tool for the creation of a Slovak middle class and a Slovak intelligentsia—a mature Slovak population that would be able not only to take over governance but also to drive the advancement of Slovak culture.

The Jewish majority's preference for Czechoslovak schools rather than Magyar or German ones by the end of the 1920s demonstrated Jewish acceptance of the status quo and the decision to pursue educational strategies in the state language.[77] It was a significant and visible component of Jewish reorientation. The decision to attend Czechoslovak schools in interwar Slovakia markedly differed from the continued preference of Prague Jews for German primary and secondary education over Czech education in the last decade of the nineteenth century. In that context Prague Jews increasingly shifted political alliances and census declarations from German to Czech but held on to their German inclinations in social and educational matters.[78] In the interwar Slovak environment, the majority of Jews tended toward Jewish nationality and politics, combined with Czechoslovak educational choices. The Union of Slovak Jews hoped to capitalize on the increase in Jewish attendance at Czechoslovak schools to redirect Jewish national choices. Hugo Roth promised that the Union of Slovak Jews would do its utmost to facilitate Jewish education in the Slovak spirit. This included financial support for the approximately one hundred Jewish university students who wanted to join the Union of Slovak Jews.[79] Many Jews who were inclined to declare Slovak as their nationality did not do so, because they were financially dependent on Zionist-funded Jewish organizations. The "Achduth" and "Mensa academica Judaica" supported only those who declared Jewish nationality.[80]

The conflict between Funk and the Union of Slovak Jews fueled local Slovak and Czechoslovak state suspicions that the Jewish national movement was in fact a cover for Magyar national activity. Slovak public opinion, not surprisingly, quickly lined up behind the Union of Slovak Jews. *Národný denník* congratulated itself ten days after Funk's outburst for having pointing to the Zionists as the promoters of Magyarization in Slovakia even earlier: it was evident to them that Jews who opposed the Union of Slovak Jews were Magyar national elements.[81] *Slovenský denník* later called Funk the "Jewish Tuka."[82]

Slovak authorities, even earlier, tended to view Jewish national politics and Zionism—combined in their shorthand as "Zionism"—as a branch of Hungarian revisionist activity in Slovakia. A 1925 preelection report discussing the Jewish national candidate from the district chief of Hlohovec in western Slovakia bears out this point:

> Dr. Eisler is not an excellent speaker and has not learned Slovak well yet. But he is the chairman of the Jewish scouts' organization and intensively occupies himself with Zionism. These young scouts speak mainly Hungarian or German amongst themselves. They maintain the Hungarian spirit and culture under the veil of Zionism. The Orthodox Jews recognize the government's interests and also the dangers that the Zionists represent as they deepen the chasm between the Jews and the local population.[83]

Slovak authorities also carried out a series of investigations of possible Hungarian irredentist activity within Jewish national sport, cultural, and educational associations in Slovakia in 1926, employing language as a basis of inquiry. The police reports expressed offense that these associations carried out their activities in Magyar and German and offered foreign language instruction in English, French, and Hebrew but did not use Slovak, the state language. The investigations, however, did not turn up any concrete evidence of antistate propaganda.[84] The police official investigating the branch of the Jewish scout association Ha-Shomer Ha-Tsair in Komárno noted that he heard only one word in Slovak: "*Pozor!*" (Attention).[85]

On the state level as well as in public opinion, the expression of Slovak suspicions and grievances against the Jews converged on the issue of Magyar language use. "There are no Jews in the world like the ones in Slovakia," acidly remarked the author of a 1929 article in *Nitrianské noviny*:

Jews living in Poland speak Polish, in Germany German, in France French, in Bohemia Czech, in Hungary Magyar—only in Slovakia do we have Jews who speak Magyar. It is a world rarity, which is likely to be what makes the Jews such great lords in Slovakia. . . . On the main street, in the coffeehouse, and in the shops you hear only Magyar spoken. You see [the Jews] reading only Magyar newspapers, they ignore Slovak cultural endeavors. [They] speak only Magyar within the family and in public. . . . We cannot explain the Jewish mentality in Slovakia in any other way than that the whole nation still regards us a nation of stupid Slovaks who must put up with every insult, like under the Magyar government.[86]

Using the Slovak language was also regarded as the fulfillment of an obligation both to the Slovak nation and to Czechoslovakia, as seen in the following evaluation of Jewish community education from the Košice-based daily *Slovenský východ*:

The Jewish Orthodox Religious Community in Košice understood its duties not only to the Slovak nation, but also to the republic. An expression of this understanding is that this community established an elementary school on Kazinczy Street using Slovak as the language of instruction. Slovak state teachers provide the instruction. The Neolog Jewish community in Košice has not forgotten Hungary, however, as we see from the fact that it has its own elementary school, in which, as the only such Jewish school in the republic, Magyar is the language of instruction.[87]

From this perspective there could be no neutral maintenance of the Magyar language among the Jewish population, at the very least for official purposes. The Slovak press sharply criticized Jews who wished to preserve the Magyar language and culture in Slovakia while at the same time putting themselves forth as loyal citizens of the state and declaring their own separate Jewish nationality:

The same Jews who cross their fingers in questions like [retaining Magyar street names in Bratislava] have just in the past few days had some congress from which they tossed a speech to the public about loyalty to the Czechoslovak Republic. They will have to forgive us if we give no [credence] to such speeches. . . . We regard the Jews as fellow citizens in the full sense of the term. That should suffice and should bring them to a better understanding of their duties to this state. It is high time that the Jews put their words into action. And when they now declare for their own nationality, let them do it consistently.[88]

The seeming inconsistency of the national orientation of Jews who declared Jewish nationality but continued to speak Magyar corroborated the distrust that Slovak state authorities as well as the local Slovak population felt for the Jews. They interpreted claims of Jewish nationality accompanied by the continued use of the Hungarian language as disingenuous. The Jewish loyalty question was framed in linguistic terms.

When the Union of Slovak Jews brought their grievance to the Bratislava police, they struck back at Funk and exposed the weaknesses of the Jewish national movement in Slovakia. They also demonstrated their confidence in the validity of the complaint and the correctness of their position on the state and the local Slovak population. Their action supports what Yeshayahu Jelínek described as the "parading of an allegedly superior loyalty to the Czechoslovak state" on the part of the pro-Slovak assimilationists and the Orthodox, who "denounced for all practical purposes other Jews as being short in loyalty."[89] Funk's outburst had been an auspicious opening for the Union of Slovak Jews to publicize and push for their program.

The 1927 police report shrewdly observed that the real motivation of the Union of Slovak Jews in lodging their grievance against Funk was to put pressure on the leadership of the Neolog Jewish community to grant their request to hold Slovak-language services in the Neolog synagogue. "It is an open secret," the report remarked, "that this request found no echo with the community board, whose members are primarily Germans and Magyars."[90]

The subsequent shift in attention to the leadership of the Neolog Jewish community of Bratislava from the Union of Slovak Jews led to a dramatic turnaround in the state's view of the much-maligned Rabbi Funk. By 1932 the state had reversed its perception of the rabbi from Magyarophile element working under the cover of Zionism to loyal Czechoslovak citizen and advocate of the lower classes. The state instead condemned the community leadership as a disloyal element that behaved in the political interests of Hungary rather than Czechoslovakia.[91] A spate of articles appeared in the statewide press in 1932 (notably in the papers *České slovo, A Zet,* and the *Slovenský večerník*), drumming up the public's interest in the question of the national orientation of Slovak Jews.[92]

The ongoing conflict between Funk and the leadership of the Neolog Jewish community erupted into open antagonism after President Masaryk's visit to Bratislava in mid-October 1930. On that occasion Dr. Viktor Stein, the president of the community, arranged Neolog participation in the program in such a way that Funk was unable to officially greet Masaryk on behalf of the Neologs as his Orthodox counterpart, Rabbi Koloman Wéber, was able to do. Stein also made it impossible for Funk to bless Masaryk, an honor enjoyed by the Orthodox rabbi Akiba Schreiber.[93]

Just one year earlier the state had conducted a pro forma investigation of Rabbi Schreiber in response to the provocative article "Trianon and Kollel" published in the Jewish national paper and organ of the Jewish Party *Jüdische Volkszeitung.*[94] The article attempted to connect the rabbi's fund-raising work to support Jewish pilgrims in Palestine coming from prewar Hungarian territories with the interwar Hungarian government's program to revise the borders set by the Treaty of Trianon. By supporting a communal construct based on the prewar

Hungarian borders, the article argued, the Kollel fostered the memory of and hope for restoration of those borders. How outspokenly "tendentious and bereft of objectivity is this act of hatred against the Kollel," condemned Rabbi Schreiber. Its lack of success is driven home by Rabbi Schreiber's distinguished participation in the president's visit. The rabbi outlined the history and purpose of the Kollel program and reminded the police commissioner that the Czechoslovak government had approved it in a German-language letter during the mid-October 1929 investigation. "'Kollel' means community (*Gemeinschaft*)," he began, "The 'Kollel' was founded by my grandfather [Rabbi Ktav Sofer[95]], the former chief rabbi in Bratislava in 1862 in Jerusalem and went by the name 'Austro-Hungarian-Bohemian-Moravian Jewish Community.' The purpose of this community is to materially support those pilgrims from the above-named lands who wish to dedicate their lives to study of the Jewish religion and the Bible in the Holy Land."[96]

The Kollel was administered by two guardians of the fund in the Kingdom of Hungary, one in Bratislava, and one in Užhorod before the war. The administration of the Kollel remained the same. Rabbi Schreiber informed the administration that members of the Kollel cared for former Austro-Hungarian citizens who chose to immigrate to Palestine after 1919. Of those immigrants, 35–40 percent were Czechoslovak citizens; 40 percent were Romanian, Yugoslav, and Austrian citizens; and 25–30 percent were Hungarian citizens. After the changes, Chief Rabbi Fuchs in Oradea oversaw leadership of Romanian citizens in the Kollel; Chief Rabbi Deutsch, in Subotica for Yugoslav citizens; Chief Rabbi Frankl, in Budapest for Hungarian citizens, Chief Rabbi Ignaz Klein, in Austria; and Chief Rabbi Akiba Schreiber in Bratislava became head of the Kollel for Slovakia. The Orthodox Jewish community had handled all approvals necessary for fund-raising in Slovakia for the Kollel with the Czechoslovak administration already in 1920. President Masaryk had himself honored the Kollel colony with a visit during his recent visit to Jerusalem in 1927, Rabbi Schreiber said.[97]

As a consequence of the attack on "our chief rabbi, head of our Kollel in Palestine, his selfless and tireless work, and his devotion to the poor," the Orthodox Jewish community resolved to break all ties to newspapers and individuals that would "degrade a Jewish leader of any society in such an irresponsible manner."[98] The Orthodox community resolved that not one of their members would read the paper, that the author of the article would be removed from the community, and that their resolution would be read in every synagogue, in every Jewish community, to every political and police administrator. "The most holy commandment of every Jew is to be a loyal citizen of the land in which he lives," the community representative wrote, "and beyond this religious injunction, every Jew in our republic is a loyal supporter of this state with deepest heartfelt feeling because in this state his equality is guaranteed." Furthermore, the head of the state was President Masaryk, whose "glorious name is recorded for all eternity in the golden letters of Jewish history."[99]

Except for this brief investigation into the Kollel triggered by the defamatory article in the *Jüdische Volkszeitung*, there is no further evidence that the Czechoslovak administration suspected the Orthodox Jewish majority of political disloyalty. It was understood that the Kollel was a religious matter that had nothing to do with border revision. The Orthodox had taken care to show their respect and acceptance of the postwar status quo from the establishment of the state forward. The Orthodox community followed proper procedure to gain approval of their new and continuing religious-communal institutions by the Czechoslovak administration. Despite the flash of suspicion, Rabbi Schreiber had the honor of blessing Masaryk rather than Rabbi Funk, who was still under investigation. Of greater consequence for Rabbi Funk's participation, however, was his conflict with the Neolog Jewish community.

Viktor Stein chose to give the official speech himself, in which he remarked that it was the fate of the Jews to "suffer in silence."[100] Masaryk responded to Stein's comment with indignation, declaring, "In our republic you have nothing to suffer from; here all can live in freedom as decent men."[101] Rabbi Funk rebuked Stein's speech on the following day, detailing a long list of the rights and privileges that the Jews in Czechoslovakia enjoyed.[102] Rabbi Funk testified that his exclusion from Masaryk's visit not only had been unjust and contrary to the obligations of his office but also constituted an anti-Czechoslovak stand. He demanded that the state examine the motivations behind Stein's actions.[103]

The state did so and concluded that Stein's "nonsensical" complaints stemmed from what they deemed his "well-known Magyar chauvinistic conviction."[104] Stein was a notorious Jewish gentry man (*džentrik*), the report stated, supported in his activities by the Lučenec millionaire Ignác Herzog, the Bratislava lawyer Koloman Dezső, and by the vice president of the Neolog Jewish community, Aladár Porzsolt, who owned an estate in Újszőny, Hungary. Porzsolt, they observed, praised Stein and the others in Hungary for steering their political activities in favor of Hungary. In addition, all of the men were allegedly freemasons.[105] By this reasoning Stein had barred Funk from Masaryk's visit out of fear that Funk would offend Stein's connections in Hungary with a very loyal speech to Czechoslovakia. In Funk's place Stein delivered a speech that the state considered grist for the mill of Hungarian interests.[106] According to the conclusion of the state investigation, Stein's meaning was quite clear when considered alongside his other dubious activities, especially the appointment of rabbis trained at the allegedly irredentist Budapest Rabbinical Seminary to positions with Neolog Jewish communities in Slovakia.[107] The state held Stein responsible for bringing these "very chauvinistic Magyars" from Hungary to serve in Slovakia.[108]

In comparison with Stein, rather than with the Union of Slovak Jews, the state found Rabbi Funk's behavior correct, if eccentric. The 1932 report went so far as to paint Funk as a beacon of democracy, a hero of the lower classes in the Neolog Jewish community, struggling for their just representation against the rich community leadership. The report enthusiastically noted that Funk called for the overthrow of the current leadership—whom Funk regarded as lukewarm to Czechoslovakia because of their property holdings in Hungary[109]—and for rewriting the community statutes, which he argued had been designed under the former regime to favor the rich.[110] For these reasons, influential community leaders were attempting to remove Funk from his position, the report concluded.[111]

Other points in Rabbi Funk's favor included his use of the Slovak language for official events and his condemnation of actions that could potentially harm the Czechoslovak state. The report emphasized that Rabbi Funk had delivered part of his address in Slovak on the occasions of Masaryk's birthday and the anniversary of the founding of the state in 1932, demonstrating his efforts to become proficient in the state language even at his advanced age. Rabbi Funk vigorously protested against Stein's filling rabbinical positions in Slovakia with graduates of the seminary in Budapest; against the Lord Rothermere's international campaign for the revision of Hungary's borders; and against the declaration made by the Hungarian minister of defense, Gyula Gömbös, in 1930 that he regarded the Jews in Slovakia to be supporters of Hungary. In addition, Rabbi Funk called on the members of the Neolog Jewish community in Bratislava to condemn Gömbös's statement and thereby show their loyalty to Czechoslovakia.[112]

The reversal of the state's view of Funk over the course of its six-year investigation corresponded with a shift in the markers that the state defined as indicators of citizen loyalty and in its techniques of observation. At first the investigation was based on internal strife within the Neolog Jewish community connected to issues of relations with the surrounding Slovak population. Later the investigation centered on problems with a more immediate bearing on external relations with Hungary: the connections of the leadership of the Neolog Jewish community with Hungary, their property holdings in Hungary, the appointment of rabbis who were Hungarian citizens trained in the rabbinical seminary in Budapest, and responses to the international Justice for Hungary campaign of Lord Rothermere and to the contentious statement of Hungarian minister of defense Gömbös in the Hungarian parliament.

A host of linguistic, social, cultural, and religious issues burdened Slovak-Jewish relations; interpreting these was an ineffective way of determining overall allegiance to the Czechoslovak state. The state could better determine the political loyalties of its Slovak Jewish citizens by considering their connections to Hungary or Hungarian Jewry and to activity that ran counter to Czechoslovak interests. Matters of citizen loyalty gained meaning in the transnational context.

The Heroes' Temple Commemoration Project

The Heroes' Temple (Hősök Temploma) lies on the corner plot of Wesselényi and Dohány Streets in central Budapest. A modest building, its minimalistic lines contrast with the Moorish grandeur of its neighbor, the monumental Dohány Street synagogue, which was consecrated with much pomp and circumstance in September 1859. Conceived in 1927 and completed in time for Rosh Hashanah services in September 1931, the Heroes' Temple serves as both a Neolog prayer hall and a site of commemoration for the ten thousand Jewish soldiers from the prewar territory of the Kingdom of Hungary who fought and died for the monarchy during World War I.

The case of the Heroes' Temple memorial project was one of the most intriguing used by the Czechoslovak state to investigate the political loyalties of the Jews in Slovakia. Perceiving the project as a potential branch of the larger Hungarian irredentist enterprise, the administration filed the documents relating to the Heroes' Temple under the heading "Hungarian Jews and the Revision of Trianon" and stamped them "classified" and "urgent." It was clear that the Czechoslovak government was deeply suspicious of a war commemoration project that extended beyond the Trianon borders of Hungary in its scope. By remembering the Jews of Slovakia and Subcarpathian Ruthenia as Hungarians, the project appeared to go hand in hand with the revisionist ambitions of the Horthy government.

The Budapest Jewish community intended to engrave the names of the 10,000 fallen Hungarian Jewish soldiers on the marble walls of the memorial, a fact the Czechoslovak state administration noted with exclamation points in its reports on the project. Physical representation of numbers and names was important to the Budapest Jewish community for proving the extent of the Hungarian Jewish wartime sacrifice. The Hungarian Jewish newspaper *Egyenlőség* had kept a running list of fallen Jewish soldiers throughout the course of the war. In 1922 the Hungarian National Statistical Bureau had calculated the figure 10,000 based on the prewar territory of Hungary as the official number of fallen Hungarian Jewish soldiers. That number was recalculated in 1927 to 5,116 based on the postwar territory, but the recalculation was taken as offensive and inaccurate by Hungarian Jews.[113] Because they regarded 10,000 as the accurate number, it was important to back it up with the personal data of soldiers from the successor states.

The Czechoslovak investigation of Slovak Jewish participation in the Heroes' Temple commemoration project began in September 1929, shortly after the chief Orthodox rabbi of Slovakia, Koloman Wéber, advised the government to be on the lookout for revisionist activity on the part of Hungarian Jewry.[114] The state proceeded to follow the activities of several rabbis and Neolog Jewish communities in Slovakia to see whether they were involved with the building of the Heroes' Temple.[115]

The Budapest Jewish community was inspired to create the Heroes' Temple memorial by a call of the Hungarian government for each religious community in the country to commemorate its own war martyrs. Within this context the building of the Heroes' Temple seemed like a perfect opportunity to simultaneously accomplish three objectives: to mourn the dead, to support the official declaration that "[Hungary] is bleeding from a thousand wounds,"[116] and to remind postwar Hungary of the loyalty and patriotism of its Jewish citizens. The latter was of particular importance after the disastrous short-lived Hungarian Soviet Republic of 1919, which had counted among its leadership many communists of Jewish origin. The Budapest Jewish community set up a commission right away to meet with the rabbis in the successor states in order to gather financial and other support for the Heroes' Temple project and to enter the personal data of the fallen soldiers.[117]

In their quest to reaffirm the loyalty and patriotism of Hungarian Jewry during the war, and to testify to their continued devotion to and identification with postwar Hungary, however, the Budapest Jewish community set its needs on a collision course with those of the Jews in Slovakia. Any involvement of the Jews in Slovakia in the Heroes' Temple project would serve only to make them more suspicious as pro-Hungarian elements in the eyes of the Czechoslovak state. It was an inevitable and irreconcilable conflict of interests. Demonstrating the loyalty of the Jews in Slovakia to Czechoslovakia depended on breaking ties with Hungary and Hungarian Jewry. In November 1929 the Czechoslovak administration advised the Jews in Slovakia to "reject the courting of their coreligionists from Hungary insofar as it concerns obvious, but unacknowledged irredentist activity," and recommended that Czechoslovak officials carefully follow Jews with Hungarian connections.[118]

Distance from Budapest is required to understand the impact and fallout of the Heroes' Temple memorial project. Viewing it from a territory that had been part of the prewar Hungarian state allows for the charting of issues emphasized by the project, especially as they facilitated a more concrete expression of altered postwar group belongings.

Recent literature on the process of commemoration asks us to consider who or what war memorials are asking us to remember. In what ways do these memorials reflect the search for meaning in war? As sites of rituals, rhetoric, and ceremonies of mourning, they speak of the connection of the past to the present, the living to the dead, and the location of the trauma of war in contemporary memory.[119] This connection is especially poignant in cases of geopolitical discontinuity. If Slovak Jews were to participate in the Heroes' Temple project with their coreligionists and former compatriots, they, too, would mourn the collapse of the Kingdom of Hungary. Their sons had fought and died for Hungary as Hungarians on the battlefield, but it was no longer possible to mourn them as such. The creation of the Czechoslovak state in which they now lived depended on the collapse of the monarchy, and its continued existence rested on keeping the revisionist ambitions of postwar Hungary at bay.

The Czechoslovak state hoped that keeping track of developments related to the Heroes' Temple memorial project would provide it with a barometer of Jewish connections to Hungary. The bulk of the investigations took place in early fall 1929, carried out by local authorities. In most cases this meant the local police.

The most detailed reports came in to Bratislava and Prague from Nitra in western Slovakia and Prešov in eastern Slovakia in the first half of November 1929. In the police report from Nitra, the head rabbi confirmed he had received a letter with the stamp of the Heroes' Temple on it in February from Péter Ujváry, who along with Samuel Glückstahl, a member of the Upper House in Hungary, was gathering the personal data of the fallen soldiers in Slovakia. Ujváry was seeking the names of fallen soldiers as well as those of subscribers to the memorial. The police investigator said that as far as it was possible for him to ascertain, none of the rabbis in the area of Nitra had joined the commission to help gather names, but that some may have given names to Ujváry because doing so represented a good opportunity to show pride in those Jewish soldiers of former Hungary. Significantly, he noted in his report that it would be a mistake to assume that the Jews in Nitra were under the influence of Hungarian Jewry, because they felt at home there, and they were convinced that life was better in the Czechoslovak Republic than in neighboring Hungary. Jews in Nitra had told the investigator that they knew their coreligionists in Hungary were "politically persecuted." As a final note, he added that Ujváry had been in the southern Slovak town of Nové Zámky and in Bratislava four years earlier (1925), trying to raise money for an "Album of Heroes" among the Jews in Neolog communities, but had not been able to collect the necessary amount.[120]

The police report from Prešov, a Neolog Jewish stronghold in eastern Slovakia, makes for convincing proof that the Jews there were not involved in the Heroes' Temple project or other suspected irredentist activity. The report exhibits a bluntly hostile position toward the local Jewish population. Sure, the report states, "Even the last Jewish barkeep in the most remote village of Šariš was an informer of the present Hungarian government. . . . In spite of this . . . it's impossible to claim that they would be subject to the influence of Hungarian irredentist circles, mainly the Revisionist League, or that they would have close ties with them."[121]

Notwithstanding his own unfriendly attitude, the author of the report recognized that the Hungarian irredentist movement, and especially the anti-Semitic Revisionist League, would hardly be an attractive forum for anti-Czechoslovak activity among the Jews in Slovakia. All of the Jews of Prešov were "100 percent Magyarized," he stressed, but Hungarian assimilation ended after the changes. In its place came Zionism, which propagated Jewish nationality and asserted that the Jews should have their own sovereign state in Palestine. In Prešov, a Dr. Karol Ferbstein spread Zionism, recruiting mainly from Magyarized Jews, who "vote for a separate Jewish nation, but are not able to rid themselves of the Hungarian mentality." The report concluded that it was better for the Jews in Czechoslovakia than it was in Hungary even before the war, which is the primary reason they were not interested in the success of any plans for revising the Trianon borders—not out of any special love or loyalty for the state.[122]

Briefer reports arrived throughout 1930 and 1931, many repeating information that was already known. Several concerned specific instances of Jewish interaction with Ujváry, Glückstahl, or the local authorities. For example, the Jewish community in Snina, in northeastern Slovakia, did gather names of fallen Jewish soldiers from their community as Ujváry requested, but despite repeated reminders the president of the Jewish community refused to send the data to Budapest. He later received a questionnaire from Ujváry that he handed over to the local officials.[123]

A report from the spring of 1930 stated that Ujváry and Glückstahl visited the Neolog Jewish community in Šahy, southwestern Slovakia, in February 1929 to request the names of the fallen soldiers. At that time the head of the Jewish religious community there, Dr. Jakub Váradi, had the requested information drawn up and sent to Budapest. However, he wanted the record to state clearly that he intended the document only to serve the purpose of piety and reverence for the dead and to prove the falsity of accusations from anti-Semitic circles that the Jewish population had not sacrificed their blood on the battlefields. He did not wish to have anything to do with further Hungarian actions. The report concluded with a list of Slovak national organizations to which Váradi belonged, including his membership on the board of the Matica Slovenska and his active role in the Agrarian Party and stating that he had come forward against the Justice for Hungary action of Lord Rothermere.[124]

To what extent was the investigation of Neolog Jews in Slovakia successful for determining levels of continuing political loyalty to Hungary? The Heroes' Temple memorial project was important in the eyes of the Czechoslovak government only for this purpose. The method, while ingenious, was far from foolproof. After all, the Heroes' Temple was a memorial for fallen Hungarian Jewish soldiers, and the sons of the Jews in Slovakia had died as Hungarian Jews. How else were they to be mourned?

As the reports show, Jews in Slovakia were not willing to be viewed as Trianon revisionists for the sake of participating in the Heroes' Temple memorial. Nevertheless, the commemoration project of the Budapest Jewish community proved attractive. The Czechoslovak government would have been wrong to assume that two of the motivations that drove the Budapest community to undertake the project—mourning the dead and fighting anti-Semitic accusations—would not appeal to the Jews in Slovakia.

However, the accusations of involvement with Hungarian revisionism aimed at the Jews in Slovakia, focusing on Neolog Jewry, took precedence. Jews in Slovakia chose to commemorate their war dead locally and modestly. Examples of their memorials include a plaque at the entrance to the Neolog cemetery in Bratislava, a pillar and rectangular concrete slab in the Neolog cemetery in Prešov, and a plaque on the wall of the Neolog synagogue in Bytča. In this way those who chose to do so could publicly pay tribute to their war dead without being connected to a project initiated by Budapest that raised the suspicion of the Czechoslovak state.

The Heroes' Temple memorial project illustrates a turning point in the history of Slovak Jewry. It was the conclusion of a formative period in which their linguistic and cultural ties to Hungary were unbound from political ones. Their peculiar position as a group had become more clearly defined in relation to Hungary, Hungarian Jewry, and the Hungarian minority in Slovakia. As the police report from Prešov had noted, Hungarian assimilation had ended after the changes, and in its place had come Zionism, which propagated Jewish nationality. Jewish nationality was the primary means by which the majority of Slovak Jews expressed their internal convictions.

Jewish nationality and Jewish national politics offered a productive way for Slovak Jews to feel, demonstrate, and act upon their reorientation as citizens of Czechoslovakia. Jewish nationality also played a significant role in the development of a particular Slovak Jewish collective identity, facilitating the delineation and management of the set of concerns peculiar to Slovak Jewry in relation to the Czechoslovak and Hungarian states and to the multinational population of Slovak, Czech, and Hungarian Jewry.

Slovak Jews appreciated the fluidity of movement among the various aspects of their group belongings that Czechoslovak citizenship allowed. They could be Czechoslovak state citizens of the Jewish nationality and speak German, Magyar, Yiddish, Czech, and Slovak, or any combination of these as they chose. The ability to affiliate with a separate Jewish nationality gave the appearance of removing them from the national fray. The majority of Slovak Jews pinned their hopes on Jewish nationality as, in the words of Rabbi Reich of Vrbové, "the only possibility of avoiding conflict with every party, every religion, and every nationality, of eliminating all misunderstandings."[125]

Affiliation with the Jewish nationality and participation in Jewish national politics also seemed to be a good way to demonstrate the severing of ties with Hungary and Hungary Jewry that Czechoslovakia was looking for as transnational evidence of Czechoslovak state loyalty among Slovak Jews. Slovak Jewish reactions to the "courting" of Hungary and Hungarian Jewry, as it was called in the case of the Heroes' Temple commemoration project, figured prominently among the suitable evidence. The Slovak Jewish press and representative organizations used the argument of belonging to a separate Jewish nationality to defend the Slovak Jewish population against the undesirable Hungarian embrace.

At the same time the Jewish national movement in Slovakia bore within it the weakness of appearing to have a Magyar national subtext as the Funk affair revealed. This was due in part to its fierce anti-assimilationist position as well as the maintenance of Magyar language usage by a number of its adherents. A Jewish national political affiliation accompanied by Magyar language usage seemed inconsistent, even if language had been officially disengaged from the Czechoslovak conception of nationality as an internal conviction in the case of the Jewish population. It fueled rather than quelled suspicions held by both the state and the surrounding Slovak population of a continuing Magyar orientation accompanied by possible antistate activity among Magyar-speaking Jews in Slovakia when this segment of the Jewish population was distinguished from the rest.

It was important for Slovak Jews to make absolutely clear to the Czechoslovak state that they did not consider themselves part of the Hungarian minority in Slovakia in a political sense. Many Slovak Jews may have continued to speak the Magyar language and even to consider themselves culturally Magyar, but this did not have a bearing on their political orientation as loyal citizens of Czechoslovakia. They disassociated the political aspect of their state and national belongings from the linguistic and cultural ones. Slovak Jews did not wish to be instrumentalized as Magyars for an irredentist cause.

Language use, once an external marker of nationality, was now politically charged as an indicator of loyalty to the bounded territorial nation. The tragic weakness of Jewish nationality lay in its illegibility; it could not be read the same way as other nationalities. Although the removal of linguistic criteria from the Czechoslovak conception of Jewish nationality had been extraordinarily productive in activating a separate Jewish national political life in Czechoslovakia, it left Jewish loyalty open to hostile interpretation.

4 Between the Nationalities

Statist Slovak Jews, Separatist Slovaks, and the Revisionist Threat

LESS THAN TWO weeks before the 1930 Czechoslovak census, the Hungarian minister of defense, Gyula Gömbös, took the floor in the Hungarian parliament to declare the Jews in the "occupied territories" to be "good Hungarian patriots." He noted his willingness to accept them into Hungary's elite Order of Heroes (Vitézi Rend), established in 1920 by the Hungarian regent Miklós Horthy and then prime minister Count Pál Teleki to honor soldiers who had served with distinction during the war.[1] Yet Gömbös argued that their coreligionists and former compatriots across the border in Hungary itself were not good Hungarians, and he would not accept them into the order. His statements in parliament came just days after more explicit remarks at the tenth-anniversary celebration of the Order of Heroes' establishment, held in the central Hungarian plains town of Kecskemét, where he defended and championed the order in the following way: "In recent days the 'Vitézi Rend' has been attacked in the *Pester Lloyd* because we exclude soldiers of Jewish confession from our ranks. I can only say, and at last permit me [to do so], that we Hungarians do remain Hungarian in at least one of our institutions."[2]

His comments were consistent with views expressed by the interwar Hungarian regime under Regent Horthy since the passage of the numerus clausus legislation in 1920. That law implied the exclusion of Jews living within the postwar Hungarian borders from the Hungarian nation on racial or national terms. But the Hungarian government saw no inconsistency in categorizing Jews in Slovakia and Subcarpathian Ruthenia as Hungarians for its irredentist cause. Vilmos Vázsonyi, former minister of justice and a respected Hungarian politician of Jewish origin, had stressed this contradiction seven years earlier, in a 1923 appeal to Prime Minister István Bethlen, stating: "The numerus clausus does not speak of religious groups [confessions] but of race. . . . This law therefore considers the Jews to be a race or a distinct nationality. And this at a time when, in Paris,

Count Teleki and Count Bethlen have declared that the Romanians and Czechs are wrong to consider the Jews a separate race, since the Jews [in Slovakia and Transylvania] are Hungarians."[3]

By 1930 Slovak Jews had grown tired of the treacherous "good Hungarian patriots" rhetoric employed by Gömbös, as well as its painful corollary: the efforts by their coreligionists across the border to entice them to declare Hungarian nationality on the census and otherwise engage in projects—like the Heroes' Temple memorial—that would identify them with Hungary and Hungarian Jewry. The mainstream Bratislava-based German-language Slovak Jewish newspaper *Jüdisches Familienblatt* firmly renounced Hungarian Jewish ambitions of this sort, its arguments reinforced by the very language of its publication. Slovak Jewish public life, including its newspaper culture, largely took place in German. German language usage, a temporary step toward the goal of acquiring the state language, was an important way for Slovak Jews to express their reorientation as citizens of Czechoslovakia, signal their renouncement of Magyarization, and demonstrate their distance from interwar Hungarian politics.

The *Jüdisches Familienblatt* derided the Association of Hungarian Jews, that "well-known group of assimilated Hungarian Jews," for issuing an appeal to world Jewry with the intent to seek international protections for Slovak Jews as a Hungarian minority. "We would refrain from the crooked logic that considers Slovak Jews a Hungarian minority," stated the *Jüdisches Familienblatt*. "If the Jews as such consider themselves a national minority, then they can only act as a *Jewish* minority. . . . We have the duty and the right to dismiss the claims of the Association of Hungarian Jews, which would put us in a false and absolutely untrue light vis-à-vis our fellow citizens and the government of our state."[4] Slovak Jews clung to Jewish minority status in order to secure their Czechoslovak statist position and protect themselves against the dangers of border revisionism. Those Slovak Jews who did not declare Jewish nationality chiefly turned directly to declarations of Czechoslovak nationality.[5] Numbers of Czechoslovak nationality declarations among Slovak Jews rose perceptibly from 1921 to 1930.

Rabbi Samuel Funk called on the Neolog Jewish community leadership, with whom he had a notorious long-standing conflict, and on Jews across Slovakia who maintained Hungarian nationality to officially disavow "the invective of the Hungarian minister [Gömbös]" and in so doing demonstrate their loyalty to the land in which they lived. When his actions found little resonance, Funk turned to Arthur Hirschler, a like-minded member of the Jewish community, to send a letter of his own to the board restating the demand for decisive action.[6] Hirschler's lengthy German-language letter stressed the need for the Jewish community to take a stand against the "shame of such a borderless insinuation." In it he drew on the by now familiar, even clichéd, tactic of comparing political and economic conditions for the Jews in Hungary and Czechoslovakia in order to emphasize Slovak Jewish gratitude and loyalty to the state. "While there [in Hungary], the numerus clausus, gentry terror, dictatorship, and cane-beatings obtain for the Jews," condemned Hirschler, "in our state four Jews were appointed public notaries out of fifteen available positions." It was the special duty of the Jewish community in the Slovak capital to take an energetic position on the matter, Hirschler argued, to serve as an example for all the other Jewish communities in Slovakia.[7]

Nevertheless, the Bratislava Neolog Jewish community leadership did not act on Hirschler's motion. It contended that the community, as a religious institution, should refrain from becoming involved in political matters. The Bratislava Orthodox Jewish community leadership arrived at a similar conclusion.[8] Another explanation for the lack of the Bratislava Neolog Jewish community leadership's action on the motion could be that it was initially made by Rabbi Funk, with whom its relationship was openly antagonistic. As for the Orthodox, their Jewish community leadership may have not felt it necessary to take the suggested stand, as the state understood their loyalty as exemplary rather than suspect.

Yet while the Neolog community board later regretted not offering an official timely renunciation of Minister of War Gömbös's statements in Hungarian parliament, the evidence does not indicate that its lack of action became a scandal in the view of the Czechoslovak state.[9] The Funk affair had not only pointed to the discrepancy between the views of that community's board and the broader membership but had also spurred the process of restructuring community statutes to enable more democratic representation. As head of the newly united Jewish Party of Slovakia and Subcarpathian Ruthenia, Julius Reisz had already sworn in 1928 to do everything in his power to paralyze the Hungarian National Party in Czechoslovakia. "It quite appears," the police report had then noted with satisfaction, "that a definite departure from the Hungarian opposition has taken place among the Jews."[10] The state already understood that with only negligible exceptions, the overwhelming majority of Slovak Jews were an undeniably loyal population and that Jewish nationality was a statist position.

Slovak Jewish loyalty to Czechoslovakia had indeed become apparent not only to the state administration but also to the Slovaks, Hungarians, and Germans. The increasingly separatist Slovak national movement resented the clear alignment of the Slovak Jewish population with the state, while the Hungarians and Germans understood Jewish nationality and Jewish national politics as a Czechoslovak statist attack on their own minority rights. "After helping the Magyars to realize their aims at domination in Slovakia," one Slovak historian writes, sympathetically representing the increasingly separatist Slovak political position of the 1930s, "[the Jews] did not hesitate to render the same service to the Czechs."[11] The Hungarian Revisionist League cited the 1930 census as an effort to completely do away with the Hungarian nationality. It claimed that the Czech census utterly misrepresented the distribution of minorities in the state. "This is all the more true in the case of the Hungarians," the organization argued in a memorandum submitted to the League of Nations, "for many Hungarians of the Jewish creed, whose mother tongue is Magyar and would like their children to attend Hungarian schools, have been classified on the Czech census as Jews."[12] Heinrich Rauchberg, professor of statistics at the University of Vienna and later at the *Deutsche Karl-Ferdinands-Universität* (the German division of the divided Czech and German sections of the Charles-Ferdinand University in Prague) before the war, focused on the problem of preserving that crucial 20 percent for the German minority in his argument against Jewish nationality. "It would be a greater injustice," he wrote, "if for a small percentage of Jews, 19 percent of the German minority would lose its language rights in some districts, than if for a mere two percent of the entire population of the state this problematic Jewish nationality is invalid."[13]

The dream of holding a neutral position in the nationalities conflict through Jewish nationality and Jewish national politics was over. By 1930 the Czechoslovak administration understood that Jews in Slovakia had become detached from Hungary and Hungarian Jewry and had rejected domestic Hungarian opposition politics. The administration recognized that they had successfully relocated their political loyalty as citizens of Czechoslovakia. Slovak Jews had consistently sought the "right path," using Jewish nationality as a political compass for their treacherous course. But far from offering an escape, even pursuing an independent Jewish position placed the Jewish population directly between the Czechs and the other nationalities as tensions rose in the 1930s. These tensions pursued the Jews to the end of the state.

Rights and Numbers

Even before the results of the 1930 census were available, Antonín Boháč of the Czechoslovak State Statistical Office was busy defending its principles and execution for both domestic and international audiences. He was compelled to do so, for ever since the first statewide census in 1921 had shown a significant decline in the number of Hungarian and German inhabitants compared with the last counts on the Austrian and Hungarian prewar censuses, the Czechoslovak administration fielded accusations that its census methods targeted national minorities.[14] If the first statewide census had been about the activation of a new concept of nationality to consolidate Czechoslovak state building, the second was about its vindication. Solving the nationalities problem in Czechoslovakia would require far more than producing demographic legitimacy for a dominant "Czechoslovak" nationality. It would involve satisfying the other nationalities and, where relevant, their increasingly hostile kin states.

Ever the scholar of demographics and population science, Boháč saw the issue not as one of methodological inaccuracy or numerical falsification, but as one of differing conceptions about what "nationality" actually meant. He urged his audiences to remember the 1872 statistical conference in St. Petersburg. Each of three experts then gave three differing answers when asked to define "nationality": (1) *political,* or equivalent to state belonging; (2) *physical,* or a racial definition of "nationality"; or (3) *psychical,* as a psychological community penetrating individual feeling and collective endeavors. "Nation" was an easier concept to define as an ethnic or political community, he wrote. No similar international agreement had been reached on the meaning of "nationality."[15] While Boháč maintained that the statistical change between 1910 and 1921 could be easily explained without attributing it to allegedly violent or illegal methods, he acknowledged that "public opinion abroad was left with the impression that the national minorities had not been treated fairly during the 1921 census."[16] The international perception of inequity had grown appreciably in the 1920s.

The Hungarian minority steadily pursued a course of action intended to draw international attention to their position. They submitted a memorandum to the president of the League of Nations Council before the census in mid-November 1930—at the same time Gyula Gömbös presented his view of the Jews in Slovakia in the Hungarian parliament—articulating standing Hungarian complaints. They later succeeded in having their position presented in the English parliament and then formally requested that the issue go to the Permanent Court of International Justice at The Hague. The English Lord Rothermere's sensationalist *Daily Mail* continued in its third year of support for the Hungarian revisionist campaign. Scholars of interwar Hungarian minority issues emphasize that the only way to bring international attention to their grievances was to keep the Hungarian minority issue on the League of Nations agenda. The German minority, for its part, launched protests following the Czechoslovak census against its allegedly cruel methods in the German-language press.[17]

Before the rise of the National Socialists to power in Germany in 1933, the dual domestic and international nature of the national minorities' problem was most pronounced in the Hungarian case. The Horthy government's determined revisionist policy merged with the considerable discontent of the Hungarian minority in eastern Czechoslovakia in a way that Weimar's interest in the German minority in the Sudeten region did not. Hungarian political parties in Czechoslovakia never warmed to what was termed "activist" participation in the political institutions of the state in interwar Czechoslovak political rhetoric, unlike their German counterparts. The German minority began to take an active part in the political life of the state in 1922, continuing until 1935 when Konrad Henlein's Nazi-subsidized Sudetendeutsch Party experienced extraordinary success among German minority voters in that year's parliamentary elections.[18] Why was there such a marked difference between the Hungarian and German relationship to Czechoslovak activist politics? To a great extent, the answer lies with their longer relationship to the territory in which they lived. It is important to remember that the Hungarian minority in Slovakia and Subcarpathian Ruthenia lived continuously on Hungarian territory until the end of the First World War.[19] The borders changed around them. They were traumatized by state dislocation.

R. W. Seton-Watson, in a confidential memorandum to President Masaryk in 1928, observed that the Hungarians and the Germans in Czechoslovakia were not treated equally. He concluded that the Hungarian position in the state was actually deteriorating. Hungarian grievances regarding questions of citizenship, education, linguistic and cultural rights, pensions and land reform, Seton-Watson acknowledged, were indeed as serious as the Hungarians claimed and required remedy.[20] He urged President Masaryk to rectify them in the jubilee year 1928 "by graceful gesture and without the appearance of yielding in any way to agitation or clamor."[21] Czechoslovakia must assure all rights guaranteed by the peace treaties to the fullest extent possible compatible with state security, Seton-Watson insisted. It was a question of moral obligation to Czechoslovakia itself and to Europe and the only way to construct a viable alternate policy to revisionism and secure the peace.[22]

Boháč felt that somewhere in all of this the collective idea of nation and nationality had changed: by 1930 "nationality" belonged to a separate category than "nation."[23] He reflected on the transformation in two articles, one in Czech and the other in English, defending the 1931 census. In his Czech-language article he considered the change to be the result of conceptual change over time, and in his English-language article he simply stated as matter of fact that "nation" and "nationality" are not identical concepts. Pointing to the difference recalled earlier census preparation debates over the relationship between language and nationality. Leading figures from the Czechoslovak State Statistical Office agreed that while the two measures were not absolutely identical, language remained the closest objective external marker of one's nationality. Boháč's observation was indicative of the greater attention Czechoslovak demographers now gave to balancing state security and minority rights. Earlier, in the interest of state building, they focused on correcting national ratios that were deemed inaccurate as recorded on the last Austrian and Hungarian censuses.

Boháč was right, of course—the collective idea of nation and nationality indeed had changed. The shift in meaning was partly his own doing. After all, his job was to ascertain the nationality of each individual inhabitant of Czechoslovakia, to count and classify the relationship of each to the state in terms of national belonging. He and his colleagues put nationality into practice not only in an environment where the national principle formed the basis of state creation and legitimacy but also for a new state that the international community intended to be the linchpin of the post–World War I east central European state system. This is where the change had taken place. Nationality was the politicized component of ethno-national belonging. It was the collective political relationship to the nation-state based on ethnic/racial criteria. Nationality, not nation, is what Boháč and his colleagues sought to quantify on the census. The census furnished the numbers upon which the nationalities within the state secured their collective national rights, whether as the bearer of state-forming legitimacy or as a national minority that had been granted collective rights under the postwar treaties.

Boháč was frustrated that his colleagues paid little attention to the actual problem of collecting this crucial data under the controversial conditions in their mixed nationality state. The prominent sociologist I. Arnošt Bláha, for instance, wrote about the basic sociological problem of nationality, presenting it as a "social phenomenon which has a subjective and objective side," or a "natural psychological social reality" derived from a collection of specific traits, but not the contested process of its actual enumeration.[24] Czechoslovak demographers again devoted much energy to the problem of defining "nationality" in their spirited pre-census debates. Yet there was little discussion of the complaints lodged by the Hungarians and Germans about the qualifications of the census takers, enumeration methods, and issues of corruption, particularly about known cases of coerced national declarations from the previous census.[25] In spite of this, Boháč was convinced in the end that the Czechoslovak State Statistical Office and the Czechoslovak government had "done their utmost to arrive at unimpeachable statistical results" and that "their efforts [had] been successful."[26] The central problem of counting, in his estimation, developed from disagreement over the meaning of "nationality" itself.

Czechoslovak demographers began discussing the principles upon which to build nationality statistics more than a year before the scheduled census took place. As in the preparations for the first statewide census, they used the concept of Jewish nationality to buttress their arguments for and against whether to count nationality directly or by linguistic criteria ("mother tongue"). On the centrality of Jewish nationality in their deliberations Boháč wrote:

> The chief motive which secured a majority for ["nationality"] was consideration for the Jewish minority. Not even the strongest supporters of the "mother tongue" could deny that the Jews form in Czechoslovakia a national minority (their representatives secured two seats in Parliament at the last general elections); nor again could they disregard the fact that the language spoken by nationally conscious Jews does not correspond to their nationality. Besides, during the negotiations for the new Constitution a promise had been made to the Jews that they should not be compelled to declare themselves as belonging to any other nationality but their own, and this was naturally regarded as binding.[27]

While to a great extent the debates rehearsed positions taken ten years earlier, the difference this time was the heightened attention to domestic and international law and the practical implications of their decisions for minority protections.

It is worth noting, given the importance of Jewish nationality in the deliberations of Czechoslovak demographers and government officials, that their point of reference always remained the Czech lands, Bohemia and Moravia, rather than Slovakia and Subcarpathian Ruthenia, where the great majority of Jews in Czechoslovakia lived. The Jewish population in Slovakia alone was more than ten thousand people greater than in Bohemia, Moravia, and Silesia combined. Jews in Slovakia comprised 4.53 percent and in Subcarpathian Ruthenia 15.39 percent of the total population, which administrators knew from the 1921 census, as compared with 1.19 percent of the total population in Bohemia, 1.43 percent in Moravia, and 1.09 percent in Silesia. If arguments for national declaration by mother tongue showed increasing concern for the danger posed by Jewish nationality for maintaining a minority language (German or Hungarian) as the second official one in a district, they should have shown more interest in Slovakia and Subcarpathian Ruthenia, where the number of Jewish national declarations was much greater. As it happened, all decisions were made within consideration of the Czech-German relationship and then applied throughout the state.[28]

Emanuel Rádl, professor of philosophy, biology, and historian of science at the Charles University in Prague, contributed to the census debate with the publication of his 1929 volume *Národnost jako vědecký problém* (Nationality as Scholarly Problem). In it he made the case for a subjective concept of nationality, which would be declared by each individual as a matter of one's own personal conviction. While the concept was similar to the then new definition of "nationality" used by Josef Mráz in designing the 1919 census of the territory of Slovakia, Rádl was able to elaborate on the idea in the context of its post–World War I development. He discussed his perspective for a wider audience in a newspaper article titled "*Kdo rozhoduje?*" (Who Decides?), which, for him, was the key issue. "Nationality is a matter of your conscience," Rádl argued. "You yourself must decide." He held that nationality could be determined neither according to some so-called racial characteristics—skin color, length of body, width of face—nor by other so-called objective external markers, like language. "No one in all the world, no government offices, no laws, and no legislative agreement, no one but you can be responsible for your own national declaration," Rádl maintained.[29]

"Has anyone thought of the consequences if the Zionists received 20 percent in a district?" asked Heinrich Rauchberg. He rejected allowing a separate "Jewish" nationality category on the census, because he equated nationality with mother tongue. Since Hebrew was a dead language and *žargon* (jargon, referring to Yiddish) merely a German dialect, he argued, it was "incorrect to construct a Jewish nationality," as there was no linguistic basis to the claim. Rauchberg resolutely confronted the protests of his colleagues that the Jews represented an exceptional case among the nationalities and should be granted Jewish nationality even if they did not speak žargon. He believed it unfair and potentially destructive to allow a category of "Jewish," as a nonlinguistic nationality, to appear on the census, where even their small percentage of declarations could drop German numbers below the required 20 percent for minority language rights.[30] Rauchberg, along with Josef Gruber, Cyril Horáček, and Antonín Boháč, had argued for national declaration according to mother tongue against support proposed for direct national declaration by Vilibald Mildschuh, Dobroslav Krejčí, and František Weyr in the census debates of 1920 through 1921.

Jan Auerhan's position was similar to that of Rauchberg. Though "nationality" has different meanings, he agreed, the concept of nationality as a community of language was customary in the Czech lands. Furthermore, Auerhan reminded his colleagues, the language law approved by the supreme court equated national and linguistic belonging. To be accurate and fair, it would be necessary to investigate all nationalities without exception according to mother tongue on the census. Auerhan argued that allowing direct national declaration would disadvantage people with a weak or socially dependent position in the state. They would be afraid to declare their true nationality, would experience pressure or coercion, and consequently would declare another nationality.[31] He saw national declaration on the basis of mother tongue as a protective measure, by which the state could fulfill its legal obligations, thus making good in the domestic and international arenas.

But where would that leave the Jewish minority? Jews would not be able to declare Jewish nationality, and Czechoslovakia would renege on guarantees it made at the Paris Peace Conference. Václav Joachim of the Ministry of the Interior argued in contrast to Rauchberg and Auerhan that Jewish nationality was part and parcel of the 1919 agreements, extended on the basis of negotiations in Paris concerning the national minorities. He reminded them that international Jewish organizations had shaped those deliberations and supported Czechoslovakia. Joachim wondered how the removal of Jewish nationality from the census might affect Czechoslovakia's standing in the international community.[32] In this he attributed a good deal of power and influence to international Jewish organizations.

"Jews must not be forced to declare for another nationality than Jewish," insisted lawyer and chair of the Jewish Party Emil Margulies in an article in the Prague-based Zionist newspaper *Selbstwehr* (Self-Defense). Margulies had himself taken part in the minority rights negotiations for east central Europe after the First World War. He argued that the demand to equate nationality with language was in fact not consistent with international law, which by all agreements secured rights for three types of minorities: religious, linguistic, and national. As a solution to the dilemma he proposed that nationality be investigated directly, alongside the question of language.[33]

The Czech-Jewish movement's newspaper *Rozvoj* (Advancement) rejected Margulies's position as artificial: first, because Zionist organizations and clubs were trying to create a "Jewish" nationality in the Sudetenland (northwest Bohemia), where it allegedly had no natural base, and, second, because Jews in Bohemia were a religious minority, not a national one. For these reasons *Rozvoj* called for an objective marker, mother tongue, to form the basis of nationality investigation on the census. Additionally, *Rozvoj* wrote that Zionism was a more pressing issue in the eastern parts of the republic, since it decreased the numbers of the German and Hungarian minorities there.[34] Here *Rozvoj* made the recurring mistake of equating Jewish nationality with Zionism, which while truer in Bohemia, still was not congruent and was even less so as one moved eastward across the republic.

Rozvoj's stance marked a significant and surprising contrast between the standard position of the Czech-Jewish movement on this issue and the Czech one itself. It was oddly similar to the German and Hungarian one, due to both its definition of the Jews solely as a religious minority and its focus on linguistic community. The Czech stance, on the other hand, represented in the widest range of Czech-language newspapers, consistently favored the Jewish national argument, or what they simply termed the "Zionist" argument, because it diminished the number of Germans and Hungarians in Czechoslovakia. The Czech paper *Večer* (Evening) bears out this point: "The Zionists are absolutely right when they demand a change in those [census] principles, which would not only damage the Jewish national movement, but also work to the disadvantage of the Czechoslovak nation, since Jews would have to declare for the Germans and Hungarians according to their mother tongue."[35]

Nevertheless, the agreement reached at long last by the statistical council and the Czechoslovak government for investigating nationality on the 1930 census was a compromise favoring declaration by mother tongue—that is, a decision supporting the German minority position—but with an exception allowed for Jewish nationality. "Nationality shall be recorded in accordance with the mother tongue," ran the enumeration instructions: "Nationality differing from that indicated by the mother tongue may be recorded only if the registered person does not speak it either in his family or in domestic life and has complete mastery of the new language. Jews, however, may always register Jewish nationality. . . . One nationality only may be recorded. In the event of anyone recording two nationalities or none at all, his nationality shall be determined on the basis of his mother tongue."[36] This constituted little change in practical terms from the definition of "nationality" used in the 1921 census, which declared, "Nationality is understood as ethnic belonging, whose main external marker is as a rule mother tongue." By that definition the census officially recorded nationality as mother tongue with the same exceptions made as described above.[37] Save for Jews in Lithuania, Jews in Czechoslovakia remained the only nationality in interwar east central Europe who could declare their nationality directly, unbound from language.[38] The Jews in Czechoslovakia were relieved. The German minority, according to Boháč, was mollified by the decision to register nationality by mother tongue as a general rule. But the Hungarian minority in Slovakia was unsatisfied and voiced their complaints in their memorandum to the League of Nations, submitted by Hungarian deputies and senators of the Czechoslovak parliament in Prague.[39]

Hungary and the 1930 Czechoslovak Census

"Beware, Jews!" warned Dr. Eugen Klein, lawyer and member of the Union of Slovak Jews in his March 1930 article for the Bratislava-based Slovak-language daily the *Slovenský dennik.* "The census should still take place only sometime in the fall, but the Hungarian papers already pen sweet words to the Jews in Slovakia, so they would declare Hungarian nationality. . . . Be careful! Don't be tempted, don't be seduced, be reasonable!" Klein used the article to point out what he considered the terrible cynicism of Hungarian public figures in both Czechoslovakia and across the border in their attempts to garner Jewish numbers. "It is peculiar impertinence," he remarked acidly, "to woo people into a camp from which they are treated to refrains like, 'The Jew is not a person, he only looks like one from afar,'" or "'From a dog there is no bacon, nor from a Jew a Magyar!'" He recalled an incident in which the Hungarian National Party refused to permit a Jew of the Hungarian camp, the esteemed Košice lawyer Dr. Halmi, to occupy the last position on the ticket, despite the fact that the chair of the party himself had proposed Dr. Halmi as a candidate. At that time, Klein emphasized, leading figures in the party declared that they absolutely did not need any Jews at all, and now with the census on the horizon those same leaders came courting. But the Jews would not let themselves be seduced, Klein concluded: "Just a small fraction of the Jews remain [in the enemy camp], where the only connection is the Hungarian language, and that is simply because they do not understand Slovak."[40]

Klein, however, was preaching to the converted. The Jews who read the *Slovenský dennik* alongside its predominantly Slovak audience would have been less likely than their coreligionists who did not understand Slovak to declare Hungarian nationality. Klein's article was another occasion for the Union of Slovak Jews to showcase its efforts to guide the Jewish population in an assimilationist direction that was favorable to the Slovaks. Articles and opinions that were intended to reach the broad spectrum of Jewish readership in the Slovak Jewish public arena would be more likely to appear in the German-language *Jüdisches Familienblatt,* the primary newspaper of the Slovak Jewish community, which articulated separation from Hungary and the Magyars in both its language use and outlook. Klein's article in the *Slovenský dennik* article confronted Slovak fears that the Jews would indeed, in spite of everything, be enticed, cajoled, or intimidated into declaring Hungarian nationality on the census, which would threaten the state and the Slovak position within it. The problem was not just that many Jews continued to speak Magyar with all the uncertain implications that carried—"We have only the Jews to thank for the fact that a great deal of Magyar is spoken in Banská Bystrica," wrote one local paper with resentment—but also that Jews in Slovakia were perceived to habitually aid others in gaining dominance over the Slovaks rather than assimilating to *them* or helping *them.* "The Jew, with only few exceptions, will not become a Slovak, because he is fundamentally an enemy of the Slavs," intoned the author of an article on the "Jewish Problem." "The fact that the Jews *do* learn Slovak is not their merit. They must, after all, speak with their customers."[41]

The recently unified Jewish Party representing Slovakia and Subcarpathian Ruthenia advised its constituency to declare Jewish nationality on the upcoming census regardless of mother tongue.[42] Julius Reisz brought the Jewish parties representing Slovakia and Subcarpathian Ruthenia together under a wide umbrella in 1928 that disavowed Zionist slogans and otherwise extricated the parties from the Zionist program, making a vote for the Jewish Party more palatable to the anti-Zionist Orthodox.[43] Speaking on the nationality issue at the annual meeting of the Jewish Party in Trenčianske Teplice, the Trenčin lawyer Dr. Adolf Süss urged Jews to ignore the propaganda swirling around them, especially now that the Jewish Party had managed to win two seats in the 1929 parliamentary elections.[44]

The Jewish Party's success in the 1929 elections stemmed from a decision made by the Prague Zionists after the disappointing 1925 elections, in which the Jewish vote was split because of the Agrarian Party's creation of a Jewish Economic Party in the east, to no longer rely on Jewish votes from Slovakia and Subcarpathian Ruthenia. A great deal of the Bohemian-based Jewish Party's earlier efforts revolved around courting Jewish votes in the east, where the Jewish population was large and compact, since Czechoslovak electoral law required 20,000 votes in one electoral constituency or all votes for that party throughout the state would be lost. Instead, Czech Zionists successfully formed a coalition with three Polish parties in the state, whose voters were concentrated in Těšín.[45] The joint ticket with the Polish middle class and Social Democratic Workers' parties had been successful, taking in a total of 104,464 votes. Two Jewish Party deputies entered the Czechoslovak parliament: Julius Reisz, head of the Jewish Party representing Slovakia and Subcarpathian Ruthenia, and the Prague Zionist Dr. Ludvik Singer, president of the Jewish National Council. After Singer's untimely death in 1931, the Bohemia Zionist Angelo Goldstein succeeded him as deputy. The electoral success led to greater internal consolidation within the party in 1931as the Jewish Parties of Czechoslovakia reunited under the leadership of Emil Margulies.[46]

In Trenčianske Teplice's Grand Hotel at the annual meeting of the Jewish Party in 1930, Reisz addressed a standing-room-only crowd on the necessity of developing independent Jewish politics as a means of Jewish national self-consciousness. In his talk he highlighted the statist and loyal nature of the Jewish Party, its strong bonds with the ruling coalition, admiration for President Masaryk, and deep appreciation that the Jews in Czechoslovakia could openly participate in public life. He followed his Slovak-language introduction and summary with an extended German-language talk, using German not only to reach the widest Jewish audience but also to underscore his anti-assimilationist Jewish national position while emphasizing the importance of the Jewish Party's alliance with the ruling majority.

"General political relations in the Czechoslovak Republic naturally influence our political position," Reisz said. "The ruling majority is comprised of 210 representatives, and the 90 opposition deputies are members of the clerical and extreme parties. For this reason it is understood that we will join the ruling majority." Of the parties in the governing coalition, Reisz believed it advantageous and logical to align with the Social Democrats, "a party close to us in ideology," so that the two Jewish Party deputies would not be isolated in parliament. Reisz and Singer joined the Social Democratic club shortly after their election. Their move evoked cries of disbelief in the Slovak press, which remarked with anti-Semitic overtones on how poorly the red cap donned by Social Democratic deputies in parliament sat on the heads of these "representatives of capital and capitalism par excellence in the Republic."[47] The decision indicated how closely the Jewish Party now aligned itself with the state's ruling majority and how unfavorably that alliance would be received in the Slovak national press. At the same time that the Slovak Jewish political stance became even more evidently statist electorally, it also turned further away from Hungary in terms of the rapidly approaching census.

"Can Minister Gömbös's statement that a Jew is not a Hungarian be considered wise when the census is taking place is Czechoslovakia?" sharply asked the organization calling itself the "Ad hoc Executive Committee of the Constituent Union of the Jews in Slovakia and Subcarpathian Ruthenia" (hereafter, Executive Committee) in its efforts to urge Jews not to register as Hungarians on the census. The question referred to his infamous remarks in the Hungarian parliament and in Kecskemét in mid-November 1930: "The Jews, who for centuries served Hungarian culture, the Jews who sacrificed 10,000 of their lives on the battlefield for Hungary, are not only *not* recognized as Hungarians, but are made into thieves and murderers and shunned like lepers."[48] The Czechoslovak administration in Bratislava collected the Magyar-language materials distributed by the Executive Committee, translated them into Slovak, and marked them with the note "Bear in mind!" The material of the Executive Committee is characterized by its outspoken style and stark condemnation of the contemporary Hungarian leadership. Writing largely in response to Gömbös's assertions, the committee instructed the Jews in Czechoslovakia's east to exact revenge—"a tooth for a tooth!"—on the Hungarian leadership by means of the census. If Gömbös could claim it was necessary to "remove Jewry from the body of the Hungarian nation like a cancer," give him what he asked for, they demanded. "If the [Hungarian authorities] cannot tolerate Jews in their midst," the Executive Committee exclaimed, "then leave them to themselves!"[49]

The 1930 census results show that many more Jews in Slovakia and Subcarpathian Ruthenia were indeed prepared to abandon their traditional alignment with Hungarian nationality in favor of Czechoslovak or Jewish nationality than had been willing to do so in 1921. An overwhelming 93 percent of the Jews in Subcarpathian Ruthenia, for instance, declared Jewish nationality in 1930, an increase of 6.19 percentage points since the previous census.[50] From a total of 16.49 percent in 1921, Hungarian nationality declarations among Jews in Slovakia fell by more than half, to 7.1 percent. The number of Czechoslovak nationality declarations by Jews in Slovakia, on the other hand, grew by one-third, from 22.27 percent to 32.19 percent.[51] For the overall population, the number of Hungarian nationality declarations dropped considerably and consistently in all but three of Slovakia's seventy-nine political districts. Czechoslovak nationality declarations rose significantly in all but eleven districts, where instead Rusyn declarations grew appreciably.[52]

In contrast to the striking change in Hungarian and Czechoslovak nationality declarations among Jews in Slovakia, Jewish nationality declarations on the territory-wide level remained nearly the same from the first statewide census to the next. The 1930 census records only a slight statistical decrease: from 54.28 percent in 1921 to 53.12 percent in 1930, a marginal difference of 1.16 percent.[53] Yet a closer look reveals greater fluctuation. District-by-district analysis of the 1930 results indicates sharp declines in declarations of Jewish nationality in fifty-nine out of seventy-nine districts, or 75 percent of the total number. Decreases in Jewish nationality were overwhelmingly accompanied by increases in Czechoslovak nationality declarations. It appears that by 1930 many Jews who had previously declared Jewish nationality now opted directly for Czechoslovak, tying themselves more closely to the state.

The remaining twenty districts, however, showed a significant rise in declarations of Jewish nationality. What explains this deviation from the overall pattern? Were there common features among the districts where Jewish nationality declarations grew that contributed to this result? Earlier, in his meticulous analysis of the 1921 census, Antonín Boháč observed that declarations of Jewish nationality were more common among Jews who lived in districts that were more densely populated by Slovaks than among Jews in more heavily Magyar districts, such as in southern Slovakia on the border with Hungary.[54] The situation was reversed by 1930. Nearly all of the twenty districts where Jewish nationality declarations sharply increased either bordered on Hungary or were otherwise located in areas with a large ethnic Magyar population.[55] Many Jewish communities in these districts were Neolog. While Jews there may not have felt comfortable declaring themselves "Czechoslovak," it may have now seemed an appropriate time to turn away from "Hungarian" to "Jewish."

Ezra Mendelsohn is correct to conclude that the substantial turn away from Hungarian nationality among Jews in Slovakia in 1930 can be attributed to both pressures from the Czechoslovak regime and the steep rise in declarations of Czechoslovak nationality.[56] But equally important was the change in their relationship with Hungary itself. This was largely a result of the intensifying Hungarian irredentist movement. Jews in Slovakia feared border revisionism. They were angered by the treatment of their fellow Jews in Hungary, who were often members of their own family, and they were embittered by the Hungarian regime's lack of appreciation for Hungarian Jewry's wartime sacrifice. And despite their tense relationship with the Slovaks and pressure from the regime, they acknowledged the relative advantages that existed for them as citizens of Czechoslovakia. They may have exaggerated the worsening position of the Jews in Hungary in their speeches, publications, and other public Czechoslovak events, but this should not detract from the reality of their position. Jews in Slovakia did not wish to bolster Magyar numbers nor the case for Hungarian revisionism.

It is important to remember, too, that declarations of Jewish nationality were not necessarily equivalent to Zionist conviction. Although the Czechoslovak administration often simplified its documentation by referring to Jewish national actors or activities as "Zionist," the Jewish national leadership and the Jewish population at large envisaged the Jewish national position more broadly. This was especially true among more traditional sections of the Jewish population in Slovakia and Subcarpathian Ruthenia who declared Jewish nationality but found Zionism antithetical to their religious beliefs. Jewish national leaders there were sensitive to the pull of Orthodoxy and Hasidism upon this population. They sought to emphasize the shared features of the Jewish national movement across the wide spectrum of the Jewish population rather than promote a specifically Zionist political agenda. As Kateřina Čapková notes, only a small percentage of those Jews who declared Jewish nationality across the state were active Zionists. One effective way to measure their active involvement in the Zionist movement is through their payment of shekels or the financial contribution of every Zionist to the World Zionist Organization (wzo). A yawning gap existed between the numbers of Jews who declared for Jewish nationality and those who paid up their shekels. Čapková points out that in 1921 only 8,685, or 4.5 percent, of the 180,855 Jews who declared Jewish nationality also contributed shekels to the wzo. In 1930 that number increased to 15,472, or 8.3 percent, shekel payers out of the 186,642 Jews who declared Jewish nationality.[57]

Jews throughout Czechoslovakia declared in greater numbers for Jewish and Czechoslovak nationality in 1930 than in 1921. They demonstrated a continuing move further away from their traditional prewar patterns of national affiliation. In Bohemia and Moravia this meant a decline in declarations of German nationality in favor of Jewish nationality rather than a rise in affiliation with Czechoslovak nationality. Jews in Bohemia showed a 5.66 percent increase in declarations of Jewish nationality from 1921 to 1930, from 14.6 percent to 20.26 percent. At the same time, their German nationality declarations dropped from 34.63 percent in 1921 to 31.01 percent, a difference of 3.62 percentage points. The change in Jewish declarations for Czechoslovak nationality equaled slightly more than a drop of 3 percentage points (3.07), from 49.49 percent to 46.42 percent. Marginally larger was the change in Moravia, where declarations of Jewish nationality rose from 47.84 percent to 51.67, a 3.83 point difference. The decline in German nationality declarations among Jews in Moravia came to 5.77 points, from 34.85 percent to 29.08 percent. Czechoslovak nationality declarations, on the other hand, rose slightly from 15.71 percent to 17.58 percent, only a 1.87 point difference.[58]

As the Hungarian and German minorities in Czechoslovakia feared, their numbers fell from 1921 to 1930. In a few significant cases this meant a drop below the 20 percent required to secure minority linguistic rights. The Hungarian Revisionist League pointed to Jewish nationality as a key culprit in the 1930 reduction of Hungarian numbers and consequent removal of Hungarian language rights in historically important districts. The league framed this argument in terms of what it considered "real national belonging," defined by mother tongue:

> We have seen that by the terms of the census decree, persons professing the Jewish faith—the only exceptions allowed—were at liberty to declare themselves members of the Jewish nation instead of that to which, by virtue of their mother tongue, *they really belonged*. Besides Jews who voluntarily declared Jewish nationality, countless others who claimed Hungarian as their mother tongue were registered as Jews. Jews who professed Slovak nationality were registered without a problem as Czechoslovak. The only hindrances were placed in the way of Hungarian Jews.[59]

The Revisionist League accused Czechoslovakia of falsely enumerating nationality according to incorrect criteria, claiming Jewish nationality to be a sham. Perhaps Boháč was right in arguing that differing conceptions of what nationality actually meant were at the heart of the dispute.

The Revisionist League also saw Jewish nationality as an invitation to corruption. It noted accordingly, "The practice followed by the Czechs of omitting to count Hungarian Jews as Hungarians is contrary to the Czechoslovak Language Law and has led to results like those recorded recently in Ungvár [in Subcarpathian Ruthenia, where the number of Hungarians dropped below 20 percent]." The argument followed that because Hungarian was the mother tongue of the majority of Jews in Ungvár, registration by Jewish nationality deprived them of their own minority linguistic rights.[60] The desire to record nationality to the advantage of the dominant Czechoslovak group undoubtedly existed. Nevertheless, the situation of Magyar-speaking Jews who intentionally and of their own will declared Jewish nationality differs qualitatively from cases of corruption that accompanied census execution across the state. Comparison with a case of census corruption from Brno, Moravia, bears out this point. Census officials there illegally changed 1,145 entries of "German" nationality into "Czechoslovak" or "Jewish" by forging the signature of the individuals in question as well as those of the census takers. Another 2,377 cases were altered, too, in order to bring the number of persons in the district declaring German nationality below the necessary 20 percent. Yet when discovered, the numbers were returned to their intended columns, bringing the German numbers back up to over 20 percent and to minority rights protections.[61]

According to the results of the 1930 census, the number of Hungarian nationality declarations dipped below 20 percent in two traditional Hungarian centers, Bratislava (Pozsony, from 23.66 to 16.16 percent) and Košice (Kassa, from 22.12 to 17.99 percent).[62] Hungarian minority language protections ended. It is fitting to take a closer look at Bratislava regarding the change. The Czechoslovak administration devoted a great deal of energy and resources to creating Bratislava as the majority Slovak capital of Slovakia since the establishment of the state, making it a Slovak national space.[63] Records from the Bratislava city council illustrate the debates and commentary surrounding the repeal of Hungarian minority linguistic rights. The record shows that Hungarian ceased to be used for official purposes in Bratislava on October 7, 1933. At that time the mayor's office took the first step of ordering trilingual street signs and other public signage to be replaced by signs in Slovak and German only.[64]

The 1930 census recorded 123,844 inhabitants of Bratislava, of whom 116,897 were Czechoslovak state citizens. Of these, 60,013 people, or 51.3 percent—a slim majority—declared Czechoslovak nationality. Numbers of German and Hungarian nationality declarations were significantly lower at 32,801 (28 percent) and 18,890 (16.16 percent), respectively. Although 14,882 people registered as Jewish by religion, only 4,747 (4 percent) also declared Jewish as their nationality.[65] "It is a matter of course that the future development of the city of Bratislava is dependent on population growth, its economic potential, and cultural development," ran the Bratislava city council's analysis of the census results. "From this perspective," the analysis continued, "we may assert that the greater part of Bratislava's population now belong to the Czechoslovak nationality, and that majority might be several thousand greater, if from the count of 10,135 individuals of the Jewish religion, which declared during the census for other than Jewish nationality, [we note that] at least half affiliated as *Slovak Jews*."[66]

"Slovak Jew" was not a separate column of nationality declaration on the 1930 census. Slovak Jews would have had to write in or otherwise make their alternate choice clear to the census taker for enumeration. Based on other evidence discussed previously, it seems fair to accept that a great number of Jews in Bratislava chose to declare themselves as "Slovak Jews." The larger point is that the Bratislava city council's analysis shows the inclination to understand not only declarations of Jewish nationality but also other Jewish declarations as "Czechoslovak." The Czechoslovak administration continued in the east central European regional tradition of using Jewish numbers as statistical material for the dominant nationality to bolster its legitimacy in the fateful calculus of the multinational state. Nevertheless, "Jewish" and even "Slovak Jew" were authentic categories of voluntary self-affiliation on the Czechoslovak census. Both were highly valued options among the polyglot Jewish population and not sham classifications.

Before discontinuing official use of the Hungarian language in Bratislava, the city council engaged in heated debate. It reflected the range of public opinion heard in the streets and in the press. The debate's fault line lay between those who argued for the continued use of Hungarian through a more liberal interpretation of the Czechoslovak language law and those who pushed for an inflexible literal interpretation. Dr. Viktor Förster, second deputy to Bratislava's mayor, Dr. Vladimír Krno, opened the discussion by requesting continued usage of Hungarian in Bratislava based on the fact that council representatives were used to conducting trilingual deliberations. Förster also argued, more controversially, that the results of the 1930 census could not be regarded as wholly accurate and therefore could not form the basis for repealing linguistic rights. Dr. Štefan Benko, head of the city notary's office, countered by rejecting claims that the census was inaccurate. He stressed that the actions taken by the mayor's office followed legislation in force across the state. Like Förster, Karol Szabola again argued for the continued usage of Hungarian within Bratislava's administrative offices based on current practice. It was simply more effective, he asserted, to leave procedures as they stood. Dr. Tibor Neumann agreed; he asked the council representative to implement a more liberal interpretation of the language law and leave minority language rights for Hungarians in their present form. After this first round of arguments, twenty-five council representatives voted to put the language law fully into practice and a minority of sixteen voted against.[67]

Discussions continued based on the mayor's decision to follow paragraph 22 of the city statutes. This allowed several other influential representatives to express their opinions on the delicate matter before the final vote. Dr. Ján Jablonický and Štefan Arkauer urged the council to leave existing language rights for the Hungarian minority in place. If the council would not agree to that course of action, they recommended that a proposal acceptable to the Hungarian-speaking city council representatives be prepared as a solution. The next set of speakers rejected this view, arguing that the steps proposed by the mayor were simply a logical consequence of the language law. Carrying through the provisions of the law, they said, posed no injustice to the Hungarian-speaking representatives. As the final speakers, Ignác Šulc and Eugen Singer, reminded the council that any changes to the language law that offered a more liberal interpretation in the case of Bratislava would naturally have to follow the correct legislative procedure. The concluding vote on the matter brought in the three previously undecided representatives for a binding vote of thirty-one for to thirteen against.[68]

Instead of moving toward a viable alternative policy to revisionism back when Seton-Watson had urged the Czechoslovak administration to do so in the jubilee year 1928—probably an unattainable goal even then—Czechoslovakia slid ever more snugly into the vice of mutually hostile relations. The Bratislava City Council's final vote only reaffirmed the convictions of the Hungarian Revisionist political movement. The movement insisted that only moving the borders would solve the worsening situation of the Hungarian minority.[69]

The New Jewish Question in Slovakia

With the steep rise in radical nationalism during the 1930s, Jews in Slovakia became ever more convinced that their fate was tied to both the territorial integrity of the state as a whole and the status quo of its organization. Theirs was a loyal statist position: championing Czechoslovakia and taking an unambiguous side in the nationalities struggle. In addition to their already decisive break with Hungary, Hungarian Jewry, and domestic Hungarian minority politics, Jews in the territory of Slovakia participated in the international boycott action against Germany and aided Jewish refugees from Nazism arriving and sojourning in Czechoslovakia. Slovak public opinion resentfully portrayed Slovak Jews as the enemy of all Slovak ambitions for their rejection of Slovak autonomist politics. When Slovak rhetoric turned to action, severe interpretations of interwar Slovak Jewish political loyalties lay at the heart of the Jewish tragedy. From an older socioeconomic and politically grounded antisemitism tied to nationality policies in prewar Hungary and their legacies in interwar Czechoslovakia, a new, more radical "Jewish Question" emerged, bound up with a broadly popular Slovak autonomist movement and energized by the Nazi rise to power in Germany.

By 1933 relations with Germany took center stage as Czechoslovakia's primary foreign and domestic policy concern. Hitler's accession to power exacerbated Czechoslovakia's already acute minority problems. The Sudeten German population, especially impressed by the Nazi fiscal program, overwhelming supported a broad pro-Nazi position in their economically depressed districts.[70] Conversely, Jewish communities and organizations across Czechoslovakia pledged solidarity with German Jewry, targeted from the start by the regime's discriminatory exclusionist policies. Their protest actions against Germany focused on boycotts, petitioning the League of Nations, and coming to the aid of the German Jewish refugees streaming into the country. The Czechoslovak branch of the Women's International Zionist Organization (WIZO) stood out for the scale of its refugee aid work between 1933 and 1939. Hanna Steiner and Marie Schmolková committed their energies to organizing and running the extensive WIZO refugee aid program in Bohemia and Moravia, while Gisi Fleishmann devoted her life to helping hundreds of refugees in Slovakia from 1933, through the German occupation, until her own deportation in 1944.[71] Kateřina Čapková strikingly observes that the ever increasing flow of refugees from Germany into Czechoslovakia was the definitive symbol of the difference between the neighboring political regimes.[72]

In April 1933 Jews across Czechoslovakia joined Great Britain, the United States, and other communities in an international boycott against Germany. The European section of the boycott movement had begun in the then Polish city of Vilna (Vilnius, Wilno) on March 20.[73] Flyers printed in Slovak and German, now Bratislava's two official languages, declared it the "holy duty of every Jew" to observe the boycott and to reject everything that could be useful to the Reich German economy. Beyond refusing to buy German products, it directed every Slovak Jew (*tunajší žid*) to "buy exclusively domestic Czechoslovak products and . . . refuse Reich German goods at all costs. Do not even attend cinema performances where Reich German films are screened."[74] This was not just about taking a stand against the conditions under which their coreligionists currently suffered in Germany; it was also about championing Czechoslovakia.

The Jewish Party held a public meeting in Bratislava in mid-May to discuss the situation of German Jewry. Their intention was also to gather signatures on the Bernheim Petition to the League of Nations drawn up on German Jewry's behalf by three representatives of the Committee of Jewish Delegations (Comité des Délégations Juives), including Emil Margulies.[75] After the three-and-a-half-hour meeting, "the participants sang the Jewish national anthem in Hebrew and calmly departed."[76] As the main speakers, Julius Reisz and Emil Margulies both argued for continued international protest against Germany. Reisz flatly characterized antisemitism in Germany as "organized for the destruction of the Jews in Germany." "Reports that the persecution of the Jews in Germany does not exist do not correspond with reality," he declared in his Slovak-language speech.

Reisz vowed that Jews would maintain their boycott until Germany changed its position about them.[77] Continuing in this vein, Margulies expressly denounced the position, prevalent in "certain Jewish circles," that Jews should respond to the events in Germany by patiently waiting for the situation to change. "Jewry must understand the position of the Jews in Germany pessimistically," he said, "because Germany's struggle against Jewry is merciless and ruthless, and will be carried through."[78] Margulies and Reisz easily persuaded the three hundred meeting attendees to unanimously accept and sign the Bernheim Petition, which contributed to the league's suspension of anti-Jewish legislation in Upper Silesia until 1937 as well as the growth of a notable international reputation for Margulies.

In his remarks Reisz reflected on why Czechoslovakia maintained its peaceful, liberal stance toward the Jewish nation in spite of the surrounding storm. It was no accident, he asserted. The main explanation for this was Masaryk himself, who "even as a university professor defended Jewish rights." The second was the character and background of the Czech and Slovak nation, which was able to understand the current situation of German Jewry because it was suppressed in Austria-Hungary. "For these reasons," Reisz concluded, "Jewry has the responsibility to contribute all its strength to the preservation of the Czechoslovak Republic. . . . We honor and cherish the Czechoslovak Republic as our beloved homeland."[79]

The growth of the anti-Czech, antistate Slovak autonomist movement reinforced Slovak Jewry's loyal statist position. The Slovak autonomist movement resented Slovak Jews' clear alignment with the inflexibly centrist Prague government.[80] "Jewry, the pillar of Magyarization, has swum over to the other side, although not to Slovak, but to Czechoslovak waters," wrote the Bratislava daily paper *Slovák,* the organ of the autonomist Slovak People's Party.[81]

In the first republic's final parliamentary election, in 1935, the Jewish Party ran together with the Czech Social Democratic Party. Margulies stepped down from his position as head of the party in protest, representing the views of the more conservative Jewish nationalists. Arnošt Frischer replaced him, serving until 1938. Angelo Goldstein and Hayim Kugel, a Zionist from Subcarpathian Ruthenia, served as deputies for the Jewish Party in parliament. Kugel was instrumental in establishing Hebrew-language schools in Subcarpathian Ruthenia, including the unique Hebrew gymnasium in Mukačevo, which was despised by the Hasidim and Czech Jewish movement. He continuously sought state funding for these schools, because Jews were a recognized national minority, but the state would not provide financial support.[82] Throughout its career in interwar Czechoslovakia, the Jewish Party strove to defend Jewish economic, social, and political rights in the state to the bitter end: dissolved in November 1938 by the newly autonomous Slovak leadership and in March 1939 with the German occupation of Bohemia and Moravia. Never as popular in Slovakia and Subcarpathian Ruthenia as in the Czech lands due to its Zionist content, it nonetheless represented the possibilities of Jewish national politics. And it was always utterly loyal to Czechoslovakia.

The severity with which the worldwide economic crisis hit Slovakia's largely agrarian economy brought heightened intensity to the question of Slovak autonomy and radicalized the so-called Jewish Question. Hlinka's Slovak People's Party, named since 1925 after its leader, Andrej Hlinka, continuously strove for Slovak autonomy within a federalized Czechoslovak framework, believing this the most effective way to address Slovakia's social problems and particular set of needs and to block the spread of secularism, atheism, and socialism. The interwar Slovak political elite consistently opposed the centralized Prague government, and the proportion of opposition voters in Slovakia remained high, at between 60 and 70 percent of the voting population.[83] In October 1932 Hlinka's Slovak People's Party joined forces with the Slovak National Party (Slovenská Národná Strana), forming an autonomous bloc with a clear anti-Czech line. In Slovakia 80 percent of sawmills lay in disuse, the number of workers had been slashed by 50 percent, and social tensions were rising.[84] It was the depth of the economic depression. The bloc represented Slovak frustrations with what one Slovak historian calls the "inconsistencies of the Czech Democracy"—that is, a policy of centralization that many Slovaks believed to be denationalizing, in conjunction with Czech actions they understood as cultural assimilation, economic discrimination, and social injustice.[85] Slovaks resented the numbers of Czech bureaucrats who remained in Slovakia even after the emergence of a Slovak élite ready to fill the necessary positions, as well as what many considered Prague's paternalistic and tactless control over Slovakia.

A new generation passionately pursued Slovak autonomy. Their movement was closely associated with a powerful Catholic Church and with a desire to see the development of a purely Slovak political and economic life.[86] In 1933 Hlinka's Slovak People's Party used the occasion of the celebratory 1,100th anniversary of the first Catholic church in Nitra to stage a mass demonstration for Slovak self-determination. The episode openly disgraced the Prague government at a time when the newly ascendant Nazi Party in Germany exploited the higher level of unemployment in ethnic German regions of the Sudetenland in their campaign to weaken and isolate Czechoslovakia.[87]

As Czechoslovakia slowly emerged from its acute economic crisis and began to rebuild, so too did polemics over Slovak-Jewish relations grip the public. Dr. Ivan Dérer, then serving as a representative of the Social Democratic Party, responded to the author Gejza Vámoš in 1934 on this issue, defending Slovak Jews against accusations ranging from "usurer" to "Magyarizer."[88] Hugo Roth resigned as head of the Union of Slovak Jews that same year. The demise of this

short-lived organization soon followed, signaling the end of Slovak-Jewish attempted rapprochement. Slovak public opinion understood Roth's resignation as
the result of attacks against him by the Slovak Jewish community. These attacks,
argued the daily *Slovák*, were really directed against the Slovaks themselves.

> Slovaks regard Dr. Roth—who even before the change of regimes contributed
> to Slovak newspapers, who even under Hungary was a member of Slovak asso-
> ciations, who in 1914 spent four weeks in the Špilberg [prison] in Brno [Mora-
> via] as a political suspect, and who saved the lives of Czechoslovak soldiers
> who fell into Austrian captivity . . . —as their own (*svojho*). Dr. Roth more
> than once proved his Slovakness (*slovenskosť*), to which the Czechoslovak
> National Council, the Slovak League and our other national organizations
> can testify; but it was not only by his memberships and his military activity
> during and after the Prevrat [that he proved his Slovakness], but through his
> educational and cultural work. He wrote the first Slovak medical books in the
> field of gynecology, as well as other literary volumes. He represented Slovak
> scholarship with dignity in Brussels, London, and Paris. He behaved very
> beautifully and effectively for the state during the Rothermere affair, when he
> spoke in the name of Slovak Jews at numerous meetings. Therefore, we must
> consider attacks directed against Dr. Roth as attacks against the Slovaks.[89]

When the Bratislava-based Slovak national daily *Národný denník* picked up
the story, it found Roth's resignation symptomatic of what it deemed the failure—and refusal—on the part of the Jews in Slovakia to join and aid the Slovak
majority in the goal of Slovak national self-determination in Slovakia. That failure, even within Roth's own assimilationist Union of Slovak Jews, seemed only
to confirm "that which we have been most aware of since the beginning of [the
organization's] activities . . . that, in every way, the Union took to paths more advantageous for its 'opponents' than for itself."[90] The Union of Slovak Jews was not
pursuing the mission outlined in its statutes—namely, to guarantee the Slovak
public that the Jews in Slovakia had established a "new, better orientation" and
had worked diligently to join the nation with which they lived under "very advantageous conditions." Instead, the *Národný denník* concluded, members of the
organization cultivated various minority interests, primarily Zionist, Hungarian, or German, within the framework of the union, which damaged the group
and its mission.[91]

The position intensified. The *Národný denník* demanded that the Union of
Slovak Jews explain why the goal of Jewish assimilation to the Slovak nation did
not take hold among their coreligionists. Why did Slovak Jews refuse to secure
their future by joining the Slovaks? Why did they not put their abilities at the service of the Slovaks? Why was it that the great majority of their coreligionists still
took a position *against* rather than *for* the Slovaks? And why had the number of
Jewish students enrolled at the German gymnasium in Bratislava actually risen

in the year since the Jews began their boycott of German products, language, and culture? The paper marveled that even if Hitler placed German Jews outside the law and declared an open struggle against them since his rise to power, the Jews still did not renounce their "German orientation." The *Národný denník* cited figures showing a rise from 341 Jewish students enrolled at the German gymnasium in the school year 1932–1933 to 361 in the school year 1933–1934, an increase of 20 students.[92] "It is this kind of fact," said the *Národný denník* writer, "which proves once again that here it is the Jews who sustain the majority of German and Hungarian schools." The report continued:

> It would be very interesting to learn which nationality these students at the German gymnasium declare—most probably Jewish nationality, which would show that this nationality regards German as its official language. In Slovakia, these Jews are the bearers and upholders of German culture with all the consequences of that actuality. And this is something that exhorts us all to attention and caution. . . .
>
> The Jews here still continue to adore [Buda]Pest and Berlin, even if here and there they kick them right in the face. Hitler's gang (*Hitlerovci*) openly and flamboyantly expresses fanatical hatred and antipathy against the Jews. Government representatives incite violence against them on the street. Pest for some time has cultivated chauvinistic anti-Jewish politics, and yet the Jews here still continue to favor Hungarian and German. Why they do it, and what they expect in terms of a peaceful existence with us and among our people remains an open question. With their professions of loyalty, they often lead the public to false conclusions concerning their actions and intentions.[93]

Roth himself listed the reasons for his resignation in a communication to the board at the May eighth meeting, reported the Bratislava *Neues Pressburger Abendblatt* later that same day. According to that paper, Roth declared the leadership of the Union of Slovak Jews to be in decline and the organization itself decaying from within. It no longer enjoyed the necessary level of trust in government circles. Furthermore, Roth maintained, the board allegedly accused him of following his own "separate ambitions." To counter, Roth said he only learned from the newspapers that the vice president of the Union of Slovak Jews had been appointed to the board of the Bratislava Neolog Jewish community.[94]

Yeshayahu Jelínek writes of Roth that he represents one face of the Jewish community in Slovakia and its tragedy. Interwar conditions in Slovakia made it impossible to fuse Jewish ethno-religious belonging and Slovak patriotism.[95] It is important to remember that the conditions that shaped the Jewish interwar experience in Slovakia included above all the post–World War I separation from Hungary and Hungarian Jewry. Slovak Jews became disabused of the assimilationist project overall based on those relationships and the political fears and expectations they bore. Additionally, no one knew when the tables might turn again, if they might face another change of regime, or how they might account for their current actions if that were to occur. They would be loyal citizens of Czechoslovakia, they would cherish the opportunities of that state belonging, they would—and largely did—learn the state language, but they would not assimilate to the Slovak cultural nation.

The civic and linguistic preconditions for that cultural or national assimilation did not exist.[96] The Slovak national movement was strongly tied to the Catholic Church and was anti-Semitic rather than espousing broader civic values, so it was not a welcoming avenue of integration. Slovak society, through historical circumstance, lacked a nonclerical elite that would open the door for Jewish cultural integration. The Slovak language lacked prestige and power.[97] According to Ladislav Lipscher, the fact that the Slovak national movement viewed the Jews as a foreign element that was diametrically opposed to the Slovaks was the single most important—and dangerous—factor in the failure of reciprocity between the two groups.[98] They would not, and could not, become Slovaks, but they could become "Slovak Jews," defined geographically rather than nationally as belonging to the territory of Slovakia within the liberal Czechoslovak state and the specific set of opportunities and challenges that reality presented. Yes, they took the persecution of German Jewry after 1933 as evidence of the failure of assimilation, as Ivan Kamenec argues, and the German Jewish crisis indeed spurred the growth of Palestine-oriented Zionism Slovakia and Subcarpathian Ruthenia.[99] Jews around the world came to understand from the experience of German Jewry that assimilation does not end antisemitism. Yet for Slovak Jews, observing the increasingly desperate situation of German Jewry reinforced what they had already learned and compounded its urgency.

Early spring 1936 marked a turning point in deteriorating Slovak-Jewish relations from rhetoric to action as Czechoslovakia prepared for war. Anti-Jewish demonstrations broke out in Bratislava in April after the premier of the French film *Le golem,* which featured Jewish characters and theme. The anti-Jewish excesses included attacks on property as well as on Jewish students by the university and in the streets.[100] Aid to the embattled Jews during the riots from members of leftist political organizations reinforced Slovak nationalist propaganda against the threat of "Judeo-Bolshevism."[101] Slovak nationalist agitation against "Judeo-Bolshevism" spiked after the Czechoslovak Treaty of Mutual Assistance with the Soviet Union concluded the previous May. More articles appeared in the Slovak national press printing false quotations from the Talmud, detailing stories of ritual murder, and quoting the elaborate Russian hoax known as the "Protocols of the Elders of Zion." The *Slovák* had recently reprinted the important Slovak author Svetozár Hurban-Vajanský's inflammatory 1881 polemic, "The Jewish Question in Slovakia," which asserted that Jewish crimes against the Slovaks included exploitation, moral and material oppression, and selling them into

Hungarian slavery.[102] "*Na Slovensku po slovensky!*" Slovak autonomists shouted. "In Slovakia speak Slovak." "After 1936," recalled Katarina Lofflerová, "a sort of phantom appeared. There was a feeling among the Jews that Masaryk is gone—so now what will happen?"[103]

The former minister of foreign affairs, Edvard Beneš, was now president of the republic, following Masaryk's retirement in 1935 at the age of eighty-five. Masaryk died in September 1937. Beneš focused a great deal of his attention on the situation of the German minority and its implications for Czechoslovakia's increasingly isolated international position. His August lecture tour in the industrial region of northwest Bohemia, the Sudetenland, coincided with the beginning of Czechoslovakia's rearmament program. At the same time, Konrad Henlein of the newly prominent Sudetendeutsch Party was in Berlin meeting with Nazi politicians and functionaries. The internationally respected Slovak Agrarian Milan Hodža became prime minister, the first Slovak to hold that position, in a strong though belated public expression of Czech and Slovak partnership in the state. Hodža met with a delegation from the Jewish Party from Slovakia shortly after his accession, declaring that according to an agreement concluded with the German minority, the Jews would also be automatically granted a share in the civil service that would be commensurate with their percentage of the population.[104]

In contrast, Karol Sidor, commander of the Hlinka Guard, proposed in March that the Jews of Slovakia and Subcarpathian Ruthenia be removed and resettled in Birobidzhan, the Jewish autonomous region of the Soviet Union set aside by Stalin. References to a Slovakia without Jews became frequent in the months that followed.[105] Sidor himself was a Polonophile, whose own interest in the "Jewish Question" began in earnest with his first visit to Poland in 1926 and who continued to be influenced by the Polish government's initiatives in this area. Sidor co-initiated the anti-Jewish riots of 1936 in Bratislava. His proposal for resettling the Jews of Slovakia and Subcarpathian Ruthenia was inspired by remarks of the Polish prime minister Josef Beck, who had said the Polish government would offer assistance to Jews who wished to emigrate from Poland.[106]

The Slovak branch of the Union of Jewish Veterans (Brit Hachajal) began training Jewish youth in military and personal self-defense maneuvers after the 1936 riots in Bratislava. They called Jewish youth to action "in view of the desperate position of Jewry as a whole."

> [We will] with all our strength and all our means join in the struggle against all plans to harm Czechoslovakia, and support all actions that serve the defense and stability of the state and its borders. . . . We live in a state where the borders protect us, where we can still breathe freely. Apart from the state loyalty to which every citizen is obliged, it behooves us in our time, and in our own interests, to take part in the defense of the state and its borders.[107]

Their position represented only the most militant take on a broadly held conviction among the Jewish population that their fate was tied to Czechoslovakia's territorial integrity. It pitted the Jewish population against an increasingly powerful Slovak national leadership. The Nazis exploited the volatile "Slovak Question" in the republic for their own purposes. They were staked out in Slovakia's backyard. Slovak-language radio broadcasts from neighboring Vienna to Bratislava after the Anschluss of Germany and Austria in March 1938 spread virulent anti-Czech and anti-Semitic propaganda to an audience that was receptive to the idea that their troubles would disappear with the elimination of the Jewish enemy and independence.[108] "At least we see eye to eye [*sme si na čistom*] with our Jews," wrote the *Slovák* in May 1938. "We know that they are our enemies, not only in terms of worldview, but they are also against us politically. Jews are against Slovak autonomy. We will remember that well, and we will remind the Jews of it when the time comes."[109]

The time came less than six months later, after the Munich Agreement fatefully marked the end of Czechoslovakia and brought the interwar state system to a close. Czechoslovakia was destroyed economically and strategically by overwhelming territorial and industrial losses, the country humiliated and demoralized by this ultimately futile sacrifice. Beneš resigned the presidency, packed his bags, and left for France on October 22, where the government would not talk with him. He left France for Britain. The elderly, Catholic, conservative, and politically uninvolved lawyer Dr. Emil Hácha sat meekly in the president's chair in Prague as successor to Beneš. Slovakia received the far-reaching autonomy it desired on October 6, now headed by a clerico-fascist regime under the Populists, its self-proclaimed only legal political party. Czecho-Slovakia annulled the 1920 Czechoslovak consitution in order to please Hitler. Its foreign minister pledged full compliance with, and reliance on, Germany "if Germany will allow this."[110]

Slovakia soon faced problems of its own territorial integrity. Under the terms of the Vienna Arbitration Award of November 1938, Hungary reannexed southern Slovakia and Subcarpathian Ruthenia. Devastated, Slovakia's newly declared autonomous leadership blamed the Jews for the Nazi-orchestrated territorial loss. Nearly one-third of the territory of Slovakia went to Hungary, with a total population of 853,670, of which 40,000 were Jews by religion (of these, 26,157 were Jews by nationality according to the 1930 census).[111] The Jews were guilty, the Slovaks explained, because they had declared Hungarian nationality. The Hungarians, on the other hand, accused the same Jews of "intense propaganda for Czechoslovakia."[112] The Jews, according to the Hungarian account, had been "disloyal" to the Hungarian nationality during the previous twenty years because of their "loyalty" to Czechoslovakia.[113]

Slovakia's autonomous government ordered the deportation of seventy-five hundred Jews without means to the territory ceded to Hungarian control while preventing Jews with more than 500,000 crowns' (US$14,802) worth of property from leaving.[114] Hungary would not let the deported Jews enter the country. For weeks they remained huddled in the late fall cold in the no-man's-land between the Slovak and Hungarian borders.[115] "The entire November action," writes Ivan Kamenec, "clearly signaled to [Slovak] Jewish citizens that the territory of autonomous Slovakia had ceased to be a safe place."[116] Slovak Jews were trapped between borders, caught in the very physical territoriality of nationhood. Their state loyalty stood helpless before changing boundaries of nationality they could not share.

Conclusion: Mapping Jewish Loyalties

THE INTERWAR CZECHOSLOVAK administration was preoccupied with the question of how to distinguish between members of minority groups who had truly become Czechoslovaks and those who had not. However, the state's concern lay less with culture or identity than with political loyalty. It was not so much that it was obligatory to give up all attachment to Hungarian or German culture—in the eyes of the state, if not the surrounding society—but to convincingly demonstrate that a transfer of political loyalties had effectively taken place in the movement from empire to nation-state.

President Masaryk himself, whose "glorious name is recorded for all eternity in the golden letters of Jewish history,"[1] played a leading role in enabling the large-scale reorientation of the Jewish population to Czechoslovakia. He is credited as the great bridge builder in the transfer of loyalties of the Jews from the old Austro-Hungarian Monarchy to the new state.[2] "Many Jews who had proudly worn the Austro-Hungarian uniform in World War I became, or saw their children become, passionate Czechoslovaks and devotees of *tatíček* Masaryk, Papa Masaryk," writes a Canadian anthropologist of Czechoslovak Jewish émigré background. "But," he adds, "typical as the switch was for many Czechoslovak Jews, it was not nearly universal. Others were too deeply [acculturated] to give up their German or Hungarian Jewish culture."[3]

Many Jews in interwar Slovakia did maintain Hungarian cultural preferences, including linguistic continuity, but even deep acculturation did not equal political ties to Horthy's Hungary and its irredentist ambitions. Few Jews continued to declare Hungarian nationality on successive interwar Czechoslovak censuses. That continuity of declaration certainly indicated a stronger attachment to and identification with Hungarian nationality than declaring Jewish or Slovak nationality while maintaining Hungarian language usage. Marking Jewish minority loyalty to the state's satisfaction required a combination of "reliable" nationality declarations combined with cutting ties to Hungary, Hungarian Jewry, and oppositional Hungarian politics. Within the hostile interwar east central European state system, minority loyalty was a matter of state security. Nationality became an important, though not exclusive, marker of loyalty and belonging to the interwar nation-state. Jewish nationality had a fundamentally statist meaning and usage in the interwar Czechoslovak context. It became an outward marker of successful reorientation of individual political loyalties to the interwar Czechoslovak state. Like the affiliation to Czech or Slovak nationality, to which many Jews had moved by 1930, the state considered Jewish nationality to be a loyal Czechoslovak position.

For Jews in Slovakia, the "right path" Vavro Šrobár urged them to seek at the state's outset appeared to be a separate one—independent from Hungary and Hungarian Jewry, but bound to the territory of Slovakia and to the opportunities available to them in Masaryk's Czechoslovakia. Slovak Jews built a new collective identity around three dominant elements connected to their experience of geopolitical reorientation from Hungary to Czechoslovakia. The first was refugee aid, welfare work, and self-help programs during the war and after, which fostered bonds of solidarity among Jews and Jewish communities in Slovakia in a range of both religious and secular ways. The second, Jewish nationality and national politics, was a position espoused by the majority of Jews in Slovakia. It promised to be an "authentic" and "neutral" route of remaining "true to ourselves" in the nationalities conflict. It also seemed to demonstrate political separation from Hungary while supporting Czechoslovak national dominance in the state. Both Hungarians and Czechoslovaks recognized that Jewish nationality was a significant point of divergence between Hungarian and Slovak Jews. Finally, the third element of reorientation involved a transformation of Jewish territoriality. This was accomplished through reorganizing Jewish communal infrastructure in Slovakia, which involved building communal institutions designed to meet the needs of the Jewish community within the new borders. Jews in Slovakia reshaped the Jewish public space to anchor themselves locally. Throughout it is important to remember the influence of continuing tensions with the surrounding Slovak population, which was caught up in its own vital and long-deferred process of national development. Jewish public space building reflected Czechoslovakia's own efforts to write and reconstruct the Slovak national story in the streets, squares, institutions, and monuments, as well as to take "linguistic possession" of the territory.[4]

At the same time, the Czechoslovak statist function of Jewish nationality placed the Jewish population squarely between the Czechs on one side and the Hungarians, Germans, and Slovaks on the other as national tensions rose precipitously in the 1930s. When Czechoslovak demographers narrowly agreed to unbundle Jewish nationality from linguistic markers, instead tying this nationality declaration alone purely to subjective internal convictions, they effectively shifted nationality from a linguistic-cultural category to an ethno-racial one. Jewish nationality was the centerpiece in this overall reconceptualization of nationality, which had become a collective political relationship to the nation-state, a means by which to quantify loyalty and reliability to the dominant political community. Hungarians and Germans understood the state's decision to count Jewish nationality without regard to language as an attack on their own language-based minority rights within the state. It seemed inconsistent to them when the state required numerical proof derived from census data for the recognition and exercise of their minority rights. After the first statewide Czechoslovak census in 1921, state demographers spent a great deal of time and effort seeking to defend their methods, including their definition of "nationality," to an increasingly hostile international community.

Slovaks saw Jewish nationality as a defense against aligning with the Slovak nation. Even when Jews in Slovakia declared Slovak nationality in significant numbers in 1930, Slovaks continued to view the Jewish population as an element at odds with their own national development. This perception grew in conjunction with the Slovak autonomist movement during the 1930s. Slovaks wanted to hear the Jewish population in Slovakia speak Slovak, not Hungarian, on the street, in coffeehouses, in schools. Slovak public opinion held speaking Slovak as the fulfillment of a Jewish obligation—and even a penance—to the Slovak nation.

In response to the escalating antisemitism that accompanied growing national tensions, Hungarian and German revisionist ambitions, and the Slovak autonomy movement, Jews in Czechoslovakia became increasingly convinced that their fate was tied to the integrity of their state's borders. And they were right. They had become intertwined with the Czechoslovak state, with its successes and its vulnerabilities. Their strategies for affirming their loyal citizenship and state belonging helped them map and travel the "right path" using the traditional and usually effective means to which they had grown accustomed in the old monarchy within the transformed post–World War I environment. Their loyalty and their numbers showed that they were not Hungarian, that they were not a threat to Czechoslovakia. On the contrary, their old "new" path aided Czechoslovakia in producing the balance of nationalities it needed.

Yet solving the nationalities problem in interwar Czechoslovakia would require far more than producing demographic legitimacy for a dominant "Czechoslovak" nationality. Times had changed. Language, nationality, and territory fused as a consequence of interwar state building. The successor states of the fallen Austro-Hungarian, Ottoman, and Russian empires were territorial manifestations of nationhood, born from the national principle. The force of irredentism aided that fusion. Irredentist ambitions within a hostile state system shaped how nationality would function in east central Europe. State sovereignty and security were at stake in the question of nationality.

Notes

Introduction

1. Austria was officially known as "the Kingdoms and Lands represented in the Reichsrat [Austrian imperial parliament in Vienna]." Kann, *History of the Habsburg Empire,* 336.

2. Rothschild, *East Central Europe,* 83–84; Mendelsohn, *Jews of East Central Europe,* 131.

3. Slovenský národný archív (SNA), f. Krajinský úrad (KÚ), box 266, inv. no. 3161.29.

4. "Eine neue Äußerung von Minister Šrobár zur Judenfrage," *Weiner Morgenzeitung,* February 19, 1920, reprinted in the *Jüdische Volkszeitung,* February 20, 1920.

5. Pierre Birnbaum and Ira Katznelson, "Emancipation and the Liberal Offer," in Birnbaum and Katznelson, *Paths of Emancipation,* 36. Nancy Sinkoff argues for the centrality of the state in the Jewish process of political modernization in *Out of the Shtetl,* 13.

6. John Efron, "The State of the Jews, the Jews and the State," in Efron, *The Jews: A History,* 273–274.This is an excellent and widely used introductory Jewish history text.

7. Magocsi, *Historical Atlas,* 61.

8. Ivan Mrva and David P. Daniel, "Slovakia during the Early Modern Era 1526–1711," in Mannová, *Concise History of Slovakia,* 141–143.

9. Ibid.

10. Miller, *Rabbis and Revolution,* 35–39. Jews from Moravia settled on manors belonging to the Pállfy, Batthyány, and Zichy families, among others, following the late seventeenth-century Turkish retreat. They founded Jewish communities in Vágújhely (today's Nové Mesto nad Vahom), Trencsén (Trenčín), Verbó (Vrbové), Holics (Holíč), Myjava (Mijava), Nyitra (Nitra), and Szenicze (Senica).

11. Ibid.

12. McCagg, *History of Habsburg Jews,* 125.

13. Halász, "A szlovák nemzeti politika és a zsidóság a dualismus idején," 44.

14. Katz, *House Divided,* 32.

15. Michael Silber, "A Jewish Minority in a Backward Economy," in Silber, *Jews in the Hungarian Economy,* 6.

16. Katz, *House Divided,* 33.

17. McCagg, *History of Habsburg Jews,* 132.

18. Katz, *House Divided,* 35.

19. McCagg, *History of Habsburg Jews,* 133–134.

20. See Bernstein, *A negyvennyolcas magyar szabadságharc és a zsidók;* and Zsoldas, *1848–1849 a magyar zsidóság életében.*

21. Pressburg became the seat of Hungarian Jewish Orthodoxy under the leadership of Rabbi Moshe Sofer, or the Hatam Sofer (1762–1839), who served as rabbi in the city

from 1806 until his death. He founded the influential yeshiva of Pressburg and led the traditionalist struggle against rapidly spreading religious reform in the early nineteenth century, opposing any changes in Judaism.

22. McCagg, *History of Habsburg Jews*, 134.

23. Elena Mannová and Roman Holec, "On the Road to Modernization, 1848–1918," in Mannová, *Concise History of Slovakia*, 196–197. The Slavic languages differentiate the term "Hungarian" as it indicates ethnic Hungarian or the Hungarian language, and as it refers to the Kingdom of Hungary or something deriving from the Kingdom of Hungary. In Slovak these terms are *"mad'ar"* (*magyar*, i.e., ethnic Hungarian), *Uhorsko* (the Kingdom of Hungary), and *uhorský* (deriving from the Kingdom of Hungary).

24. Ibid.

25. Kontler, *History of Hungary*, 257–259.

26. Livia Rothkirchen, "Slovakia: I. 1848–1918," in Jewish Publication Society of America (JPSA), *Jews of Czechoslovakia*, 1:72.

27. Katz, *House Divided*, 37.

28. Rothkirchen, "Slovakia: I. 1848–1918," 1:73.

29. Katz, *House Divided*, 38–39; McCagg, *History of Habsburg Jews*, 135.

30. Karady, "Religious Divisions," 162.

31. McCagg, *History of Habsburg Jews*, 135.

32. Kann, *History of the Habsburg Empire*, 338.

33. McCagg, *History of Habsburg Jews*, 135; "A népesség anyanyelve és magyarul tudása 1900-ban és 1910-ben," *Magyar Statisztikai Évkönyv. Új Folyam XXIII. 1915* (Budapest, 1918), 15, chart 11. Ethnic Hungarians comprised only 45.4 percent of the Hungarian kingdom's total population in 1900 and 48.1 percent in 1910.

34. Jelínek, *Carpathian Diaspora*, 9; Mendelsohn, *Jews of East Central Europe*, 88.

35. Karady, "Religious Divisions," 162. Victor Karady terms this the "assimilationist social contract" in his pivotal study.

36. Kieval, *Making of Czech Jewry*, 4, 8, 198–203. Kieval coined the term "secondary acculturation" to designate the process of change and adaptation of Bohemian Jewry from a largely rural population to an urban one, which shifted from espousing a cosmopolitan cultural orientation to a nationally overdetermined one in the era of late nineteenth-century national development and conflict.

37. Jews, counted according to religion, equaled 932,458 of the total population, or 4.5 percent, in 1910. Of these, 705,488, or 75.7 percent, declared Hungarian as their mother tongue on the 1910 Hungarian census. Nevertheless, 21.8 percent declared "German" (Yiddish was counted as German), 0.6 percent "Slovak," 0.1 percent "Romanian," 0.3 percent "Ruthenian," 1.1 percent "Croatian," and 0.4 percent "Other." "A népesség anyanyelve vallások szerint 1910-ben," *Magyar Statisztikai Évkönyv*, 20, chart 13.

38. Rachamimov, "Collective Identifications," 182–183. See Rachamimov's excellent discussion distinguishing "loyalty" from "identity" and historiographical approaches to understanding gradations of late nineteenth-century Jewish collective identity.

39. Jelínek, "In Search of Identity," 216.

40. Katz, *House Divided*. See Katz's authoritative discussion and analysis of the Hungarian Jewish Congress of 1868, including its origins and implications.

41. "Neology (Neologism)," *Encyclopedia Judaica* (New York: Macmillan, 1971), 951–954; Kinga Frojimovics and Rita Horváth, "Jews and Nationalism in Hungary," *European Legacy* 7, no. 5: 642; Leonard Mars, "Discontinuity, Tradition, and Innova-

tion: Anthropological Reflections on Jewish Identity in Contemporary Hungary," *Social Compass* 46 (1999): 26.

42. Karady, "Religious Divisions," 163.

43. Kieval, "Negotiating Czechoslovakia," 113.

44. Karady, "Religious Divisions," 170.

45. Ibid.

46. McCagg, *History of Habsburg Jews,* 190. A Neolog count completed just after the First World War found that 292,155 (65.5 percent) of the 444,567 Jews within the new borders were Neolog; 130,373 (29.2 percent) were Orthodox; and 22,373 (5.3 percent) were Status Quo Ante. Of the 955,452 Jews in Hungary in 1911 at least half were Orthodox.

47. Aryeh Sole, "Subcarpathian Ruthenia: 1918–1938," in JPSA, *Jews of Czechoslovakia,* 1:140.

48. Halász, "A szlovák régió zsidó lakosságának anyanyelvi megoszlása az 1891., 1900. és 1910. évi népszámlálások adatainak tükrében, megyénként," in "A szlovák nemzeti politika és a zsidóság a dualismus idején," 54, table 6; "Náboženství a cirkve," *Deset let československé republiky. Svazek první* (Prague, 1928), 442; Vratislav Bušek, "Poměr státu k církvím v Československé republice," in Janda, *Československá vlastivěda díl V. Stát,* 355–356. In 1920, 165 out of the 217 Jewish religious communities in Slovakia belonged to the newly established Organization of Autonomous Orthodox Jewish Communities.

49. Karady, "Religious Divisions," 165.

50. Rothkirchen, "Slovakia: I. 1848–1918," 1:76.

51. Jelínek, *Židia na Slovensku,* 17.

52. Rothkirchen, "Slovakia: I. 1848–1918," 1:76.

53. Jelínek, *Židia na Slovensku,* 28.

54. Mannová and Holec, "On the Road to Modernization," 233; Rothkirchen, "Slovakia: I. 1848–1918," 1:73.

55. R. W. Seton-Watson, "The Slovaks" letter to the *Spectator,* November 2, 1907; and R. W. Seton-Watson, "The Future of Bohemia" lecture delivered at King's College, London, July 6, 1915 in honor of the quincentenary of the death of the fifteenth-century Czech religious reformer Jan Hus, both in Rychlík et al., *R. W. Seton-Watson and His Relations,* 126–128, 254.

56. Leff, *National Conflict,* 24.

57. Rothkirchen, "Slovakia: I. 1848–1918," 1:73.

58. Ľubomír Lipták, "Slovakia in the 20th Century," in Mannová, *Concise History of Slovakia,* 199.

59. Szabó, "'Židovaká otázka' na Slovensku v prvých rokoch československej republiky," 60–62.

60. Ibid., 62–63.

61. Jelínek, *Židia na Slovensku,* 19.

62. Rothkirchen, "Slovakia: I. 1848–1918," 1:77; Michael K. Silber, "Bratislava," YIVO Encyclopedia of Jews in Eastern Europe, 2010, http://www.yivoencyclopedia.org/article.aspx/Bratislava.

63. Hanebrink, *In Defense of Christian Hungary,* 23. See Hanebrink's excellent study for the development, nature, and implications of political Catholicism in Hungary.

64. Mannová and Holec, "On the Road to Modernization," 213; Lipscher, *Židia v slovenskom štáte,* 11–13.

65. Rothkirchen, "Slovakia: I. 1848–1918," 1:78.

66. Szabó, "'Židováká otázka' na Slovensku v prvých rokoch československej republiky," 59.

67. SNA, f. MPS, box 258, inv. no. 2424, July 21, 1919; and inv. nos. 339–341.

68. Borský, "Jewish Communities," 122–123.

69. Borský, *Synagogue Architecture in Slovakia,* 83. The rebbes were Rabbi Avraham Shalom Halberstamm from Stropkov (Prešov region in northeastern Slovakia) and Rabbi Shmuel Angel of Radomyśl (southeastern Galicia, Poland).

70. "Poměr obyvatelstva israelského náboženského vyznání a židovské národnosti," *Sčítání lidu, 1921* (Praha, 1924), 65* část textová, table 57.

71. Boháč, *Národnostní mapa republiky československé,* 148–155; Mendelsohn, *Jews of East Central Europe,* 142–143.

72. Mendelsohn, *Jews of East Central Europe,* 144–145.

73. Boháč, *Národnostní mapa republiky československé,* 148–155; Mendelsohn, *Jews of East Central Europe,* 142–143.

74. Mendelsohn, *Jews of East Central Europe,* 144–145.

75. Jelínek, *Carpathian Diaspora,* 1–3; Šoltés, *Tri jazyky, štyri konfesie,* 7–15.

76. Jelínek, *Carpathian Diaspora,* 10–11.

77. Mendelsohn, *Jews of East Central Europe,* 144–145; Jelínek, *Carpathian Diaspora,* 124.

78. Kieval, "Negotiating Czechoslovakia," 104; see Cohen, *Politics of Ethnic Survival,* 233–273, on Czech nationalist resentment of the Jews for their pro-German position in an era of heightened ethnic conflict.

79. Kieval, "Negotiating Czechoslovakia," 119.

80. Karady, *Jews of Europe,* 210. Karady calls this "acculturational attraction."

81. *Österreichische Statistik,* vol. 63, pt. 3 (1902), 178; Čapková, *Češi, Němci, Žide?,* 93–105. Čapková's thorough and excellent study has been published in English translation by Berghahn Books under the title *Czechs, Germans, Jews? National Identity and the Jews of Bohemia* (2012).

82. Kieval, "Negotiating Czechoslovakia," 106.

83. Čapková, *Češi, Němci, Žide?,* 267.

84. Ibid., 268–269; see Mendelsohn, *Jews of East Central Europe,* 139, on the low level of antisemitism in Bohemia and Moravia.

85. Lipscher, *Židia v slovenskom štáte,* 14.

86. Ibid., 15.

87. "Sväz Slovenských Židov–zpráva," SNA, f. PR, box 14, folder 751; Hradská, "Postavenie Židov na Slovensku v prvej československej republike," 132–133.

88. *Allgemeine Jüdische Zeitung,* June 18, 1937.

89. Jelínek, *Carpathian Diaspora,* 131, 147.

90. Ibid., 130–131.

91. Ibid., 151.

92. Such scholarship including McCagg, *History of Habsburg Jewry;* McCagg, *Jewish Nobles and Geniuses;* Karády, *Önazonositás, Sorsválasztás;* Rozenblit, *Reconstructing a National Identity;* Silber, *Jews in the Hungarian Economy;* Lupovitch, *Jews at the Crossroads;* and Konrád, "Jews and Politics in Hungary."

93. Jelínek, *Davidova hviezda pod Tatrami,* 8–10. This group includes Zionist Samuel Bettelheim; historian and genealogist Rabbi Max Schay; Rabbi Mayer M. Stein of Trnava;

publisher, editor, and historian Hugo Gold; and journalists David Gross and David Hoffmann.

94. Jelínek, "In Search of Identity," 207.

95. Mendelsohn, *Modern Jewish Politics,* 103–104.

96. Laqueur, *History of Zionism,* 70–83.

97. Rozenblit, *Reconstructing a National Identity,* 36.

98. Ibid.

99. Kieval, *Making of Czech Jewry,* 93–153, 200.

100. Adolf Soltész, "A Sionizmus," *Egyenlőség,* July 11, 1897.

101. "Memorandum of the Jews of Hungary to the Jews throughout the World," the Central Hungarian Jewish Association (Magyar Zsidó Központi Szövetség), YIVO, RG348 Wolf-Mowshowitch collection, box 18, folder 160.

102. Karády, "Religious Divisions," 162.

103. Schweitzer, "Miért nem kellett Herzl a magyar zsidóknak?," 45.

104. McCagg, *History of Habsburg Jews,* 194.

105. Ibid.

106. Silber, "Bratislava"; Haber, *Die Anfänge des Zionismus in Ungarn.* The Mizrachi Orthodox Jewish movement's motto was "the *Land of Israel* for the People of Israel according to the Torah of Israel." The movement was able to adopt Zionism by rejecting its secular aspects, instead focusing on religious interpretations of its central principles.

107. Janowsky, *Jews and Minority Rights,* 212.

108. Michael Stanislawski, "Russian Jewry, the Russian State, and the Dynamics of Jewish Emancipation," in Birnbaum and Katznelson, *Paths of Emancipation,* 281.

109. "His Majesty's Government views with favour the establishment in Palestine of a national home for the Jewish people, and will use their best endeavours to facilitate the achievement of this object, it being clearly understood that nothing shall be done which may prejudice the civil and religious rights of existing non-Jewish communities in Palestine, or the rights and political status enjoyed by Jews in any other country." Mendes-Flohr and Reinharz, *Jew in the Modern World,* 582.

110. Janowsky, *Jews and Minority Rights,* 243.

111. Aharon Moshe Rabinowicz, "The Jewish Minority," in JPSA, *Jews of Czechoslovakia,* 1:157.

112. Crhová, "Jewish Politics," 279.

113. Rozenblit, *Reconstructing a National Identity,* 144.

114. Ibid., 143.

115. Ibid.

116. Kieval, "Negotiating Czechoslovakia," 110.

117. Rychnovsky, *Masaryk a židovstvi,* 75; Rabinowicz, "Jewish Minority," 1:159.

118. Aharon Moshe Rabinowicz, "The Jewish Party," in JPSA, *Jews of Czechoslovakia,* 1:260.

119. "Stažnost Sväzu Slovenských Židov," SNA, f. PR, box 556.

1. From Hungary to Czechoslovakia

1. Žilina was the seat of the Slovak government from the issuance of the Martin Declaration by the Slovak National Council on October 30, 1918 (two days after the

proclamation of Czechoslovakia in Prague) until March 1919, when Bratislava became the capital of Slovakia. Leff, *National Conflict,* 40–41.

2. SNA, f. MPS, box 17, inv. nos. 135–137; Rothkirchen, "Slovakia: II., 1918–1938," 1:86.

3. Lacko, *Prevrat 1918,* 5–6.

4. Ibid., 7.

5. Ibid., 3–4.

6. The Jewish People's Union for Slovakia (JPU) is the English translation used throughout the text for the Jewish self-defense organization Ľudový zväz židov pre Slovensko/Volksverband der Juden für die Slovakei, founded March 25, 1919 in Piešťany (Pőstyén), which would become the Slovak section of the Jewish Party before the first parliamentary elections in 1920. SNA, f. MPS, box 258, inv. no. 886.

7. SNA, f. MPS, box 17, inv. nos. 135–137.

8. The title "*župan*" is translated as "county administrator" throughout the text.

9. SNA, f. MPS, box 17, inv. no. 136.

10. Kieval, *Making of Czech Jewry,* 185–186.

11. Roshwald, *Ethnic Nationalism,* 162.

12. Lipták, "Slovakia in the 20th Century," 245. Czechs alone formed only 49 percent of the total Czechoslovak state population without the Slovaks. Whereas, according to the 1921 Czechoslovak census, "Czechoslovaks" formed 65.51percent of the total Czechoslovak state population, and "Germans" 23.36 percent.

13. Ibid.

14. In the introduction to their book *Homelands,* Nick Baron and Peter Gatrell contend that fluctuating "populations . . . formed a crucial part of the period's experimental and combustible politics of state-building, which laid the foundations of contemporary eastern Europe" (3).

15. The full text of the telegram is reprinted in the appendix to Rabinowicz, "Jewish Minority," 1:248.

16. Jelínek, *Dávidova hviezda pod Tatrami,* 123.

17. The American Jewish Joint Distribution Committee (AJDC) was founded shortly after the outbreak of World War I in 1914 to assist Jews in Palestine. The organization soon expanded its relief activities to aid Jewish war sufferers in Russia and Austria-Hungary. While the JDC mission has historically been to bring aid and relief to Jews and Jewish communities around the world, today the organization also provides nonsectarian disaster relief.

18. "Czecho-Slovakia: The Relief Work in 1919," JDC New York archives, New York collection of the years 1919–1921, folder "Czechoslovakia January through July 1920," item id. no. 217787, 5.

19. Kieval, *Making of Czech Jewry,* 74.

20. Ibid., 188–189.

21. The May 1919 attack on the Klinger family in Prague is a notable example. Iggers, *Women of Prague,* 316–318.

22. Rothschild, *East Central Europe,* 77.

23. Jerzy Tomaszewski, "Židovská Otázka na Slovensku v Roku 1919," in Kamenec, Mannová, and Kowalská, *Historik v čase a priestore,* 173, 175.

24. Jelínek, *Dávidova hviezda pod Tatrami,* 125.

25. Lipták, "Slovakia in the 20th Century," 239.

26. Nurmi, *Slovakia—Playground for Nationalism,* 38.

27. Jelínek, "In Search of Identity," 209.

28. Jelínek, *Dávidova hviezda pod Tatrami*, 128–129.

29. Rabinowicz, "Jewish Minority," 1:248.

30. The full text of the telegram is reprinted in the appendix to ibid., 1:223–225.

31. Original English-language letter from Vavro Šrobár to the Republique Tcheco-slovaque Legation a Londres, September 14, 1919. Full text of the document in Rabino-wicz, "Jewish Minority," 1:226–227.

32. Šrobár, *Z môjho života*, 55–59.

33. Lipták, "Slovakia in the 20th Century," 239.

34. Ibid.

35. Hanák, *Corvina History of Hungary*, 164.

36. Kontler, *History of Hungary*, 328.

37. Hanák, *Corvina History of Hungary*, 164–165.

38. Leff, *National Conflict*, 40–41.

39. Lipták, "Slovakia in the 20th Century," 239.

40. Bugge, "Making of a Slovak City," 218.

41. Ibid., 213.

42. Lipták, "Slovakia in the 20th Century," 243.

43. Bugge, "Making of a Slovak City," 221.

44. For detailed discussion of the series of revolutions in Hungary see Kontler, *History of Hungary*, chapter 7, "In Search of an Identity," 324–344; Völgyés, *Hungary in Revolution;* Siklós, *Revolution in Hungary;* and Tőkés, *Béla Kun*.

45. "Jüdische Brüder!," Volksverband der Jüden für die Slovakei. SNA, f. MPS, box 258, inv. no. 885.

46. SNA, f. MPS, box 258, inv. no. 884–885.

47. Materials concerning Jewish refugee matters in wartime Hungary are located in the Hungarian National Archives (Magyar Országos Levéltár [MOL]), Ministry of the Interior (Belügyminiszterium) K148, Presidential Files (Elnöki Iratok), 1914–1918. Files pertaining to Austrian Jewish refugee movement, accommodation, and local Jewish community aid are collected in MOL, K148, box 494, file 37.

48. Rozenblit, *Reconstructing a National Identity*, 59.

49. Rechter, *Jews of Vienna*, 75.

50. YIVO, RG 335.2, AJRF collection, box 1, folder 1, inventory page 99.

51. Ibid., 103.

52. Ibid., 99.

53. Ibid., 102–106.

54. Bárkány and Dojč, *Židovské náboženské obce na Slovensku*, 40; Menyhért, *Szlovenszkói Zsidó Hitközségek Története*, 53.

55. YIVO, RG 335.2, AJRF box 1, folder 1, inventory page 103.

56. SNA, f. MPS, box 258, inv. no. 885.

57. The JPU founded the *Jüdische Volkszeitung* in Bratislava in August 1919 as a Jewish national mouthpiece.

58. Rabbi Samuel Reich, "Positive Arbeit," *Jüdische Volkszeitung*, August 27, 1920. About two hundred Jewish teachers took part in the Slovak-language summer course. Rothkirchen, "Slovakia II: 1918–1938," 1:88.

59. Janowsky, *Jews and Minority Rights*, 369.

60. Rychnovsky, *Masaryk a židovstvi*, 75; Rabinowicz, "Jewish Minority," 1:159.

61. SNA, f. MPS, box 258, inv. no. 884–885.

62. Max Brod, "Orthodoxie, Zionismus, Nationaljudentum," *Jüdische Volkszeitung*, November 28, 1919.

63. YIVO, RG335.2, AJRF, box 1, folder 1, inventory page 103.

64. SNA, f. MPS, box 258, inv. no. 2424, July 21, 1919.

65. Ibid., inv. nos. 339–341.

66. Ibid., box 17, inv. no. 37, January 19, 1920.

67. Ibid., inv. no. 511, February 20, 1920.

68. Ibid.

69. Rozenblit, *Reconstructing a National Identity*, 66.

70. Marrus, *Unwanted*, 65.

71. Magocsi, *Historical Atlas*, 125–127.

72. SNA, f. MPS, box 392, inv. no. 611, January 22, 1921.

73. Ibid., box 278, October 27, 1919.

74. Ibid., box 392, inv. no. 609, March 11, 1921.

75. Baron and Gatrell, *Homelands*, 3.

76. Gatrell, *Whole Empire Walking*, 11.

77. Baron and Gatrell, *Homelands*, 4.

78. SNA, f. MPS, box 278, inv. no. 346.

79. JPU to the MPS in Bratislava, October 31, 1919, in ibid., inv. no. 358.

80. Ibid.

81. SNA, f. MPS, box 278, inv. no. 356

82. To be a citizen of the new Czechoslovak state, one had to fall into at least one of the following four categories: (1) persons who had received right of residency in the former Austro-Hungarian Monarchy on the territory of the contemporary Czechoslovak state before January 1, 1910; (2) persons who were former citizens of the German Empire who had their permanent residence in territories that fell to Czechoslovakia; (3) persons who were former German, Austrian, or Hungarian citizens born on the territory of contemporary Czechoslovakia who as children had German citizenship and their permanent address on contemporary Czechoslovak territory; or Austrian or Hungarian citizens who had right of residency on Czechoslovak territory before the war, even if they did not reside or have right of residency there when this law came into effect; or (4) persons who before October 28, 1918, had the right of residency within the former Austro-Hungarian Monarchy outside of Czechoslovak territory but became employees of the Czechoslovak state. *Ústavní zákon ze dne 9. dubna 1920, kterým se doplňují a mění dosavadní ustanovaní o nabývání a pozbývání státního občanství a práva domovského v republice Československé*. In the appendix to Hajn, *Problém ochrany menšin*, 264.

83. SNA, f. MPS, box 278, inv. no. 578.

84. Ibid., inv. no. 365.

85. Ibid., inv. no. 463.

86. "Příslušníci Polští a Ukrajinští v Č.S.R.," December 6, 1921, in ibid., box 400, inv. no. 622.

87. Lesser, *Welcoming the Undesirables*, 23–25. Lesser's is a valuable study of the growing stream of Jewish immigration from east central Europe to Brazil in the early twentieth century. Brazil was a popular destination for Jewish refugees leaving Czechoslovakia. This would be a fascinating area for more research.

88. "Polští uprichlíci, nebezpečenství zavlečni a neštovic" from the vládní poradce pro zdravotnictví, August 5, 1920, SNA, f. MPS, box 394, inv. no. 950.

89. Ibid.

90. Palestina Amt to the MPS in Bratislava, August 13, 1920, in ibid., inv. no. 965. The Palestine Office aided in all areas of immigration preparation and documentation for Jews immigrating to British Mandate Palestine.

91. Joint Distribution Committee (JDC), *Reports Received by the JDC,* 108.

92. Palestina Amt to the MPS in Bratislava, August 13, 1920, SNA, f. MPS, box 394, inv. no. 965.

93. Rabbi Wéber's work on behalf of the Jewish refugees in Hungary was celebrated during the war. He was known as an outspoken defender of the refugees among the administration.

94. JDC, *Reports Received by the JDC,* 118.

95. Letter from the Ústredná kancelária orthodoxných židovských obci na Slovensku v Bratislave to the Kapitanský úrad, August 23, 1920, SNA, f. MPS, box 394, inv. no. 949.

96. Letter from the Hlavní policejní kapitanát v Bratislavě to the MPS: "Židovští úprichlíci z Polska Internování," August 28, 1920, ibid., inv. no. 948.

97. Ibid., inv. no. 943, August 30, 1920.

98. "Ubytování polských uprchlíků v barákovém táboře na Slamených boudách," September 29, 1920, in ibid., inv. no. 958.

99. AJDC in Košice to the Militär Commando Sanitäts Chef in Bratislava, August 13, 1920, in ibid., inv. no. 952.

100. "Zákaz vstupu dalších židovských utečencov z Polska," from zasadnutia bratislavského administratívného výboru to the MPS, February 21, 1921, Archív hlavného mesta SR Bratislavy (AMB), f. MB, box 2325, inv. no. 99.

101. Ibid.

102. "Příslušníci polští a ukrajinští v Č.S.R.," December 6, 1921, SNA, f. MPS, box 400, inv. no. 622.

103. Letter from the Ministerstvo sociální péče Republiky československé in Prague to the MPS in Bratislava, February 17, 1921, in ibid., box 393, inv. no. 482.

104. Ibid., inv. no. 494.

2. Nationality Is an Internal Conviction

1. Josef Mráz (1882–1934) was one of the cofounders of the Czechoslovak State Statistical Office, who had begun his work as a statistician for the Provincial Statistical Office of the Bohemian kingdom. He is noted for his work on the first census in Slovakia (1919), as well as on statistical theory and agricultural statistics. Federální statistický úřad, *70 let československé státní statistiky,* 194. Žilina was the provisional capital of Slovakia from December 12, 1918, through February 4, 1919, when Bratislava became the capital. Bugge, "Making of a Slovak City," 221.

2. From the report by Josef Mráz, "Prozatímní sčítání lidu na Slovensku," February 8, 1919, SNA, f. MPS, box 277, inv. no. 101.

3. "Prozatímní sčítání lidu na Slovensku," in ibid., inv. no. 76; emphasis added.

4. R. W. Seton-Watson, *Racial Problems in Hungary* (New York: Howard Fertig, 1972).

5. "Great Moravia," a large Slavic state said to have existed for nearly seventy years between 833 and 900, was an important component of the Czechoslovak romantic national idea as well as the development of Slovak nationalism. Considered to have bridged the western Slavs with the Slavonic tribes in the Balkans and with Byzantium, the weakening state collapsed under attack by the Magyar tribes who settled in the Danube Basin in approximately 896. The Czech and Slovak tribes then underwent separate development.

6. Šrobár, *Osvobodené Slovensko*, 7–8.

7. Štúr was a nineteenth-century Slovak linguist, leader of the Slovak national movement, and member of the Hungarian parliament.

8. Šrobár, *Osvobodené Slovensko*, 11.

9. Rothschild, *East Central Europe*, 76.

10. Leff, *National Conflict*, 35.

11. "Prozatímní sčítání lidu na Slovensku," sna, f. mps, box 277, inv. no. 74. In this transitional period before the signing of the Treaty of Trianon, Slovakia was often denoted as the "occupied territory of the former Kingdom of Hungary."

12. See Scott, *Seeing Like a State*, for thinking about ways the state "sees" the population and makes it "legible."

13. Klineberger, *Národ a národnost*, 53.

14. Mendelsohn, *On Modern Jewish Politics*, 128.

15. "Let us follow our own path . . . let all men speak well or ill of our nation, our literature, our language: they are ours, they are ourselves, and let that be enough." B. Suphan, ed., *Johann Gottfried Herder, Sämmtliche Werke* (Berlin: Weidmann), in Smith, *Nationalism*, 27.

16. Kedourie, *Nationalism*, 68.

17. Ibid.

18. Tilly, *Formation of National States*, 6.

19. Smith, *Nationalism*, 11.

20. Connor, *Ethnonationalism*, 197.

21. Gellner, *Nations and Nationalism*, 7.

22. Rozenblit, *Reconstructing a National Identity*, 7.

23. Smith, *Nationalism*, 12.

24. Ibid., 13.

25. Herzl, *Jewish State*, 145.

26. Brubaker, *Nationalism Reframed*, 7.

27. Ibid., 16.

28. Dominique Arel, "Language Categories in Censuses," in Kertzer and Arel, *Census and Identity*, 95.

29. David Kertzer and Dominique Arel, "Censuses, Identity Formation, and the Struggle for Political Power," in Kertzer and Arel, *Census and Identity*, 26; and Arel, "Language Categories in Censuses," 97.

30. Jan Auerhan, "Kolik je čechoslováků?," *ČSV* II (1921): 49, and Antonín Boháč, "Slovensko ve světle statistiky-kniha Josefa Mráza," *ČSV* II (1921): 225–226.

31. Cyril Horáček, "Národnostní statistika," *ČSV* II (1921): 187.

32. Mráz, *Slovensko ve světle statistiky*, 33.

33. Ibid.; exclamation points in the original.

34. Arel, "Language Categories in Censuses," 93.
35. Auerhan, "Kolik je čechoslovaků?"; Mráz, "Dva důkazy o falešnosti maďarských dat o řeči mateřské na základě dat o znalosti řečí"; and Horáček, "Národnostní statistika," all in *ČSV* II (1921).
36. Jan Auerhan (1880–1942) worked as a statistician for the Provincial Statistical Office of the Bohemian kingdom from 1906 and became the undersecretary to the president of the Czechoslovak State Statistical Office at its founding in January 1919. He is most noted for his work in the demographic and anthro-geographic fields, the study of Czech and Slovak minorities abroad, and minority questions more generally. Federální statistický úřad, *70 let československé státní statistiky*, 186.
37. Auerhan, "Kolik je čechoslovaků?," *ČSV* II (1921): 51.
38. SNA, f. MPS, box 277, inv. no. 76; emphasis added.
39. Károly Keleti (born 1833, Pozsony [Pressburg, Bratislava]; died 1892, Budapest) *Életrajzi lexikon.* www.kereso.hu-yrk-Ryrgenwm/7502.
40. Boháč, "Národnost či jazyk?," *ČSV* II (1921): 50.
41. Ibid., 49. Keleti published his views on nationality in 1880 in the *Statistische Monatschrift* under the title "Zur Frage der Volkszählung." Horáček, "Národnostní statistika," *ČSV* I (1920): 187.
42. Antonín Boháč (1882–1950) is regarded as the founder of Czechoslovak demographics, especially with regard to questions of nationality. He was a member of the Czechoslovak delegation to the Paris Peace Conference in 1919 and worked for the Czechoslovak State Statistical Office upon his return. Boháč was the deputy chairman of the Society for the Study of Nationality Questions. Federální statistický úřad, *70 let československé státní statistiky*, 195. Boháč was also associate professor of demography at the Charles University Faculty of Science, where he lectured on the "Basics of Population Science." He introduced the usage of punch card technology for processing Czechoslovak census data. "Historie statistiky v Čechách po roce 1918," Czech Statistical Office, *http://www.czso.cz/csu/redakce.nsf/i/historie_statistiky_v_cechach_po_roce_1918.*
43. Federální statistický úřad, 50.
44. Úřad statistický, *Sčítání lidu v republice československé ze dne 15. února 1921*, 77* (čast textová).
45. SNA, f. MPS, box 277. This carton contains the original handwritten forms used for collecting the raw data for the 1919 census.
46. Sčítání lidu na Slovensku 1919. "Anketa mezi popisujícími pověřníky," in ibid., box 380, inv. nos. 7, 8–9.
47. "Sčitanie ľudu," *Národnie noviny* (Turčiansky Svätý Martin), August 22, 1919.
48. Ibid.
49. "Slováci!," *Šarišské hlasy* (Prešov), August 24, 1919.
50. Mráz, "O předběžném sčítání lidu na Slovensku roku 1919," *ČSV* II (1921): 133–134.
51. "O Maďarech, Němcích a židech," SNA, f. MPS, box 380, inv. no. 4.
52. "O opravných návrzích pro příští sčítání," in ibid., 7.
53. "O nepřístojnostech při sčítání," in ibid., 5; Josef Mráz, "O předběžném sčítání lidu na Slovensku roku 1919," *ČSV* II (1921): 135.
54. Leff, *National Conflict*, 23.
55. The Slavic languages differentiate the term "Hungarian" as it indicates ethnic Hungarian or the Hungarian language and as it refers to the Kingdom of Hungary or

something deriving from the Kingdom of Hungary. In Slovak these terms are "*mad'ar*" (*magyar*, i.e., ethnic Hungarian), *Uhorsko* (the Kingdom of Hungary), and *uhorský* (deriving from the Kingdom of Hungary).

56. "*Hutorit'*" is a form of "*hovorit*," to speak.

57. Mráz, "O předběžném sčítání lidu na Slovensku roku 1919," 135.

58. "O Mad'arech, Němcích a židech," SNA, f. MPS, box 380, inv. no. 4.

59. Mráz, "O předběžném sčítání lidu na Slovensku roku 1919," 129. Unfortunately, the demographic breakdown of those who chose "Other" on the 1919 Slovak census is unavailable, so the conclusion that the majority of Jews declared for Jewish nationality comes from census-taker reports and their insistence that it be included as a separate column on the next census. See footnote: Státní úřad statistický, *Sčítání lidu v republice československé ze dne 15. února 1921, 77**.

60. Slovaks who declared as Slovak, according to the options presented on the 1919 Slovak census, were recorded as "Czechoslovak." Slovaks were not recorded as "Slovak" until the 1930 statewide census.

61. Jelínek, *Davidova hviezda pod Tatrami*, 184.

62. Crhová, "Jewish Politics in Central Europe," 275.

63. Friedmann, *Mravnost či oportunita?*, 29–30.

64. Rothkirchen, "Slovakia II: 1918–1938," 1:87–90; and Memorandum to the MPS on the letterhead of the Ústredný volebný výbor sdružených židovských strán na Slovensku, SNA, f. MPS, box 71, inv. no. 243.

65. Rabinowicz, "Jewish Minority," 1:157–161; and Crhová, "Jewish Politics," 277–279.

66. "Allgemeine Tagung der Judenheit in der Slovakei," *Jüdische Volkszeitung* [JVZ], February 13, 1920.

67. Ibid.

68. Rabinowicz, "Jewish Minority," 1:201.

69. Rothkirchen, "Slovakia II: 1918–1938," 1:90.

70. Rothschild, *East Central Europe*, 93–94.

71. Leff, *National Conflict*, 53, 74.

72. Čapková, *Češi, Němci, Židé?*, 242.

73. *Preßburger Zeitung*, January 21, 1920.

74. "Die jüdischer Wahlbewegung," JVZ, January 30, 1920.

75. "Allgemeine Tagung der Judenheit in der Slovakei," JVZ, February 13, 1920.

76. "Die Bedeutung der jüdischen Wahlpartei," JVZ, April 16, 1920.

77. "An die jüdischen Wähler und Wählerinnen!," JVZ, March 19, 1920. The Jewish Hospital Society (Jüdischer Krankenhaus Verein) made a point of expressing its independence from all party politics. SNA, fond PR, box 36, folder 660, inv. no.678.

78. Crhová, "Jewish Politics," 282.

79. Report of the Associated Jewish Parties, SNA, f. MPS, box 89, inv. no. 244.

80. Emil Waldstein, "Unsere Volkabstimmung," JVZ, April 30, 1920.

81. Ibid.

82. "Der jüdische Kongreß in Brünn," JVZ, June 18, 1920.

83. "Der Deligiertentag des Volksverbandes," JVZ, November 5, 1920.

84. Rothkirchen, "Slovakia II: 1918–1938," in JPSA, *Jews of Czechoslovakia*, 1:91.

85. Čapková, *Češi, Němci, Židé?*, 242.

86. SNA, f. MPS, box 89, February 5, 1922.

87. "Das Komitee der Konservativ-jüdischen Partei beim Minister Mičura," *Jüdische Presse*, April 28, 1922; SNA, f. MPS, box 71.

88. SNA, f. MPS, box 89, inv. nos. 545–547. The Orthodox Jewish communities of Slovakia did not want to be a part of the federation of Jewish communities' project introduced by the national Jews.

89. Leo Landman discusses the functioning of the concept of *Dina D'Malkhuta Dina*, the law of the kingdom (the state) is the law in the modern Jewish world, in *Jewish Law in the Diaspora*, 135–148.

90. Janowsky, *Nationalities and National Minorities*, 151.

91. Mendelsohn, *On Modern Jewish Politics*, 38.

92. "Ein Slovakischer Schriftsteller über die Judenfrage," JVZ, September 10, 1920; and Karel Kálal, "Rozmnožme národ," *Slovenský dennik*, August 27, 1920.

93. "Ein Slovakischer Schriftsteller über die Judenfrage," JVZ, September 10, 1920.

94. Úřad statistický, *Sčítání lidu v republice československé ze dne 15. února 1921*, 77* (část textová).

95. The Czechoslovak constitution, *Ústavní listina Československé republiky* (hereafter, Ústava 1920), was ratified on February 29, 1920.

96. Ústava 1920, Article 128. Articles governing minority protections include 128 through 134.

97. František Weyr, "Ústava československé republiky," in Janda, *Československá vlastivěda díl V. Stát*, 162.

98. Hajn, ed., *Problém ochrany menšín*, 261–262.

99. Ústava 1920, Article 132.

100. According to Article 7 of the treaty of St. Germain-en-Laye, signed on September 10, 1919, "Czechoslovak" was the official language of Czechoslovakia, with two branches, Czech and Slovak. Included in the 1920 Czechoslovak Constitution, Language Law of February 29, 1920.

101. Law of February 29, 1920, Articles 2 and 5.

102. Boháč, "Národnost či mateřský jazyk?," ČSV I (1920): 274.

103. Ibid., 273.

104. Boháč, *Národnostní mapa republiky československé*, 16.

105. Proponents of direct national declaration included Professors Mildschuh, Krejčí, and Weyr; proponents of mother tongue declaration included Professors Rauchberg, Gruber, Horáček, and Boháč. Boháč, *Národnostní mapa republiky československé*, 15.

106. Ibid., 16.

107. Jews by religion numbered 354,342 in total, or 1.35 percent of the population of Czechoslovakia, with their numbers substantially increasing moving from west to east; from .8 percent of the population of Bohemia to 13.4 percent of the population of Subcarpathian Ruthenia. Státní úřad statistický, *Sčítání lidu v republice československé ze dne 15. února 1921*, 65* část textová, table 57: Poměr obyvatelstva israelského náboženského vyznání a židovské národnosti.

108. Persons declaring German nationality in the 1921 Czechoslovak census numbered 3,123,568 in total, or 23.4 percent of the population of Czechoslovakia. *Sčítání lidu*, 60*, table 50: Národnost československých státních příslušníků.

109. The relationship between the national minority and its kin state is explained by Rogers Brubaker in his *Nationalism Reframed*: "A state becomes an external national

'homeland' for 'its' ethnic diaspora when political or cultural elites define ethnonational kin in other states as members of one and the same nation, claim that they 'belong,' in some sense, to the state, and assert that their condition must be monitored and their interests protected and promoted by the state; and when the state actually does take action in the name of monitoring, promoting, or protecting the interests of it ethnonational kin abroad" (58).

110. Boháč, *Národnost a sčítání lidu*, 3.

111. "Mateřského jazyka nikoliv národnosti," October 8, 1920, SNA, f. MPS, box 37, inv. no. 158.

112. *Sčítání lidu, 1921*, 77* část textová.

113. Horáček, "Dnešní stav národnostní a jazykové otázky u nás," *Československá vlastivěda díl V. Stát*, 210. He refers to statute number 86/30.

114. Ibid.

115. Kertzer and Arel, "Censuses, Identity Formation," 2, 3; Scott, *Seeing Like a State*, 2–3, 76–77, 81.

116. Kertzer and Arel, "Censuses, Identity Formation," 2, 3.

117. These materials are located in SNA, f. MPS, boxes 380, 381, and 385.

118. SNA, f. MPS, box 381, attached to inv. no. 122, Nové Zámky, February 9, 1921.

119. "Mit írjanak a zsidók a 11-es rovatba?," *Magyar Ujság*, Bratislava, February 15, 1921; SNA, f. MPS, box 380, inv. no. 587.

120. "Politische Selbstbestimmung (Volkszählung und Wahlen)," JVZ, February 4, 1921.

121. Ibid.

122. *Sčítání lidu, 1921* (Praha, 1924), 65* část textová, table 57.

123. *Magyar Statisztikai Évkönyv. Új Folyam XXIII. 1915* (Budapest, 1918), 20, chart 13, "A népesség anyanyelve vallások szerint 1910-ben." On the 1910 census in the Kingdom of Hungary, 75.5 percent of the Jewish population declared Hungarian to be their mother tongue. In 1921, 76 percent of the Jews in Slovakia opted away from traditional German and Hungarian national alliances by declaring "Jewish" and "Czechoslovak." *Sčítání lidu, 1921*, 65* část textová, table 57.

124. Boháč, *Národnostní mapa republiky československé*, 149.

125. Ibid., 18.

126. *Sčítání lidu, 1921*, 69* část textová.

127. Ibid., 75*.

128. *Sčítání lidu, 1921*, 77* část textová. There was also a precipitous rise in declarations of Russian nationality in 1921, stemming from the Rusyn population.

129. SNA, f. PR, box 556, inv. no. 73.

3. Contested Loyalty

1. "Maďarská propaganda v kongesových židovských obcích na Slovensku," *Lidové listy*, February 1, 1925, SNA, f. PR, box 556, inv. no. 22.

2. See introduction.

3. "Náboženství a cirkve," *Deset let československé republiky. Svazek první*, 442; Vratislav Bušek, "Poměr státu k církvím v Československé republice," in Janda, *Československá vlastivěda díl V. Stát*, 355–356. The 52 Neolog and Status Quo Ante communi-

ties came together under the name Sväz židovských náboženských obcí na Slovensku Jeschurun. Out of the 217 Jewish religious communities in Slovakia, 165 belonged to the Organization of Autonomous Orthodox Jewish Communities.

4. Hanebrink, *In Defense of Christian Hungary*; and Hanebrink, "Transnational Culture War," 80.

5. Katzenburg, "Hungarian Jewry in Modern Times," in Braham, *Hungarian-Jewish Studies*, 155.

6. M. Kovács, *Liberal Professions*, 50–51.

7. Borský, "Jewish Communities," 122–123.

8. Menyhért, *Szlovenszkói Zsidó Hitközségek Története*, 53. The official number recorded in the 1921 statewide census is 47,882, or 7.93 percent of the total population of Košice. The unofficial total compiled by aid organizations accounted for refugee inflows and regional in-migration to the city.

9. From the interview with Erzsébet Weiss conducted by Éva Kovács in the later 1980s for her 1991 dissertation, "A Kassai Zsidóság Etnikai Identitása." Kovács conducted interviews in Košice and Budapest between 1986 and 1990 with Magyar-speaking Jews who lived in Košice during the interwar period.

10. "Der feierenden Republik zum Gruß," *Jüdisches Familienblatt* (JFB) (Bratislava), October 26, 1928.

11. "Die Entwicklung der jüdischen Gemeinden in der Slowakei während der letzen 10 Jahre," *JFB*, October 26, 1928.

12. The following two excellent articles explore the process and challenges of creating a Slovak national space after the First World War: Bugge, "Making of a Slovak City," and Lipták, "Rok 1918 a rekonštukcia historickej pamäti," 180–191.

13. "Entwicklung," *JFB*, October 26, 1928.

14. See "Catalogue of Synagogues in Slovakia," in Borský, *Synagogue Architecture*, 110–139, which offers a comprehensive index of extant and demolished synagogues in Slovakia based on Borský's exhaustive documentation project *Synagoga Slovaca*, conducted from 2000 to 2006.

15. "Das Feier des 28. Oktober in den Gemeinden. Festrede des Dr. Viktor Stein," *JFB*, November 9, 1928.

16. From the interview with János Vass conducted by Éva Kovács.

17. Johnson, *Slovakia, 1918–1938*, 86. The percentage of Jewish students attending Magyar schools sank from 43.2 percent in the 1921–1922 school year to 19.7 percent in 1930–1931. Attendance at German schools rose from 13.3 percent in 1921/1922 to 18.4 percent in 1930–1931.

18. The Czechoslovak constitution guaranteed that in towns or districts where there lived a national minority comprising a considerable fraction (20 percent) of the population, the language of that minority was to be used simultaneously with "Czechoslovak" for all official notices of the courts, offices, and organs of the state; the instruction in and administration of schools for members of the national minority was to be given in their language; and all educational and cultural institutions set up for that national minority were to be administered in their language. From the Law of February 29, 1920, Articles 2 and 5.

19. According to the First Vienna Arbitration of November 2, 1938, Hungary's borders were redrawn to include a territory of 12,103 square kilometers from southern Slovakia

and Subcarpathian Ruthenia. Košice (Kassa, Kaschau) lay within these borders. The quoted text is from the interview with Dr. Gábor Sarlós conducted by Éva Kovács.

20. From the interview with Jenő Silber conducted by Éva Kovács.

21. The Ha-shomer Ha-tsair movement in the territory of Slovakia was founded after the First World War with the help of Polish Zionist youth in cooperation with the Kadima movement in Subcarpathian Ruthenia. Its goal was to prepare Jewish youth for life in Palestine. See Mešťan, *Hašomer Hacair.*

22. From the interview with Jenő Silber conducted by Éva Kovács.

23. The United Jewish Party of Slovakia and Subcarpathian Ruthenia was established on March 18, 1928, in Košice from the Jewish Party and the Jewish Economic Party.

24. Interview with Julius Reisz in the *Kassai Napló,* November 27, 1928.

25. "Slovakisches Judentum," *JFB,* February 10, 1928.

26. Ibid.

27. Ibid.

28. Hradská, "Postavenie Židov na Slovensku v prvej československej republike," 132.

29. Ľudovit Štúr (1815–1856) was a central figure in the Slovak national awakening in the mid-nineteenth century. He is best known for codifying the written Slovak language based on the central Slovak dialect. He was a pedagogue, poet, publicist, and statesman who served in the Hungarian Diet from 1846 to 1848.

30. Svätopluk was the legendary ninth-century ruler of Great Moravia, a territory encompassing today's Slovakia. The Slovak National Awakening movement wrote of him as the "Slovak King" in works from the eighteenth century forward.

31. Roth, *Ku Pôde a Skutočnosti,* 8.

32. "Sväz slovenských židov-zpráva." "*Slovenskí Židia žili storočia na Slovensku spolu so Slovákmi a boli práve tak utláčaní ako oni,*" SNA, f. PR, box 14, folder 751.

33. Ibid.

34. The term "Zionists" here refers to those Jews who wished to establish a Jewish homeland in Palestine, while "national Jews" were those who sought to secure Jewish economic, social, political, and religious rights as a national minority in Czechoslovakia.

35. Roth, *Ku Pôde a Skutočnosti,* 33.

36. Leo Spielberger, "Slovenskó zsidósága," in Ujvári, *Magyar Zsidó Lexikon,* 855–857.

37. Mária M. Kovács explains why Jews in Hungary refused international minority protections in "Ambiguities of External Minority Protection," 43–48.

38. Spielberger, "Slovenskó zsidósága," in Ujvári, *Magyar Zsidó Lexikon,* 855–857.

39. Borský, *Synagogue Architecture,* 123.

40. Menyhért, *Szlovenszkói Zsidó Hitközségek Története,* 66.

41. Gruber, *National Geographic Jewish Heritage Travel,* 195; "Dom umenia—neologická synagóga," Miestny úrad Košice—Staré Mesto. http://www.kosice-city.sk/clanky-detail/4dom-umenia-neologicka-synagoga.

42. Bárkány and Dojč, *Židovské náboženské obce na Slovensku,* 376.

43. Menyhért, *Szlovenszkói Zsidó Hitközségek Története,* 65.

44. Ibid.

45. Erika Heet, "Lajos Kozma, Hungarian Modernist," http://www.dwell.com/articles/lajos-kozma-hungarian-modernist.html.

46. Borský, *Synagogue Architecture,* 123.

47. Ruth Ellen Gruber, "Lipót Baumhorn Tour," http://www.centropa.org/?nID=60 &tID=26.

48. Borský, *Synagogue Architecture,* 119–120.

49. Lipták, "Collective Identity," 124–125; Lipták, "Rok 1918 a rekonštrukcia historickej pamäti," 181.

50. Kieval, "Negotiating Czechoslovakia," 113. Kieval eloquently considers my analyses of the transformation of the landscape in this piece, referring to my "Building Slovak Jewry: Material Evidence of Reorientation as Citizens of Czechoslovakia," a paper delivered at the Association for Jewish Studies Annual Conference, December 2007; and "'Abandon Your Role as Exponents of the Magyars': Contested Jewish Loyalty in Interwar (Czecho)Slovakia," *Association for Jewish Studies Review* 33, no. 2 (November 2009): 341–362.

51. Gruber, *Virtually Jewish,* 156. Gruber discusses museum establishment as a ritual in itself, the exhibits of which designate what must be remembered and how.

52. Ményhert, *Szlovenszkói Zsidó Hitközségek Története,* 150.

53. Kónya and Landa, *Stručné Dejiny Prešovských Židov,* 40.

54. Peter Bugge uses this term in his analysis of the "Czechoslovakization" of Bratislava. Bugge, "Making of a Slovak City," 221.

55. Jelínek, "In Search of an Identity," 207.

56. These were in fact the main arguments of the Jewish national movement in Slovakia against all other Jewish political groups. The Czechoslovak state understood that the Zionist struggle against the Union of Slovak Jews stemmed from the threat it posed to winning a Jewish national mandate in parliament. SNA, f. PR, box 556, inv. nos. 69–70.

57. The Jewish Party received a total of 98,845 votes in 1925. *Manuel Statistique de la République Tchécoslovaque III,* 256, table XI 3, "Votes valuables, exprimés aux élections pour la Chambre des Députés, en Tchécoslovaquie, en novembre 1925 et mandates attributes."

58. "Kongruová náboženská obce židovská v Bratislave-Stažnost sväzu slovenských židov," SNA, f. PR, box 556, inv. nos. 1–3.

59. Ibid.

60. "Neolog žid. cirkevná obec v Bratislave-vnutorné rozpory," November 12, 1932, in ibid.

61. "Stažnost sväzu slovenských židov," in ibid.

62. Ibid.

63. Ibid.

64. Ibid.

65. Ibid.

66. Ibid.

67. Ibid.

68. SNA, f. PR, box 556, inv. nos. 69–70.

69. "Glossen," *JFB,* August 12, 1927.

70. "Memorandum of the Jews of Hungary to the Jews throughout the World," Magyar Zsidó Központi Szövetség, YIVO, RG348 Wolf-Mowshowitch collection, box 18, folder 160.

71. "Glossen," *JFB,* August 12, 1927.

72. Ibid.

73. "Sväz slovenských židov," *Národný denník,* November 9, 1926.

74. See introduction.

75. Josef Mráz had complained about the "immaturity of the [Slovak] population" in relation to the struggle to find reliable census takers in 1919. "Prozatímní sčítání lidu na Slovensku," SNA, f. MPS, box 277, inv. no. 80. One of the greatest difficulties faced by Slovakia was the lack of nationally conscious educated Slovaks who were able to take over the running of the infrastructure, civil service, and professions, since preparation for those jobs had required Magyarization during the Dual Monarchy period.

76. Johnson, *Slovakia, 1918–1938,* 128.

77. Ibid., 186. The percentage of Jewish students attending Czechoslovak gymnasia in Slovakia increased incrementally throughout the 1920s, reaching 61.9 percent by the 1930–1931 school year.

78. Cohen, *Politics of Ethnic Survival,* 224–225.

79. "Stažnost sväzu slovenských židov," SNA, f. PR, box 556.

80. Ibid.

81. "Sväz slovenských židov," *Národný denník,* November 9, 1926.

82. "Pán rabín Funk vo 'Slováku'," *Slovenský dennik,* September 12, 1928.

83. Štátný oblastný archív Bratislave, fond Župný úrad v Bratislave, file 8833/1925, in Crhová, "Jewish Politics in Central Europe," 289–290.

84. Report submitted in Bratislava, February 25, 1926, SNA, f. PR, box 79, inv. no. 836. The reports concerning possible irredentist activity within Jewish national associations in Slovakia are located in carton 79 and date from 1926.

85. Report submitted in Komárno, March 9, 1926, in ibid., inv. no. 842.

86. "Židia u nás," in *Nitrianské noviny,* April 28, 1929.

87. "Židia v Košiciach," in *Slovenský východ (Košice),* November 19, 1929. Interestingly, the example of the Orthodox elementary school in Košice also shows an auspicious overlap between Slovak linguistic-political pressures and the fulfillment of religious obligation. From the Orthodox Jewish perspective, hiring non-Jewish Slovak teachers ensured that the students at the Orthodox school never saw their Jewish teachers breaking the Sabbath during Saturday classes. A former student of the Orthodox school on Kazinczy Street in Košice, the same school to which the author of the article referred, recalled asking why the teachers at his school were Christian. The answer was that the religious community did not want the children to see their Jewish teacher pick up the chalk and write on the blackboard on Saturday, like in the Neolog school. From an interview with Jenő Silber conducted by Éva Kovács for her 1991 thesis, "A Kassai Zsidóság Etnikai Identitása."

88. "Židia na Slovensku," in *Národný denník,* June 2, 1929.

89. Jelínek, "In Search of Identity," 215.

90. SNA, f. PR, box 556, inv. no. 5.

91. "Neolog žid. cirkevná obec v Bratislave-vnutorné rozpory," November 12, 1932, SNA, f. PR, box 556.

92. Ibid.

93. Report filed November 6, 1930, in ibid. Rabbi Akiba Schreiber was a descendent of Rabbi Moshe Schreiber (the Hatam Sofer), belonging to the Schreiber dynasty of Orthodox rabbis. He served from 1906 to 1939, when he emigrated to Jerusalem, where he died in 1959.

94. A Kollel is a group of people studying Talmud who are supported by other Jews.

95. Rabbi Avraham Shmuel Binyomin Sofer, also known as Ktav Sofer (March 13, 1815-December 31, 1871), succeeded the Hatam Sofer as chief rabbi of Pressburg (Pozsony, later Bratislava).

96. SNA, f. KÚ, box 266, inv. no. 58564, October 19, 1929.

97. Ibid.

98. Ibid., box 556, inv. no. 561–562, July 23, 1929.

99. Ibid.

100. SNA, f. PR, box 556.

101. Ibid., inv. no.125. The full text of both Stein's and Masaryk's comments can be found in the October 24, 1930, article "Das slovakische Judentum begrüßt den Staatspräsidenten," in the *Jüdisches Familienblatt*.

102. SNA, f. PR, box 556, inv. nos. 125–128. This is a copy of the text of Funk's speech.

103. Report filed November 6, 1930, SNA, f. PR, box 556.

104. Ibid.

105. Ibid.

106. Ibid.

107. The most publicized of these was the installation of Rabbi Dr. Resovski, formerly the rabbi of Abony in Hungary, as the rabbi of Lučenec (Losonc). Materials relating to this matter, including a police report and newspaper clippings from the Magyar and Slovak press are located in SNA/PR/557. The head of the Rabbinical Association in Slovakia, the Orthodox Rabbi Stein of Trnava (Nagyszombat), believed that the election of Rabbi Resovski would have a disastrous impact on the development of the loyal inclination among Jews in Slovakia and that it would set a precedent for other places where the hostile influence of Budapest worked behind the scenes. "Vol'ba rabína v Lučenci," March 12, 1929, SNA, f. PR, box 557.

108. Ibid.

109. Funk testified that Stein, Dezső, and Porzsolt would always officially take a stand against the Hungarian government but that they were bound to Hungary by their property holdings in southern Slovakia. "Neologické žid. Náboženské obec v Bratislave-činnost," SNA, f. KU, box 266.

110. "Neolog žid. cirkevná obec v Bratislave-vnutorné rozpory," November 12, 1932, SNA, f. PR, box 556.

111. Ibid. Funk was pensioned off in 1934 for the following reasons: (1) he was unable to agree and cooperate with the community board; (2) he was physically and intellectually unable to carry out his obligations; (3) he would not oversee the production of kosher meat in the community nor give his *hechsher* (stamp of approval) to it; (4) he went to the local police headquarters and accused members of the community of being irredentist and Magyarone (including the complaint that Aladár Porzsolt held an estate in Hungary, an estate that had been passed on to him by his parents); and (5) he had not mastered the state language. From the report on Funk's dismissal submitted by Porzsolt on March 26, 1934, to the minister of Schools and National Education in Prague, SNA, f. PR, box 556.

112. SNA, f. PR, box 556; and "Neologické žid. Náboženské obec v Bratislave-činnost," SNA, f. KU, box 266.

113. Vér Andor "Világháború," in Ujvári, *Magyar Zsidó Lexikon*, 950.

114. AMZV, sekce II, řada III, box 326, 113601/29.

115. Ibid.

116. Frojimovics et al., *Jewish Budapest*, 294.

117. SNA, f. PR, box 558, inv. nos. 56.347/29.
118. Ibid.
119. Winter, *Sites of Memory.*
120. SNA, f. KU, box 266, inv. 1602/29.
121. Ibid., inv. no. 3161/29.
122. Ibid.
123. AMZV, II, III, 326, 1.470. March 25, 1930.
124. Ibid., 5279. April 14, 1930.
125. Rabbi Samuel Reich, "Die Bedeutung der jüdischen Wahlpartei," *JVZ*, April 16, 1920.

4. Between the Nationalities

1. "An den Vorstand der israelitischen Religionsgemeinde in Bratislava," SNA, f. PR, box 556, inv. no. 163, December 1, 1930; Erik Naberhuis, "The Hungarian Vitéz Order," http://www.austro-hungarian-army.co.uk/vitez.html.
2. Dočasný výkonný výbor utvárajúcej sa židovskej jenoty na Slovensku a Podkarpatskej Rusi, "Žide, plať'!," SNA, f. PR, box 556, inv. no. 181.
3. *Pax a Droit* 6 (June 1923), cited in Mendelsohn, *Jews of East Central Europe,* 105. Vázsonyi is remembered by Hungarian Jews as a truly democratic politician who always defended the Jewish community in cases of high politics. Frojimovics et al., *Jewish Budapest,* 541.
4. "Magyarisch-jüdische Verblendung," *JFB*, Bratislava, January 2, 1931. The article refers to the "Memorandum of the Jews of Hungary to the Jews throughout the World" distributed by the Central Hungarian Jewish Association (Magyar Zsidó Központi Szövetség), YIVO, RG348 Wolf-Mowshowitch collection, box 18, folder 160.
5. On the 1921 Czechoslovak statewide census, 54.28 percent of Jews in Slovakia declared Jewish nationality; 22.27 percent, Czechoslovak nationality; 16.49 percent, Hungarian nationality; and 6.68 percent, German nationality. *Sčítání lidu, 1921,* 90 část textová, tables 104 and 105 combined.
6. "Minister honvédov Gömbös—činnost," February 23, 1931, SNA, f. KÚ, box 266, inv. no. 10600.
7. "An den Vorstand der israelitischen Religionsgemeinde in Bratislava," December 1, 1930, SNA, f. PR, box 556, inv. no. 161–164.
8. "Neologická židovská náboženská obec v Bratislave—činnost'," March 25, 1931, SNA, f. KÚ, box 266, inv. no. 17439.
9. "Resolucia," November 29, 1932, SNA, f. PR, box 556, inv. no. 223.
10. SNA, f. KÚ, box 115, inv. no. 12473 and 19373. The Jewish Party of Slovakia and Subcarpathian Ruthenia was established on March 18, 1928, in Košice.
11. Mikuš, *Slovakia,* 96.
12. Hungarian Frontier Adjustment League [Magyar revíziós liga], *Memorandum Concerning the Situation of the Hungarian Minority in Czechoslovakia,* 32.
13. Boháč, "Národnost při druhém sčítání lidu," 18.
14. Ibid., 14, 16. Boháč designed both the 1921 and the 1930 census.
15. Boháč, "Nationality and the New Czechoslovak Census," 106, 108. Boháč discusses the outcomes of the 1872 St. Petersburg congress in his article "Národnost či jazyk?," *ČSV* II ročník (Prague, 1921), 50. This debate is discussed in detail in chapter 2.

16. Boháč, "Nationality and the New Czechoslovak Census," 105.

17. Boháč, "Národnost při druhém sčítání lidu," 14; and Boháč, "Nationality and the New Czechoslovak Census," 106. See Miklós Zeider, "The League of Nations and Hungarian Minority Petitions," and Ferenc Eiler, "'Minority Foreign Policy': The Role of Czechoslovakia's Hungarian Minority in the European Minorities Congress, 1925–1938," in Eiler and Hájková, *Czech and Hungarian Minority Policy*, 85–115, and 117–140.

18. Rothschild, *East Central Europe*, 99–100.

19. Jan Rychlík, "The Situation of the Hungarian Minority in Czechoslovakia, 1918–1938," in Eiler and Hájková, *Czech and Hungarian Minority Policy*, 29.

20. Seton-Watson, "The Situation in Slovakia and the Magyar Minority," in Rychlík, Marzik, and Bielik, *R. W. Seton-Watson and His Relations*, 413.

21. Ibid., 407.

22. Ibid., 413.

23. Boháč, "Národnost při druhém sčítání lidu," 14.

24. Ibid.

25. Tara Zahra provides a thorough analysis of cases where Germans were forced to declare as Czechs and other methods by which, she argues, Germans were made into Czechs in 1921 in *Kidnapped Souls*, 118–123.

26. Boháč, "Nationality and the New Czechoslovak Census," 115.

27. Ibid., 109. The two representatives of the Jewish Party elected to parliament in 1929 were Dr. Ludvik Singer of Prague and Dr. Julius Reisz of Bratislava.

28. According to article 2 of the 1920 Czechoslovak language law, if in a court district there were living at least 20 percent of Czechoslovak citizens of the same language that was different from Czech or Slovak according to the most recent population census, the state administration, courts, offices of public prosecutors, and organs of local self-government were obliged to use that language as the second official one.

29. Emanuel Rádl, *Národnost jako vědecký problem* (Prague, 1929); Emanuel Rádl, "Kdo rozhoduje?," *Právu lidu*, February 16, 1930.

30. Antonín Boháč, "Národnost při druhém sčítání lidu," 17–18. Boháč enumerates all main lines of argumentation.

31. Ibid., 21. Auerhan elaborated on his position in an interview with the Czech newspaper *České slovo* on February 9, 1930.

32. Boháč, "Národnost při druhém sčítání lidu," 18.

33. Kateřina Čapková, "Margulies, Emil," YIVO Encyclopedia of Jews in Eastern Europe, 2010, http://www.yivoencyclopedia.org/article.aspx/Margulies_Emil; Boháč, "Národnost při druhém sčítání lidu," 25.

34. "Sčítání," *Rozvoj*, February 21, 1930.

35. *Večer*, February 17, 1930.

36. Boháč, "Nationality and the New Czechoslovak Census," 111.

37. *Sčítání lídu, 1921*, 77* část textová.

38. See Mendelsohn, "Lithuania," in *Jews of East Central Europe*, 212–239.

39. Boháč, "Nationality and the New Czechoslovak Census," 111.

40. Eugen Klein, "Varuj Žide," *Slovenský dennik*, March 1, 1930.

41. "Židovský problém," *Pohranský Hlásnik*, no. 34, August 22, 1930.

42. The Jewish Party officially unified to represent all of Czechoslovakia in January 1931 after a series of meetings in Moravská Ostrava. More than one hundred delegates

and guests from across the country attended the opening convention. Rabinowicz, "Jewish Party," JPSA, *Jews of Czechoslovakia*, 2:283.

43. Čapková, *Češi, Němci, Židé?*, 243.

44. "Landesparteileitungssitzung der Jüdischer Partei für die Slovakei in Trenč. Teplice," *JVZ*, Bratislava, August 22, 1930.

45. Čapková, *Češi, Němci, Židé?*, 243.

46. Rabinowicz, "Jewish Party," 279–280.

47. "Židia u soc. demokratov," *Národný denník*, Bratislava, December 6, 1929. Deteriorating Czechoslovak-Polish relations made continued Polish-Jewish electoral cooperation inappropriate. Crhová, "Jewish Politics," 297.

48. "Dočasný výkonný výbor utvárajúcej sa židovskej jednoty na Slovensku a Podkarpatskej Rusi," "Nemôžeš byť vitézom, lebo nie si Maďarom! Žid je len žid!," SNA, f. PR, box 556, inv. no. 177.

49. "Dočasný výkonný výbor utvárajúcej sa židovskej jednoty na Slovensku a Podkarpatskej Rusi, "Žide, plať! (Zmysel', Tu je doba odplaty)," SNA, f. PR, box 556, inv. no. 182.

50. Rabinowicz, "Jewish Party," 285. In absolute numbers, this meant that 94,000 out of the 101,000 Jewish inhabitants by religion in Subcarpathian Ruthenia in 1930 declared Jewish nationality in contrast with the 80,000 out of 93,000 Jewish inhabitants by religion in 1921.

51. *Sčítání lidu, 1921* (Praha, 1924), 90 čast textová, tables 104 and 105 combined: "Israelité československé státní přislušnosti podle národnosti," and *Sčítání lidu v republice Československé ze dne 1. Prosince 1930. Čast 1*, 105.

52. "Dodatok V. Retrospektívny prehl'ad o národnosti resp. materinskej reči obyvatel'stva politických okresov od r. 1880 v číslach pomerných," 164–167. Hungarian nationality declarations increased by 2.26 percent in Bratislava's outlying district, by .02 percent in Nové Mesto nad Váhom, and by.08 percent in Myjava. The eleven districts where Czechoslovak nationality declarations decreased due to rising Ruthene declarations included Bratislava's outlying district, Bardejov, Stará Ľubovňa, Nové Mesto nad Váhom, Liptovský Svätý Mikuláš, Púchov, Sabinov, Skalica, Stropkov, Zvolen, and Žilina.

53. Rothkirchen, "Slovakia: II, 1918–1938," 1:102.

54. Boháč, *Národnostní mapa republiky československé*,16.

55. Exceptions included Žilina and Nová Baňa. "Dodatok V. Retrospektívny prehl'ad o národnosti resp. materinskej reči obyvatel'stva politických okresov od r. 1880 v číslach pomerných," 164–167.

56. Mendelsohn, *Jews of East Central Europe*, 160.

57. Čapková, *Češi, Němci, Židé?*, 49–50.

58. Friedmann, *Einige Zahlen über die tschechoslovakischen Juden*, 23, 25.

59. Hungarian Frontier Adjustment League [Magyar reviziós liga], *Memorandum Concerning the Situation of the Hungarian Minority in Czechoslovakia* (Sárkány LTD., Budapest, 1934), 71; emphasis added.

60. Ibid., 73.

61. Zahra, *Kidnapped Souls*, 125–126.

62. "Dodatok V. Retrospektívny prehl'ad o národnosti resp. materinskej reči obyvatel'stva politických okresov od r. 1880 v číslach pomerných," 164–167.

63. See Bugge, "Making of a Slovak City," and Lipták, "Rok 1918 a rekonštrukcia historickej pamäti."

64. "Usnesenie mestskej rady v záležitosti výsledkov sčítania ľudu z roku 1930," AMB, f. MB, box 2490, inv. no.: 11.972/prez. 1933.

65. "Obyvateľstvo," AMB, f. MB, box 2537. A study focusing on nationality choices among Jews in Bratislava would be very interesting.

66. Ibid.; emphasis added.

67. "Usnesenie mestskej rady v záležitosti výsledkov sčítania ľudu z roku 1930," AMB, f. MB, box 2490, inv. no.: 11.972/prez. 1933.

68. Ibid.

69. *Memorandum Concerning the Situation of the Hungarian Minority in Czechoslovakia*, 89.

70. Rothschild, *East Central Europe*, 123.

71. Irma Polak, "The Zionist Women's Movement," in JPSA, *Jews of Czechoslovakia*, 2:145; Dina Porat, "Fleischmann, Gisela," YIVO Encyclopedia of Jews in Eastern Europe, 2010, http://www.yivoencyclopedia.org/article.aspx/Fleischmann_Gisela.

72. Čapková, *Češi, Němci, Židé?*, 259. See also the excellent volume coauthored by Kateřina Čapková and Michal Frankl, *Nejisté útočiště: Československo a uprchlíci před nacismem, 1933–1938*, which polemicizes the conventional perception of Czechoslovakia as "island of freedom, democracy, and tolerance" in the 1930s.

73. Levin, *Holocaust*, 60.

74. SNA, f. PR, box 235, folder 212, inv. no. 397.

75. The Bernheim Petition, named after its signer Franz Bernheim, who was fired from his warehouse job in Upper Silesia after the Nazi accession to power and moved to Prague, is known as the only favorable League of Nations action on a Jewish claim. Submitted on May 17, 1933, by Emil Margulies, the petition temporarily suspended Nazi anti-Jewish legislation against the Jews of Upper Silesia on the grounds that it violated the league-guaranteed German-Polish Convention of 1922. Nazi legislation came back into effect in 1937 when the league convention expired. The Comité des Délégations Juives was formed at the Paris Peace Conference in 1919. David Engel, "Minorities Treaties," YIVO Encyclopedia of Jews in Eastern Europe, 2010, http://www.yivoencyclopedia.org/article.aspx/Minorities_Treaties. See the full text of the Bernheim Petition at the American Jewish Yearbook Archives, *www.ajcarchives.org/AJC_DATA/Files/1933_1934_4_YRAppendices.pdf*.

76. SNA, f. PR, box 235, folder 212, inv. no. 134.

77. Ibid., inv. no. 132.

78. Ibid., inv. no. 133.

79. Ibid., inv. no. 132.

80. Prague feared that risking flexibility in the Slovak position would lead directly to the extinction of the state. Leff, *National Conflict*, 136.

81. "Židia na Slovensku v minulosti a teraz," *Slovák*, September 9, 1933, no. 204.

82. Čapková, *Češi, Němci, Židé?*, 245.

83. Lipták, "Slovakia in the 20th Century," 247–248.

84. Ibid., 253.

85. See Mikuš, *Slovakia*, 6–39.

86. Rothschild, *East Central Europe*, 120.

87. Rothkirchen, "Slovakia: II, 1918–1938," 1:105.

88. Ibid., 106–107.

89. "Českí socialisti a mad'arskí Židia," *Slovák*, Bratislava, May 19, 1934.

90. "Na jaké cesty sa to dostal Sväz slovenských židov?," *Národný denník*, Bratislava, May 15, 1934.

91. Ibid.

92. "Čo je s vývojom asimilačného hnutia Židovstva na Slovensku?," *Národný denník*, Bratislava, May 25, 1934. The Nazification of the German community in Slovakia in 1937 forced Jewish students to withdraw from the German gymnasium. Jelínek, "In Search of Identity," 217–218.

93. Ibid.

94. "Was geht in dem Verband der jüdischen Slowaken vor? Warum hat der Obmann Primarius Dr. Hugo Roth adgedankt?," *Neues Pressburger Abendblatt*, Bratislava, May 8, 1934.

95. Jelínek, *Dávidova hviezda pod Tatrami*, 179.

96. Lipscher, *Židia v slovenskom štáte*, 14.

97. All of these missing elements signified a lack of what Victor Karady has called "acculturational attraction." Karady, *Jews of Europe*, 210.

98. Lipscher, *Židia v slovenskom štáte*, 15.

99. Kamenec, *Po stopách tragédia*, 14.

100. Ibid., 17; Rothkirchen, "Slovakia: II, 1918–1938," 1:108. The riots took place on April 24–27, 1936.

101. Jelínek, "In Search of Identity," 218.

102. Rothkirchen, "Slovakia: II, 1918–1938," 1:108.

103. Oral history with Katarina Lofflerová, conducted by Martin Korcok in Bratislava in 2004 for *www.centropa.org*, *Jewish Witness to a European Century*, http://www.centropa.org/biography/katarina-lofflerova.

104. The Orbis publishing house translated and distributed Beneš's August 1936 speeches, in "various languages in the hope that they will contribute to the formation abroad of a just opinion of Czechoslovakia," as *The Problems of Czechoslovakia* in 1936. Also *Československé dějiny v datech*, 410; and Jelínek, "In Search of Identity," 222–223.

105. "Nech sa st'ahujú Židia do Palestíny a Birobidžanu," *Slovák*, March 12, 1937; Kamenec, *Po stopách tragédia*, 18; Jelínek, "In Search of Identity," 224; Rothkirchen, "Slovakia: II, 1918–1938," 1:109.

106. Katuninec, "Karol Sidor and the Jewish Question," 340–341.

107. SNA, f. PR, box 144, inv. no. 803.

108. See Delfiner, *Vienna Broadcasts to Slovakia*.

109. *Slovák*, Bratislava, May 18, 1938.

110. Rothschild, *East Central Europe*, 132–133.

111. Rothkirchen, "Slovakia: II., 1918–1938," 1:114.

112. Lipscher, *Židia v slovenskom štáte*,18. Lipscher writes that this explanation does not hold up to the census results. The Hungarian accusation appears in a telegram of the Hungarian embassy in Prague from October 1, 1938, also cited in Lipscher, 18.

113. Rothkirchen, "Slovakia: II., 1918–1938," 1:114.

114. Nižňanský, *Holokaust na Slovensku*, 228–230.

115. Rothkirchen, "Slovakia: II., 1918–1938," 1:116.

116. Kamenec, *Po stopách tragédia*, 29.

Conclusion

1. SNA, f. PR, box 556, inv. no. 561–562, July 23, 1929.

2. Rabinowicz, "Jewish Minority," 1:166–167.

3. Ivan Davidson Kalmar, "Forgetting and Identity: Ethnic Engineering and the Jews of Czechoslovakia," a 2005 paper presented at the Centre for Russian and East European Studies, University of Toronto, in Heitlinger, *In the Shadows,* 147.

4. Bugge uses this term in his analysis of the "Czechoslovakization" of Bratislava, "Making of a Slovak City," 221.

Bibliography

Primary Sources

Archival Material

Czech Republic

Archív Ministerstva zahraničních věcí ČR (AMZV), Prague
    II. sekce 1918–1939, III. řada
Archív Národního muzea
    Pozůstalost Antonína Boháče

Hungary

Magyar Országos Levéltár (MOL; Hungarian National Archives), Budapest
    Belügyminiszterium K148, Elnöki Iratok, 1914–1918
    Menekültek ügyei
    Egyesületi ügyei
    Egyházi és közoktatási ügyei

Slovakia

Archív hlavného mesta SR Bratislavy (AMB)
    Fond Mesto Bratislavy
Slovenský národný archív, Bratislava (SNA)
    Oddelenie nových fondov, 1918–1968
    Fond Krajinský úrad (KÚ)
    Fond Ministerstvo s plnou mocou pre správu Slovenska (MPS)
    Fond Policajné riaditel'stvo (PR)

United States

Joint Distribution Committee Archives (JDC), New York
    New York collection of the years 1919–1921
YIVO Institute for Jewish Research, New York
    Record Group 335.2; American Joint Reconstruction Foundation (AJRF)
    Record Group 00000348 Lucien Wolf and David Mowshowitch papers, [ca. 1869–1959]

Newspapers

České slovo, Prague
Dr. Bloch's Österreichische Wochenschrift (ÖW), Vienna
Egyenlőség, Budapest

Judaica, Bratislava
Der Jüdische Herold, Dunajská Streda
Jüdische Nachrichten, Prešov
Jüdische Presse, Bratislava
Jüdische Volkszeitung (JVZ), Bratislava
Jüdische Zeitung (JZ), Vienna
Jüdisches Familienblatt (JFB), Bratislava
Kassai Napló, Košice
Lidové listy, Prague
Magyar Ujság, Budapest
Múlt és Jövő, Budapest
Národnie noviny, Turčiansky Svätý Martin
Národný denník, Bratislava
Neues Pressburger Abendblatt, Bratislava
Nitrianské noviny, Nitra
Preßburger Zeitung, Bratislava
Rozvoj, Pardubice
Šarišské hlasy, Prešov
Selbstwehr, Prague
Slovák, Bratislava
Slovenský denník, Bratislava
Slovenský východ, Košice
Ungarländische Jüdische Zeitung (UJZ), Budapest
Večer, Prague

Printed Primary Sources

American Jewish Committee. *Jews in the Eastern War Zone.* New York, 1916.
Boháč, Antonín. *Národnost a sčítání lidu.* Prague, 1930.
——. "Národnost při druhém sčítání lidu." *Statistický obzor,* XII Ročník. Prague, 1931: 14–30.
——. *Národnostní mapa republiky československé. Podrobný popis národnostních hranic, ostrovů a menšin.* Prague, 1926.
——. "Nationality and the New Czechoslovak Census." *Slavonic and East European Review* 10, no. 28 (1931): 105–115.
Československý statističní věstník (ČSV), Prague, 1919–1921
Deset let československé republiky. Svazek I. Prague, 1928.
Friedmann, Franz [František]. *Einige Zahlen über die tschechoslovakischen Juden.* Prague,1933.
——. *Mravnost či oportunita? Několik poznámek k anketě akad. Spolku "Kapper" v Brně.* Prague, 1927.
Hajn, Alois. *Problém ochrany menšin.* Prague, 1923.
Hungarian Frontier Adjustment League. *Memorandum Concerning the Situation of the Hungarian Minority in Czechoslovakia.* Budapest: Sárkány, 1934.
Janda, Bohumil, ed. *Československá vlastivěda. Díl V. Stát.* Prague: Sfinx, 1931.
Joint Distribution Committee (JDC). *Reports Received by the Joint Distribution Committee of Funds for Jewish War Sufferers.* New York, 1916.
Klineberger, Bohdan. *Národ a národnost.* Prague, 1919.

Magyar Statisztikai Évkönyv. Új Folyam XXIII. 1915. Budapest, 1918.
Manuel Statistique de la Republique Tchécoslovaque I–III. Prague, 1925–1928.
Mráz, Josef. *Slovensko ve světle statistiky.* Prague, 1921.
"Náboženství a cirkve." *Deset let československé republiky. Svazek I.* Prague, 1928.
Rádl, Emanuel. "Kdo rozhoduje?" *Právu lidu,* February 16, 1930.
——. *Národnost jako vědecký problém.* Prague, 1929.
Roth, Hugo. *Ku Pôde a Skutočnosti.* Bratislava: Tlačou ÚČ. Tlačiarne "Universum" v Bratislave, 1927.
Šrobár, Vavro. *Osvobodené Slovensko. Pamäti z Rokov, 1918–1920.* Sväzok Prvý. Prague, 1928.
——. *Z môjho života.* Prague: Fr. Borový, 1946.
Ujvári, Péter, ed. *Magyar Zsidó Lexikon.* Budapest: A Magyar Zsidó Lexikon Kiadása, 1929.
Úřad statistický. "Dodatok V. Retrospektívny prehl'ad o národnosti resp. materinskej reči obyvatel'stva politických okresov od r. 1880 v číslach pomerných." *Štátistický Lexikon Obcí v Republike Československej, III. Krajna Slovenská,* Vydaný ministerstvom vnútra a štátnym úradom štatistickým na základe výsledkov sčítania l'udu z 1. decembra 1930. Prague, 1930.
——. *Sčítání lidu v republice československé ze dne 15. února 1921.* Prague, 1924.
——. *Sčítání lidu v republice Československé ze dne 1. Prosince 1930. Čast 1.* Prague, 1934.
Ústavní listina Československé republiky [Constitutional Charter of the Czechoslovak Republic]. February 29, 1920. Available in English online at the Internet Archive's Open Library, https://openlibrary.org/books/OL23290715M/The_constitution_of _the_Czechoslovak_Republic.

Secondary Sources

Bárkány, Eugen, and L'udovít Dojč. *Židovské náboženské obce na Slovensku.*Bratislava: Vesna, 1991.
Baron, Nick, and Peter Gatrell. *Homelands: War Population and Statehood in Eastern Europe and Russia, 1918–1924.* London: Anthem, 2004.
Beneš, Edvard. *The Problems of Czechoslovakia: Speeches of the President of the Republic, Dr. Edward Beneš, in Northern Bohemia.* Prague: Orbis, 1936.
Bernstein, Béla. *A negyvennyolcas magyar szabadságharc és a zsidók.* Budapest: Múlt és Jövő Kiadó, 1998.
Birnbaum, Pierre, and Ira Katznelson, eds. *Paths of Emancipation: Jews, States, and Citizenship.* Princeton, NJ: Princeton University Press, 1995.
Borský, Maroš. "Jewish Communities and Their Urban Context: A Case Study of Košice, Prešov, and Bardejov." In *Architektúra and Urbanizmus* 38, no. 3–4 (2004): 115–138.
——. *Synagogue Architecture in Slovakia: A Memoiral Landscape of a Lost Community.* Bratislava: Jewish Heritage Foundation/Menorah, 2007.
Braham, Randolph L., ed. *Hungarian-Jewish Studies.* New York: World Federation of Hungarian Jews, 1966.
Brubaker, Rogers. *Nationalism Reframed: Nationhood and the National Question in the New Europe.* Cambridge, UK: Cambridge University Press, 1996.

Bugge, Peter. "The Making of a Slovak City: The Czechoslovak Renaming of Pressburg/ Pozsony/Prešporok, 1918–19." In *Austrian History Yearbook* 35 (2004): 205–227.

Čapková, Kateřina. *Češi, Němci, Židé? Národní identita Židů v Čechách, 1918–1938.* Prague—Litomyšl, Czech Republic: Paseka, 2005.

———. *Czechs, Germans, Jews? National Identity and the Jews of Bohemia.* New York: Berghahn Books, 2012.

Čapková, Kateřina, and Michal Frankl. *Nejisté útočiště: Československo a uprchlíci před nacismem, 1933–1938.* Prague: Paseka, 2008.

Československé dějiny v datech. Prague: Nakladatelství Svoboda, 1986.

Cohen, Gary. *The Politics of Ethnic Survival: Germans in Prague, 1861–1914.* Princeton, NJ: Princeton University Press, 1981.

Connor, Walker. *Ethnonationalism: The Quest for Understanding.* Princeton, NJ: Princeton University Press, 1994.

Crhová, Marie. "Jewish Politics in Central Europe: The Case of the Jewish Party in Interwar Czechoslovakia." In *Jewish Studies at Central European University II, 1999–2001,* edited by András Kovács and Eszter Andor. Budapest: Central European University, 2002.

Efron, John, Steven Weitzman, and Matthias Lehmann. *The Jews: A History,* 2nd ed. Boston: Pearson, 2014.

Eiler, Ferenc, and Dagmar Hájková, eds. *Czech and Hungarian Minority Policy in Central Europe, 1918–1938:* Prague: Masarykův ústav a [Archív] Akademie věd ČR; Budapest: MTA Etnikai-nemzeti Kisebbségkutató Intézete, 2009.

Delfiner, Henry. *The Vienna Broadcasts to Slovakia, 1938–1939: A Case Study in Subversion.* New York: Columbia University Press, 1974.

Federální statistický úřad. *70 let československé státní statistiky.* Prague, 1989.

Frojimovics, Kinga, and Rita Horváth. "Jews and Nationalism in Hungary." *European Legacy* 7, no. 5 (2002): 641–644.

Frojimovics, Kinga, Géza Komoróczy, Viktória Pusztai, and Andrea Strbik, eds. *Jewish Budapest: Monuments, Rites, History.* Budapest: Central European University Press, 1999.

Gatrell, Peter. *A Whole Empire Walking: Refugees in Russia during World War I.* Bloomington: Indiana University Press, 1999.

Gellner, Ernest. *Nations and Nationalism.* Ithaca, NY: Cornell University Press, 1983.

Gruber, Ruth Ellen. *National Geographic Jewish Heritage Travel: A Guide to Eastern Europe.* National Geographic, 2007.

———. *Virtually Jewish: Reinventing Jewish Culture in Europe.* Berkeley: University of California Press, 2002).

Haber, Peter. *Die Anfänge des Zionismus in Ungarn (1897–1904.)* Köln: Böhlau Verlag, 2001.

Halász, Iván."A szlovák nemzeti politika és a zsidóság a dualismus idején." *Limes* 1 (Spring 1999): 43–58.

Hanák, Péter, ed. *The Corvina History of Hungary: From Earliest Times until the Present Day.* Budapest: Corvina Books, 1991.

Hanebrink, Paul. *In Defense of Christian Hungary.* Ithaca, NY: Cornell University Press, 2006.

———. "Transnational Culture War: Christianity, Nation, and the Judeo-Bolshevik Myth in Hungary, 1890–1920." *Journal of Modern History* (March 2008): 55–80.

Heitlinger, Alena. *In the Shadows of the Holocaust and Communism: Czech and Slovak Jews since 1945*. New Brunswick, NJ: Transaction, 2006.

Herzl, Theodor. *The Jewish State*. New York: American Zionist Emergency Council, 1946.

Hoensch, Jörg K., Stanislav Biman, Ľubomír Lipták, eds. *Emancipácia Židov—antisemitizmus—prenasledovanie v Nemecku, Rakúsko-Uhorsku, v českých zemiach a na Slovensku*. Bratislava: Veda, Vydavateľstvo SAV, 1999.

Hradská, Katerína. "Postavenie Židov na Slovensku v prvej československej republike." In Hoensch et al., *Emancipácia Židov—antisemitizmus*, 131–138.

Iggers, Wilma A. *Women of Prague*. Providence, RI: Berghahn Books, 1995.

Janowsky, Oscar. *The Jews and Minority Rights (1898–1919)*. New York: Columbia University Press, 1933.

————. *Nationalities and National Minorities (With Special Reference to East Central Europe)*. New York: Macmillan, 1945.

Jelínek, Yeshayahu A. *The Carpathian Diaspora: The Jews of Subcarpathian Rus' and Mukachevo, 1848–1948*. New York: East European Monographs, 2007.

————. *Davidova hviezda pod Tatrami*. Prague: Ján Mlynárik, 2009.

————. "In Search of Identity: Slovakian Jewry and Nationalism (1918–1938)." In, *A Social and Economic History of Central European Jewry*, edited by Yahuda Don and Victor Karady, 207–228. New Brunswick, NJ: Transaction, 1989.

————. *Židia na Slovensku v 19. a 20. storočí*, I. Časť. Bratislava: Edícia Judaica Slovaca, 1999.

Jewish Publication Society of America (JPSA). *The Jews of Czechoslovakia: Historical Studies and Surveys*, Vol. 1. Philadelphia: Jewish Publication Society of America, 1968.

————. *The Jews of Czechoslovakia: Historical Studies and Surveys*, Vol. 2. Philadelphia: Jewish Publication Society of America, 1971.

Johnson, Owen V. *Slovakia, 1918–1938: Education and the Making of a Nation*. New York: Distributed by Columbia University Press, 1985.

Kamenec, Ivan, Elena Mannová, and Eva Kowalská, eds. *Historik v čase a priestore. Laudatio Ľubomírovi Liptákovi*. Bratislava: VEDA, 2000.

————. *Po stopách tragédie*. Bratislava: Archa, 1991.

Kann, Robert A. *A History of the Habsburg Empire, 1526–1918*. Berkeley: University of California Press, 1977.

Karády, Victor. *The Jews of Europe in the Modern Era: A Socio-Historical Outline*. Budapest: CEU Press, 2004.

————. *Önazonositás, Sorsválasztás: A zsidó csoportazonosság történelmi alakváltozásai Magyarországon*. Budapest: Új Mandatum, 2001.

————. "Religious Divisions, Socio-Economic Stratification and the Modernization of Hungarian Jewry after the Emancipation." In Silber, *Jews in the Hungarian Economy*, 161–186.

Katuninec, Milan. "Karol Sidor and the Jewish Question." In *Holokaust ako Historický a Morálny Problém v Minulosti a v Súčasnosti*, edited by Monika Vrzgulová and Daniela Richterová, 118–126. Bratislava: Dokumentačné stredisko holokaustu, 2008.

Katz, Jacob. *A House Divided: Orthodoxy and Schism in Nineteenth-Century Central European Jewry*. Translated by Ziporah Brody. Hanover, NH: Brandeis University Press, 1998.

Kedourie, Elie. *Nationalism*. London: Hutchinson, 1961.

Kertzer, David, and Dominique Arel, eds. *Census and Identity. The Politics of Race, Ethnicity, and Language in National Censuses*. Cambridge, UK: Cambridge University Press, 2002.

Kieval, Hillel J. *The Making of Czech Jewry: National Conflict and Jewish Society in Bohemia, 1870–1918*. Oxford, UK: Oxford University Press, 1988.

———. "Negotiating Czechoslovakia: The Challenges of Jewish Citizenship in a Multiethnic Nation-State." In *Insiders and Outsiders: Dilemmas of East European Jewry*, edited by Richard I. Cohen, Jonathan Frankel, and Stefani Hoffman, 103–119. Oxford, UK: Littman Library of Jewish Civilization, 2010.

Konrád, Miklós. "Jews and Politics in Hungary in the Dualist Era, 1867–1914." *East European Jewish Affairs* 39, no. 2 (August 2009): 167–186.

Kontler, László. *A History of Hungary: Millennium in Central Europe*. New York: Palgrave Macmillan, 2002.

Kónya, Peter, and Dezider Landa. *Stručné dejiny Prešovských židov*. Prešov, Slovakia, 1995.

Kovács, András, and Eszter Andor, eds. *Jewish Studies at the Central European University II. 1999–2001*. Budapest: Central European University Press, 2002.

Kovács, Éva. "A Kassai Zsidóság Etnikai Identitása a Két Világháború Között (1918–1938)." [The Ethnic Identity of Kassa (Košice) Jewry between the Two World Wars]. PhD diss., ELTE, 1991.

Kovács, Mária M. "The Ambiguities of External Minority Protection: The Hungarian *Numerus Clausus* Debate." *East European Jewish Affairs* 36, no. 1 (June 2006): 43–48.

———. *Liberal Professions and Illiberal Politics: Hungary from the Habsburgs to the Holocaust*. New York: Oxford University Press, 1994.

Lacko, Martin. *Prevrat 1918 v obci Modrová*. Bratislava, 2001.

Landman, Leo. *Jewish Law in the Diaspora: Confrontation and Accommodation*. Philadelphia: Dropsie College for Hebrew and Cognate Learning, 1968.

Laqueur, Walter. *A History of Zionism*. New York: Schocken Books, 1976.

Leff, Carol Skalnik. *National Conflict in Czechoslovakia: The Making and Remaking of a State, 1918–1987*. Princeton, NJ: Princeton University Press, 1988.

Lesser, Jeff. *Welcoming the Undesirables: Brazil and the Jewish Question*. Berkeley: University of California Press, 1995.

Levin, Nora. *The Holocaust: The Destruction of European Jewry*. New York: Schocken Books, 1973.

Lipscher, Ladislav. *Židia v slovenskom štáte, 1939–1945*. Banská Bystrica, Slovakia: PrintServis, 1992.

Lipták, Ľubomir. "Collective Identity and Public Spaces." In *Collective Identities in Central Europe and Modern Times*, edited by Moritz Csáky and Elena Mannová, 121–136. Bratislava: Institute of History of the Slovak Academy of Sciences, 1999.

———. "Rok 1918 a rekonštukcia historickej pamäti v mestách na Slovensku." In *Acta Contemporanea k pětašedesátinám Viléma Prečana*, 180–191. Ústav pro soudobé dějiny AV ČR: Praha, 1998.

———. "Slovakia in the 20th Century," in Mannová, *Concise History of Slovakia*. 256–301.

Lupovitch, Howard N. *Jews at the Crossroads: Tradition and Accommodation during the Golden Age of the Hungarian Nobility, 1729–1878.* Budapest: Central European University Press, 2007.

Magocsi, Paul Robert. *Historical Atlas of Central Europe,* rev. and exp. ed. A History of East Central Europe, Vol. 1. Seattle: University of Washington Press, 2002.

Mannová, Elena, ed., *A Concise History of Slovakia.* Bratislava: Historický ústav SAV, 2000.

Mannová, Elena, and Roman Holec, "On the Road to Modernization, 1848–1918," in Mannová, *Concise History of Slovakia,* 196–197.

Marrus, Michael. *The Unwanted: European Refugees from the First World War through the Cold War.* 2nd ed. Philadelphia: Temple University Press, 2002.

Mars, Leonard. "Discontinuity, Tradition, and Innovation: Anthropological Reflections on Jewish Identity in Contemporary Hungary." *Social Compass* 46 (1999).

McCagg, William O., Jr. *A History of Habsburg Jews, 1670–1918.* Bloomington: Indiana University Press, 1989.

Mendelsohn, Ezra. *The Jews of East Central Europe between the World Wars.* Bloomington: Indiana University Press, 1983.

———. *On Modern Jewish Politics.* New York: Oxford University Press, 1993.

Menyhért, Lányi. *Jewish Nobles and Geniuses in Modern Hungary.* New York: Distributed by Columbia University Press, 1972.

———. *Slovenszkói Zsidó Hitközségek Története.* Kassa [Košice]: Athenaeum, 1933.

Mendes-Flohr, Paul, and Jehuda Reinharz, eds. *The Jew in the Modern World,* 2nd ed. Oxford, UK: Oxford University Press, 1995.

Mešťan, Pavol, ed. *HaŠomer Hacair Dejiny Hnutia.* Bratislava: SNM Múzeum židovskej kultury, 2001.

Mikuš, Joseph A. *Slovakia: A Political History, 1918–1950.* Milwaukee: Marquette University Press, 1963.

Miller, Michael Laurence. *Rabbis and Revolution: The Jews of Moravia in the Age of Emancipation.* Stanford, CT: Stanford University Press, 2011.

Nižňanský, Eduard, ed. *Holokaust na Slovensku, Obdobie autonómie (6.10.1938–14.3.1939) Dokumenty.* Bratislava: Milan Šimečka Foundation, Židovská náboženská obec Bratislava, 2001.

Nurmi, Ismo. *Slovakia—A Playground for Nationalism and National Identity: Manifestations of the National Identity of the Slovaks, 1918–1920.* Helsinki: Suomen Historiallinen Seura, 1999.

Rabinowicz, Aharon Moshe. "The Jewish Minority," in JPSA, *Jews of Czechoslovakia,* 155–265.

———. "The Jewish Party," in JPSA, *Jews of Czechoslovakia,* 2: 253–346.

Rachamimov, Alon. "Collective Identifications and Austro-Hungarian Jews (1914–1918): The Contradictions and Travails of Avigdor Hamieri." In Cole and Unowsky, *Limits of Loyalty,* 178–198.

Rechter, David. *The Jews of Vienna and the First World War.* London: Littman Library of Jewish Civilization, 2001.

Roshwald, Aviel. *Ethnic Nationalism and the Fall of Empires. Central Europe, Russia, and the Middle East, 1914–1923.* London: Routledge, 2001.

Rothkirchen, Livia. "Slovakia: I. 1848–1918," in Jewish Publication Society of America (JPSA), *Jews of Czechoslovakia,* 1: 72.(00b)

Rothschild, Joseph. *East Central Europe between the Two World Wars.* A History of East Central Europe, Vol. 9. Seattle: University of Washington Press, 1974.

Rozenblit, Marsha. *Reconstructing a National Identity: The Jews of Habsburg Austria during World War One.* New York: Oxford University Press, 2001.

Rychlík, Jan, Thomas D. Marzik, and Miroslav Bielik, eds. *R. W. Seton-Watson and His Relations with the Czechs and Slovaks.* Prague: Ústav T.G. Masaryka, Matica Slovenska,1995.

Rychnovsky, Ernst. *Masaryk a židovstvi.* Praha, 1931.

Schweitzer, Gábor. "Miért nem kellett Herzl a magyar zsidóknak?" *Budapest Negyed* (Spring 1995): 45–55.

Scott, James C. *Seeing Like a State: How Certain Schemes to Improve the Human Condition Have Failed.* New Haven, CT: Yale University Press, 1998.

Seton-Watson, R. W. *Racial Problems in Hungary.* New York: Howard Fertig, 1972.

Siklós, András. *Revolution in Hungary and the Dissolution of the Multinational State, 1918.* Budapest: Akadémiai Kiadó, 1988.

Silber, Michael, ed. *Jews in the Hungarian Economy, 1760–1945.* Jerusalem: Magnes Press, 1992.

Sinkoff, Nancy. *Out of the Shtetl: Making Jews Modern in the Polish Borderlands.* Providence, RI: Brown Judaic Studies, 2004.

Smith, Anthony. *Nationalism: Theory, Ideology, History.* Malden, MA: Blackwell, 2001.

Šoltés, Peter. *Tri jazyky, štyri konfesie: Etnická a konfesionálna pluralita na Zemplíne, Spiši a v Šariši.* Bratislava: Historický ústav SAV, 2009.

Szabó, Miroslav. "'Židovaká otázka' na Slovensku v prvých rokoch československej republiky." *Střed/Center* (February 2011): 59–81.

Tilly, Charles. *The Formation of National States in Western Europe.* Princeton, NJ: Princeton University Press, 1975.

Tökés, Rudolf L. *Béla Kun and the Hungarian Soviet Republic.* New York: Praeger, 1967.

Völgyés, Ivan, ed. *Hungary in Revolution, 1918–1919: Nine Essays.* Lincoln: University of Nebraska Press, 1971.

Winter, Jay. *Sites of Memory, Sites of Mourning.* Cambridge, UK: Cambridge University Press, 1995.

Zahra, Tara. *Kidnapped Souls: National Indifference and the Battle for Children in the Bohemian Lands.* Ithaca, NY: Cornell University Press, 2008.

Zsoldas, Jenő, ed. *1848–1849 a magyar zsidóság életében.* Budapest: Múlt és Jövő Kiadó, 1998.

Internet Sources

"Bernheim Petition." American Jewish Yearbook Archives. *www.ajcarchives.org/AJC _DATA/Files/1933_1934_4_YRAppendices.pdf.*

Čapková, Kateřina. "Margulies, Emil." YIVO Encyclopedia of Jews in Eastern Europe, 2010. http://www.yivoencyclopedia.org/article.aspx/Margulies_Emil.

Czech Statistical Office. "Historie statistiky v Čechách po roce 1918." *http://www.czso.cz /csu/redakce.nsf/i/historie_statistiky_v_cechach_po_roce_1918.*

"Dom umenia—neologická synagóga." Miestny úrad Košice—Staré Mesto. http://www .kosice-city.sk/clanky-detail/4dom-umenia-neologicka-synagoga.

Életrajzi lexikon. www.kereso.hu-yrk-Ryrgenwm/7502.

Engel, David. "Minorities Treaties." YIVO Encyclopedia of Jews in Eastern Europe, 2010. http://www.yivoencyclopedia.org/article.aspx/Minorities_Treaties.

Gruber, Ruth Ellen. "Lipót Baumhorn Tour." http://www.centropa.org/?nID=60&tID=26.

Heet, Erika. "Lajos Kozma, Hungarian Modernist. " http://www.dwell.com/articles/lajos -kozma-hungarian-modernist.html.

Korcok, Martin. "Katarina Lofflerová." Oral history for *www.centropa.org. Jewish Witness to a European Century.* http://www.centropa.org/biography/katarina-lofflerova.

Naberhuis, Erik. "The Hungarian Vitéz Order." *http://www.austro-hungarian-army.co .uk/vitez.html.*

Porat, Dina. "Fleischmann, Gisela." YIVO Encyclopedia of Jews in Eastern Europe, 2010. http://www.yivoencyclopedia.org/article.aspx/Fleischmann_Gisela.

Silber, Michael K. "Bratislava." YIVO Encyclopedia of Jews in Eastern Europe, 2010. http://www.yivoencyclopedia.org/article.aspx/Bratislava.

Index

acculturation, 15, 93; antisemitism as discouragement to, 69; linguistic, 8; secondary, 7, 20, 148n36; Slovak expectation of rapid acculturation, 16

Agrarian Party, 67, 112, 126

American Jewish Joint Distribution Committee (AJDC), 26, 32, 152n17; goals of, 33–34; JPU cooperation with, 34–35; refugee aid and, 38, 43, 44

antisemitism, 2, 11, 33, 112; anti-Jewish violence, 5, 23–27, 28, 32; in Bohemia and Moravia, 15; campaign against "Jewish privilege," 12; in Germany, 134–135; Hungarian government protection from, 7; in Hungary, 16, 19, 87, 90, 102, 133; Jews forced to "dissimilate" by, 18–19; Magyarization and, 10; Masaryk's opposition to, 26; of Revisionist League, 111; of Slovak autonomist movement, 139, 141; in Slovakia, 28, 66

Arel, Dominique, 56

Arkauer, Štefan, 133

Assembly of Jewish Notables, 3

assimilation, 70, 93, 99; cultural, 136, 139; forced, 49; Hungarian, 2, 112, 113; Jewish nationalism as response to, 18; linguistic, 53, 56, 71; to Slovak nation, 69, 137; social, 7, 8, 86; Zionist opposition to, 100

assimilationism, 5, 67, 76, 100, 148n35; antisemitism as discouragement to, 69; as negligible movement in Slovakia, 16; Neolog Judaism and, 8; Slovak Jews' turn away from, 138–139; Union of Slovak Jews and, 97, 102, 125, 137

Associated Jewish Parties, 63–67, 70, 100

atheism, 136

Auerhan, Jan, 56, 123, 157n36

Ausgleich (Austro-Hungarian Compromise, 1867), 6, 9

Austerlitz, Teodor, 96

Austria, 1, 18, 147n1; Anschluss with Nazi Germany, 141; language counted in censuses, 52; Prussian victory over (1866), 6; refugee relief in, 33; tolerant political tradition of, 15; Zionism in, 20

Austria-Hungary, Dual Monarchy of, 1, 46, 143, 145; collapse and dissolution of, *xviii*, 20, 29, 49, 87; creation of, 6; Magyar elites' power within, 6–7; refugee policy of, 39, 40; Zionism in, 19. *See also* Habsburg Monarchy

Autoemanzipation (Self-Emancipation) (Pinsker), 18

Balfour Declaration, 20

"Bar Kochba" (Zionist organization), 19

Bárkány, Eugen, 96

Baumhorn, Lipót, 95

Beck, Josef, 140

Beneš, Edvard, 1, 31, 49, 100, 140, 141

Benko, Štefan, 132

Bernheim, Franz, 169n75

Bernheim Petition, 134, 135, 169n75

Bethlen, István, 115

Bettelheim, Sámuel (Samu), 19, 150n93

bilinguality, 9

Birnbaum, Pierre, 2

Birobidzhan, 140

Bláha, I. Arnošt, 120–121

blood libel, 26

Boháč, Antonín, 13, 58, 123, 130, 157n42; on counting mother tongue in census, 71–72; Czechoslovak census (1921) and,

REBEKAH KLEIN-PEJŠOVÁ is Jewish Studies Assistant Professor of History at Purdue University. Her recent publications include articles in *Austrian History Yearbook, AJS Review,* and *Shofar.* She lives with her husband and two daughters in West Lafayette, Indiana.